James C. Morris

Revelation
and Daniel

Considered together

Copyright © 2022, James C. Morris

Revelation and Daniel: Considered together

Scripture taken from the New King James Version.
Copyright © 1979, 1980, 1982 by Thomas Nelson, Inc.
Used by permission. All rights reserved.

Bible text from the New King James Version is not to be reproduced in copies or otherwise by any means except as permitted in writing by Thomas Nelson, Inc., Attn: Bible Rights and Permissions, P.O. Box 141000, Nashville, TN 37214-1000.

ISBN: 978-1-945774-89-8

Dispensational Publishing House, Inc.
220 Paseo del Pueblo Norte
Taos, NM 87571

www.dispensationalpublishing.com

Ordering Information: Quantity sales. Special discounts are available on quantity purchases by churches, associations, and others. For details, contact the publisher at the address above or at our toll-free number: 1-844-321-4202

Orders by U.S. trade bookstores and wholesalers. Please contact the publisher: 1-844-321-4202

1 2 3 4 5 6 7 8 9

TABLE OF CONTENTS

INTRODUCTION | 1

REVELATION 1 | 7

REVELATION 2 AND 3 | 17
The letters to the Seven Churches

REVELATION 4 | 43

REVELATION 5 | 51
A scroll sealed with seven seals

REVELATION 6 | 57

REVELATION 7 | 69

REVELATION 8 | 75

REVELATION 9 | 81
The first woe

REVELATION 10 | 89

DANIEL 1 | 97

DANIEL 2	103
DANIEL 3	115
DANIEL 4	121
DANIEL 5	129
DANIEL 6	135
DANIEL 7	141
DANIEL 8	155
DANIEL 9	169
DANIEL 10	185
DANIEL 11	191
DANIEL 12	221
REVELATION 11	231
REVELATION 12	241
REVELATION 13	251
REVELATION 14	261

A Lamb stands on mount Zion with 144,000

Revelation 15 | 269

Revelation 16 | 273

Revelation 17 | 281

Revelation 18 | 291

Revelation 19 | 297

Revelation 20 | 311

Revelation 21 | 327

Revelation 22 | 335

Appendix | 343
*Why Historians Date
the Revelation to the
Reign of Domitian*

Introduction

The book of Revelation is undoubtedly the most difficult to understand of all the books in the Bible. While all of the Bible contains multiple levels of truth, in most of it the surface level has meaning in itself, while there is also an underlying, deeper, level of truth. The one that lies on thesurface is almost always instructive in and by itself. But in the Revelation, this surface level often disappears. For the meanings of some of the visions are not explained at all.

For this reason, many imagine the Revelation is impossible to understand, and claim it is not worth studying. But as a guard against that reaction, our God opened this book with a message unlike anything found in any other book in the entire Bible. For, immediately after the title and the statement of the source of this book, we find the words, **"Blessed is he who reads and those who hear the words of this prophecy, and keep those things which are written in it; for the time is near."** (Revelation 1:3) So this is the only book in the entire Bible that contains an explicitly stated blessing to those who read it and hear (that is, give heed to) its message.

Everything our God has bothered to tell us, He has told us for a reason. And no one can dismiss anything He has said without loss to their own souls. And in this case, we are specifically told the reason. As He had said much earlier, **"Surely the Lord GOD does nothing, Unless He reveals His secret to His servants the prophets."** (Amos 3:7) Even so, in the Revelation, its purpose is plainly stated. It was **"to show His servants--things which must shortly take place."** (Revelation 1:1) But who are the ones to whom have been revealed the **"things which must shortly take place"**? **"His servants."**

When our Lord was here in bodily form, **"the disciples came and said to Him, 'Why do You speak to them in parables?' He answered and said to them, 'Because it has been given to you to know the mysteries of the kingdom of heaven, but to them it has not been given.'"** (Matthew 13:10-11) So, although our God has chosen to reveal these things to **"His servants,"** they are *family secrets* of the house of God, and are thus intentionally hidden from those who choose to not believe.

And because these things are intentionally hidden from unbelievers, the ancient scribes who toiled at copying out these words (many of whom were themselves unbelievers) found this the most difficult of all the books of the Bible to copy. Being unable to understand what was said, they often assumed that the words, as they stood on the page they were copying, could not be the actual words given by God. So they "corrected" the text they were copying. Although evil hearts sometimes intentionally changed what had been said by God, most of this, at least in the case of the Revelation, was done in an honest, but misguided, effort to "correct" what seemed to the scribes to be obvious errors that had been made in preparing the source texts from which they were copying. This has led to more differences between the manuscripts of the Revelation than of any other book of the Bible.

Scholars have expended much labor in their attempts to reconstruct the true original text of this book. But most modern scholars have given undue credence to two ancient manuscripts that, although they are thought to be much older than any other surviving Greek manuscripts, are admitted by almost all to contain convincing evidence of having been intentionally made different from the source texts from which they had been copied.

So, in my opinion, the most satisfactory reconstruction of the original text of the Revelation is not a modern one, but one made in the 1800s by William Kelly in his book, "Lectures on the Revelation." (This nineteenth century writer should not be confused with the twentieth century writer by the same name.) This book is available in many larger libraries, and is also available at no cost for online reading or download at: https://www.stempublishing.com. And as a side note, this book is also an excellent refutation of the many errors of Historicism.

The Revelation also differs from other books of the Bible in that it explicitly states its divisions. For toward the end of the first chapter, John was told to **"Write the things which you have seen, and the things which are, and the things which will take place after this."** (Revelation 1:19) What John had "seen" was the vision recorded in the previous ten verses. **"The things which are"** are the letters to the seven churches in chapters 2 and 3, and **"the things which will take place after this"** are the rest of the book, as can be clearly seen in Revelation 4:1, where John was told, **"Come up here, and I will show you things which must take place after this."**

But there is another feature of the book of Revelation that, while not entirely unique to this book, is developed in a unique way. And that is its references to another book of the Bible. That other book is not named, as the scriptures often do when they refer to something previously said by God. But, like the rest of this mysterious book, the references to this other book are hidden in symbolic language.

We are first shown a **"sealed" "scroll,"** and told that no one, other than the **"lamb as though it had been slain,"** was worthy to open its seals. And as we think of this **"sealed" "scroll,"** we remember that there had previously been a prophecy, the book of Daniel, given by the inspiration of God, that had been sealed at His direct command. And who but God himself is worthy to open a seal placed at His own command? So no one but the **"lamb as though it had been slain,"** being God himself, was worthy to open the seals on the book of Daniel.

Then, as each of the **"seven seals"** was opened, there followed a vision whose meaning is still being debated. But no one can doubt that, whatever these visions represent in detail, they unquestionably reveal massive destruction on a scale so far reaching as to at least seem to involve a world wide collapse of the entire existing social order. And this shows how the prophecies in Daniel can still take place, even though the nations of which they speak seem to have disappeared a long time ago. For in recent decades, we have watched as one modern nation after another has collapsed. And each time one of them fell, the old, natural, nations almost immediately reappeared, as if by magic. They had been there all along, right where they had always been. But modern politics had masked both their identities and their borders. So we can easily see how a world wide collapse of the entire social order will make room for the old, natural, order to suddenly rise again in its place.

Then, after the seals had been opened, the prophet, John, was shown **"a little book"** that was now **"open."** And he was told to **"eat"** it. That is, to digest it, to read and study it until he knew it so well it became simply a part of himself. And throughout the rest of the book of Revelation, almost all the symbols are drawn directly from the book of Daniel. And that is why it is my contention that both the **"sealed" "scroll"** and **"the little book"** that was **"open,"** represent the book of Daniel. And that is also why this commentary is titled, **"Revelation and Daniel, Considered Together."** The order of our consideration will be, first, the first ten chapters of the Revelation, up to the point where John was told to **"eat"** the **"little book."** Then we will go back and **"eat" "the little book"** of Daniel, before continuing with the last part of the book of Revelation.

But now we need to ask, if this interpretation is correct, why was the book of Daniel first called **"a scroll,"** and then called **"a book"**? The Hebrew scriptures were written on scrolls. But the gentiles bound their writings into books. As long as the prophecy of Daniel remained sealed, it was a Hebrew document. So it was depicted as a scroll. But once the seals had been opened, all, including gentiles, could understand it, so it was then depicted as a book, rather than as a scroll. All of this, of course, is interpretation. So I cannot positively say that it is correct. But to me, this seems to be what the Holy Spirit is indicating in this symbolism.

Finally, in interpreting these important parts of the word of God, I have applied two rules derived from examining the rest of scripture. Throughout the Bible, from one end to the other, every dream or vision for which we are given an inspired interpretation, had a meaning entirely different from what had been seen. But at the same time, the numbers in the vision were always literal.

A typical illustration of this is the dreams of the butler and baker interpreted by Joseph and then fulfilled in Genesis 40:9-22. In the first dream, the three branches were three days, and in the second dream, the three baskets were three days. And the interpretations of these two dreams, which, although they were entirely different from what had been seen, were fulfilled a literal three days later.

On the other hand, again throughout the Bible without a single exception, explicit statements of coming events for which we have an inspired statement of their fulfillment, were always fulfilled literally, down to the tiniest detail. (Of course, taking into consideration the usage of obvious figures of speech.) A typical example of this is the words **"Even my own familiar friend in whom I trusted, Who ate my bread, Has lifted up his heel against me."** (Psalm 41:9) We all know how this was literally fulfilled in Judas, one of the twelve, who betrayed our Lord. (John 13:18, 18:1-5)

From these two principles, which run without exception throughout all of scripture, I have derived two rules for interpreting Bible prophecy. The first is that prophetic dreams or visions are never images, videos, as it were, of coming events. Instead, they are visual symbols of these events. Thus, the visions in the Revelation are not "a primitive man's attempt to describe modern battle tanks and helicopters," as some have impiously styled them. Instead, they are visual symbols of coming events. And we can find the meanings of these symbols only in the inspired word of God itself.

And the second rule I have derived from these principles is that explicit statements of coming events always mean exactly what they say. And this applies even to explicit statements that are made within a vision. A typical application of this rule is to be found in Revelation 20:7, where we read, **"Now when the thousand years have expired, Satan will be released from his prison."** Although this statement is made within a vision, it is an explicit statement of a coming event, made in plain language. And therefore denying that this will actually happen is nothing short of unbelief.

And I need to point out that this commentary does not have the authority and certainty of my previous book. "Keys to Bible Prophecy," published by Dispensational Publishing House, Taos, NM. (ISBN # 978-1-945774-33-1) This is because everything our God has said is certain and sure. But whenever we interpret what He said, we inject a possibility of error. My previous book was mainly about explicitly stated prophecies made in plain language, and thus contained numerous unequivocal statements about coming events. But this book, since it is about visions that are not accompanied by an inspired interpretation, must, of necessity, involve a considerable amount of interpretation.

And even when we are strongly persuaded that we have interpreted a given passage correctly, we can never be absolutely certain that our interpretation is correct.

This book is sent out for the prayerful consideration of my brethren, and with the prayer that it might be a blessing to their souls.

- James C. Morris

REVELATION 1

"The Revelation of Jesus Christ, which God gave Him to show His servants--things which must shortly take place. And He sent and signified *it* by His angel to His servant John, who bore witness to the word of God, and to the testimony of Jesus Christ, to all things that he saw. Blessed is he who reads and those who hear the words of this prophecy, and keep those things which are written in it; for the time is near." (Revelation 1:1-3)

The first clause here, **"The Revelation of Jesus Christ,"** indicates that this book is about Him. This is again stated near the end of the book, where we read that **"The testimony of Jesus is the spirit of prophecy."** (Revelation 19:10) It has been observed that, if we do not see Jesus in a prophecy, we have missed its very spirit, much less its details. But a further explanation of this opening clause is in the second clause, **"which God gave Him."** So God gave this book to Jesus Christ. But why did God give it to Him? **"To show His servants–things which must shortly take place."**

Many have made bad use of the word **"shortly"** here, insisting that this word should be interpreted in human terms. They insist that it means that the things in this book were to take place within a few years of the time it was given. But this word should be interpreted on a divine time scale, not a human one. For **"with the Lord one day is as a thousand years, and a thousand years as one day."** (2 Peter 3:8)

Some complain that this answer is "unsatisfying." But this is not a human answer. When this statement is examined in its context, its meaning becomes absolutely clear. The Holy Spirit said this in answer to **"scoffers"** who **"will come in the last days, walking according to their own lusts, and saying, 'Where is the promise of His coming? For since the fathers fell asleep, all things continue as they were from the beginning of creation.'"** (2 Peter 3:3-4)

The Holy Spirit's answer was:

> "For this they willfully forget: *that* by the word of God the heavens were of old, and the earth standing out of water and in the water, by *which* the world *that* then existed perished, being flooded with water. But the heavens and the earth *which* are now preserved by the same word, are reserved for fire until the day of judgment and perdition of ungodly men. But, beloved, do not forget this one thing, *that* with the Lord one day *is* as a thousand years, and a thousand years as one day. The Lord is not slack concerning *His* promise, as some count slackness, but is longsuffering toward us, not willing that any should perish but *that* all should come to repentance. But the day of the Lord will come as a thief in the night, in *which* the heavens will pass away with a great noise, and the elements will melt with fervent heat; both the earth and the works that are in it will be burned up." (2 Peter 3:5-10)

Thus we see that the statement **"with the Lord one day is as a thousand years, and a thousand years as one day"** was a *divine* explanation for apparent delay in the fulfillment of prophecy. This is also stated in the Old Testament, where, in speaking of judgment, the Holy Spirit said, **"a thousand years in Your sight Are like yesterday when it is past, And like a watch in the night."** (Psalm 90:4, see verses 3-9) God's answer is that **"The Lord is not slack concerning His promise, as some count slackness, but is longsuffering toward us, not willing that any should perish but that all should come to repentance."** So we see that, as the things in this book must indeed **"shortly come to pass,"** yet, on a *divine* time scale, it has only been a couple of days since God said this.

But now, after the declaration of the subject of this book, and that these things **"must shortly come to pass,"** we are given its pedigree. **"And He sent and signified it by His angel to His servant John, who bore witness to the word of God, and to the testimony of Jesus Christ, to all things that he saw."** So, after God gave this Revelation to Jesus Christ, Jesus sent it **"by His angel to His servant John."** And John **"bore witness to"** it.

And then this opening statement ends with the blessing we noticed in the introduction. **"Blessed is he who reads and those who hear the words of this prophecy, and keep those things which are written in it; for the time is near."** So, as we have noticed, this book contains a special blessing to those who read it, heed it, and keep it. As we noted earlier, this is a caution against those who insist that this book is not profitable. Instead, as we are told in another place, **"And so we have the prophetic word confirmed, which you do well to heed as a light that shines in a dark place, until the day dawns and the morning star rises in your hearts; knowing this first, that no prophecy of Scripture is of any private interpretation, for prophecy never came by the will of man, but holy men of God spoke** *as they were* **moved by the Holy Spirit."** (2 Peter 1:19-21)

So, contrary to the cavils of unbelief, we are explicitly told that we **"do well to heed"** Bible prophecy, and a special blessing is pronounced on those that read, heed, and keep the book of Revelation.

After this opening statement comes John's salutation: **"John, to the seven churches which are in Asia: Grace to you and peace from Him who is and who was and who is to come, and from the seven Spirits who are before His throne, and from Jesus Christ, the faithful witness, the firstborn from the dead, and the ruler over the kings of the earth."** (Revelation 1:4-5a)

This book is actually an epistle, from John to seven specific churches in the Roman province of Asia, which was in the western part of what is now Turkey. Each of these seven churches is individually addressed in the separate messages in chapters 2 and 3. But this epistle was not merely from John. It was also from **"Him who is and who was and who is to come,"** that is, from God Himself. But it was also from **"the seven Spirits who are before His throne."**

What are these **"seven Spirits"**? We are not told. But **"the seven Spirits of God"** are explicitly mentioned in Revelation 3:1, 4:5, and 5:6. And **"four spirits of heaven"** are mentioned in Zechariah 6:5. Although **"four spirits"** plus the trinity make seven, these, like the trinity itself, are mysteries whose meanings are not revealed. And we do well to refrain from delving into things which our God has not revealed, even if He has mentioned them.

Finally, this epistle is also **"from Jesus Christ, the faithful witness, the firstborn from the dead, and the ruler over the kings of the earth."** So this epistle is not only from John, but from the entire Godhead.

This mention of the faithfulness and power of our Lord Jesus causes the Spirit to break out in a wonderful doxology, **"To Him who loved us and washed us from our sins in His own blood, and has made us kings and priests to His God and Father, to Him be glory and dominion forever and ever. Amen."** (Revelation 1:5b-6)

And then we find the wonderful declaration, **"Behold, He is coming with clouds, and every eye will see Him, even they who pierced Him. And all the tribes of the earth will mourn because of Him. Even so, Amen."** (Revelation 1:7)

The same people we have noticed, who make such bad use of the words **"must shortly take place"** in verse 1, make similar bad use of the words **"even they who pierced Him"** in verse 7. They insist that this means that the actual individuals **"who pierced Him"** would see Him when He came **"with clouds."** So they reason that this means that it had to happen within the lifetimes of the individuals **"who pierced Him."** But the error of this claim is obvious when we realize that there can be zero question that not **"every eye"** saw our Lord at any time even close to A.D. 70, when these people insist that the Revelation was fulfilled.

And then we read, **" 'I am the Alpha and the Omega, *the* Beginning and *the* End,' says the Lord, 'who is and who was and who is to come, the Almighty.' "** (Revelation 1:8) This great statement of the identity of the true source of the Revelation closes the opening words of this important book of the Bible.

"I, John, both your brother and companion in the tribulation and kingdom and patience of Jesus Christ, was on the

island that is called Patmos for the word of God and for the testimony of Jesus Christ." (Revelation 1:9)

This fact, that this book was revealed through John, is mentioned three times in this first chapter; in verses 1-2, in verse 4, and again here in verse 9. And in the end of the book, it is mentioned twice more; in chapter 21:2 and 22:8. So our God told us this no less than five times. In addition, the words **"I saw"** are repeated thirty-three times in this book. (Revelation 1:12, 17, 4:4, 5:1, 2, 6:1, 9, 7:1, 2, 8:2, 9:1, 17, 10:1, 5, 13:1, 2, 3,11, 14:6, 15:1, 2, 16:13, 17:3, 6, 18:1, 19:11, 19, 20:1, 4, 11, 12, and 21:1, 22) So the Holy Spirit, who inspired these words, made a great point of the fact that this was revealed through John. But He also explicitly told where John was when this was revealed to him, and why he was there.

John **"was on the island that is called Patmos for the word of God and for the testimony of Jesus Christ."** Why is this important? As is clearly demonstrated in the appendix to this book, there is overwhelming historical evidence that it was the Emperor Domatian who condemned John to Patmos. In actual fact, there are few historical facts more absolutely established than this. For it was clearly stated by multiple writers thought to be from the second through the fourth centuries, including at least three that included details stated by none of the others, proving that none of these had gotten his information only from the others. Two other writers from this period stated details that could be interpreted to mean John was sent to Patmos by an earlier emperor, but that is not a necessary conclusion from what either of them said. One writer from before the fifth century clearly contradicted this. But the thing *that* writer is most famous for is having made *many* historical errors.

And why is the fact that John was condemned to Patmos by Domatian important? Because Domatian did not even come into power until well after Jerusalem had been destroyed. So the fact that John **"was on the island that is called Patmos for the word of God and for the testimony of Jesus Christ"** is proof that the Revelation could not even possibly be a prophecy about the destruction of Jerusalem, as is falsely claimed by some.

> "I was in the Spirit on the Lord's Day, and I heard behind me a loud voice, as of a trumpet, saying, 'I am the Alpha and the Omega, the First and the Last,' and, 'What you see, write in a book and send *it* to the seven churches which are in Asia: to Ephesus, to Smyrna, to Pergamos, to Thyatira, to Sardis, to Philadelphia, and to Laodicea.' "(Revelation 1:10-11)

The detail that John was **"in the Spirit"** shows that these things did not come from his own mind, but that they actually came from the Spirit of God. And this opening vision, at least, was **"on the Lord's Day."**

John suddenly heard, behind himself, **"a loud voice, as of a trumpet."** This voice said two things. First, the speaker identified Himself. **"I am the Alpha and the Omega, the First and the Last."** So these words came directly from the Lord Himself. And then He said, **"What you see, write in a book and send *it* to the seven churches which are in Asia: to Ephesus, to Smyrna, to Pergamos, to Thyatira, to Sardis, to Philadelphia, and to Laodicea."**

Why does this number seven come up so often in scripture? It is found 461 times in the Bible, although 75 of these are parts of the statement of a larger number. So the number seven stands alone 386 times in the Bible, including 53 times in the Revelation. Again, the word "seventh" is found 122 times in the Bible, including 5 times in the Revelation. Many of us have concluded that in the scriptures, the number seven represents perfection. If this is correct, then the seven spirits before the throne and the seven spirits of God would represent the perfection of God, and the seven churches would be a perfect representation of the church.

These seven churches are then expanded upon in the vision seen when the prophet turned to see the voice that spoke to him.

> "Then I turned to see the voice that spoke with me. And having turned I saw seven golden lampstands, and in the midst of the seven lampstands *One* like the Son of Man, clothed with a garment down to the feet and girded about the chest with a golden band. His head and hair *were* white like wool,

as white as snow, and His eyes like a flame of fire; His feet *were* like fine brass, as if refined in a furnace, and His voice as the sound of many waters; He had in His right hand seven stars, out of His mouth went a sharp two-edged sword, and His countenance *was* like the sun shining in its strength." (Revelation 1:12-16)

Here, in **"One like the Son of Man,"** we see the Lord in Judicial robes. That is, He now presents Himself, neither as **"the Lamb of God,"** nor as **"the Lion of the tribe of Judah,"** but as **"the judge of all the earth."** For He was **"clothed with a garment down to the feet and girded about the chest with a golden band."**

As gold seems to be a symbol of Divine righteousness, The **"golden band"** which was **"girded about"** His **"chest,"** that is, around His heart, would speak of divine righteousness restraining His feelings of love for the churches that He is judging. For a judge cannot allow emotions to affect the righteousness of his judgment.

The judicial nature of this representation is further seen in the facts that **"His eyes"** were **"like a flame of fire,"** and

"His feet *were* like fine brass, as if refined in a furnace." "His eyes," that is, His vision, burned through everything, that is, nothing could be hidden from His sight.

And **"fine brass"** seems to represent judicial punishment. We can observe the symbolic difference between brass and gold in the two altars in the tabernacle and later in the temple. The brazen altar was the place where animals were sacrificed, speaking of judgment, while the golden altar was the place where incense was burned, speaking of worship. And the significance of the fact that it was His feet that **"*were* like fine brass"** can be seen in Psalm 91:13 and Malachi 4:3, where we read of the Lord trampling the wicked.

But here, this **"One like the Son of Man"** is not only seen as a judge, but as the Almighty God himself. For he is seen with hair as **"white as snow,"** indicating both His purity and His great age. For we saw this same white hair on **"the Ancient of Days"** in Daniel 7:9. And **"His countenance *was* like the sun shining in its strength."** We remember that our God dwells in **"unapproachable light."** (1 Timothy

6:16) Finally, **"out of His mouth went a sharp two-edged sword."** We remember that the scriptures refer to the word of God as a sword. See, for instance, Ephesians 6:17 and Hebrews 4:12.

But, in the midst of all this awesome glory, significant detail is buried. Not only was He standing **"in the midst of the seven lampstands,"** but also **"He had in His right hand seven stars."** Some imagine that the details of a prophecy are not important. But here the Holy Spirit takes care to make sure we notice these details. For He points them out, saying, **"The mystery of the seven stars which you saw in My right hand, and the seven golden lampstands: The seven stars are the angels of the seven churches, and the seven lampstands which you saw are the seven churches."** (Revelation 1:20)

Here we need to stop and take notice of the Greek word transliterated **"angels."** [1] In modern English, this word has come to mean a spirit sent from heaven. And it is sometimes used this way in the scriptures. But that is not the basic, essential, meaning of this word in the Greek language. For in the Greek, it simply meant a messenger. So, rather than spiritual beings assigned to oversee various churches, the seven messengers mentioned here were the human messengers of the seven churches.

The effect of this awesome vision on the prophet was typical. **"And when I saw Him, I fell at His feet as dead."** (Revelation 1:17a) We see such reactions in Leviticus 9:24, Numbers 22:31, 1 Kings 18:39, 1 Chronicles 21:16, Ezekiel 1:28, 3:23, and 43:3, and Daniel 10:7. But, even as John's reaction was typical, so was the Lord's. **"But He laid His right hand on me, saying to me, 'Do not be afraid.'"** (Revelation 1:17b) This message, **"Do not be afraid,"** was also given in Daniel 10:12, Luke 1:13, 1:30, and 2:10.

But then, the speaker says, **"I am the First and the Last. I *am* He who lives, and was dead, and behold, I am alive forevermore. Amen. And I have the keys of Hades and of Death.'"** (Revelation 1:17c-18) So this was unquestionably a vision of our Lord Jesus himself, judging in the midst of the seven churches, and holding their respective messengers in His right hand.

---

1 This Greek word is αγγελοι, a plural of αγγελος, aggelos in our alphabet, word number 32 in Strong's Greek Dictionary.

And then John was given the command we noticed in the introduction. **"Write the things which you have seen, and the things which are, and the things which will take place after this."** (Revelation 1:19) John was to write the vision we have just been examining. But then he was to write two more things. He was also to write **"the things which are, and the things which will take place after this."** These are the three divisions of the book of Revelation, as is made clear by the opening words of chapter 4. **"After these things I looked, and behold, a door *standing* open in heaven. And the first voice which I heard *was* like a trumpet speaking with me, saying, 'Come up here, and I will show you things which must take place after this.'"** (Revelation 4:1)

The Greek words translated **"take place after this"** in these two passages (Revelation 1:19 and Revelation 4:1) are identical. And the Greek word translated **"this"** [2] in each of these passages is plural. So in both places it should have been translated **"these,"** rather than **"this."** And the meaning would be much clearer if the word **"*things*"** were added in each case, making it read, **"the things which will take place after these *things*."** (With the word **"*things*"** being in italics to show that it had been added to complete the sense.)

So in Revelation 1:19, John was actually told to **"Write the things which you have seen, and the things which are, and the things which will take place after these *things*."** And in Revelation 4:1, John was actually told, **"Come up here, and I will show you things which must take place after these *things*."**

So the part of the Revelation beginning with chapter 4 is not the **"things which must take place"** after the time at which the Revelation was given, but **"the things which must take place"** after **"the things which are,"** which are the things contained in chapters 2 and 3.

---

2   This Greek word is ταυτα, *tauta* in our alphabet, word number 5023 in Strong's Greek Dictionary. This Greek word is the dative plural neuter form of the Greek word ουτος, *houtos* in our alphabet, word number 3778 in Strong's Greek Dictionary, which means *this*.

 # REVELATION 2 AND 3

The letters to the Seven Churches

In Revelation two and three, the Holy Spirit addressed seven letters to seven churches in the Roman province of Asia. There can be no question that all of these were actual churches that existed at that time. But why were these particular churches addressed? Why, for instance, did these letters include neither Jerusalem, the early center of Christianity, nor Rome, the largest city in the world? And why were only seven churches addressed? There seems to be something more involved here than just seven letters to seven particular churches.

We remember that in the historical books of the Bible, vast spans of time are often passed over in just a few verses, while the stories of certain individuals fill many chapters. So the point of these divinely inspired records is not just to satisfy the curiosity of the readers. Rather, certain stories were selected for inclusion, while most others were left out. We are not left to our own imaginations as to why this was done. For we are explicitly told that **"whatever things were written before were written for our learning, that we through the patience and comfort of the Scriptures might have hope."** (Romans 15:4) Even so, the letters to the seven churches must have a far greater significance than simply letters to a few specific churches that existed thousands of years ago. But what is that significance?

We find our first hint about this in two statements from the first chapter. In verse 1 we read, **"The Revelation of Jesus Christ, which God gave Him to show His servants – things which must shortly take place."**

And then in verse 19 we read, **"Write the things which you have seen, and the things which are, and the things which will take place after this."**

So the book itself is about **"things which must shortly take place."** And, as we have noticed, it is in three divisions. The first division was the things which John had just seen, that is, the vision of Jesus, seen as a judge in the midst of seven churches. The second division was **"the things which are."** And the third division was **"the things which will take place after this."** Then, immediately after the end of the seven letters, the next thing we read is **"After these things I looked, and behold, a door *standing* open in heaven. And the first voice which I heard *was* like a trumpet speaking with me, saying, 'Come up here, and I will show you things which must take place after this.'"** (Revelation 4:1)

I have no explanation for why the translators of the NKJV, which we are using, rendered the last word in both Revelation 1:19 and Revelation 4:1 as **"this."** For, as we have noticed, the Greek word translated **"this"** in both of these places is plainly plural, so in English, both of these places should read, **"take place after these *things*,"** not **"take place after this,"** as the NKJV renders them. I have repeated this here to stress the importance of this point. For it is critical to understanding the book of Revelation.

So in the first place, the entire book is about **"things which must shortly take place,"** and the third division is about **"things which will take place after these *things*."** That is, **"things which will take place after" "the things which are."**

This is the first distinct hint in the text of the Revelation, that the seven letters represent something more than just individual messages to seven local churches that existed thousands of years ago.

This rendering of the Greek word ταυτα as **"this,"** rather than **"these *things*,"** is an unfortunate error which occurs in several translations. For it masks what the Holy Spirit actually said in these two passages. From chapter 4 onward, the Revelation is about things that were to take place after what was revealed in chapters 2 and 3. But the things presented after chapter 3 have still not all happened, even to this day. So Revelation 1:19 and 4:1 together form a distinct hint that these seven letters speak of the period from when the Revelation was given until a time that has not yet arrived.

The next hint of this we will notice is in verse 19 of chapter 2, where we read, concerning the church of Thyatira, **"I know your works, love, service, faith, and your patience; and as for your works, the last are more than the first."** Here we see a time progression clearly implied. For the last works are said to be more than the first works.

So we have two distinctly stated hints that these letters speak of a period of time. But then, in this same series, we have three more, not mere hints, but distinct statements of, a passing of time.

The first of these is in verse 4 of chapter 2, where the church of Ephesus was told that **"you have left your first love."** Then, in verse 10 of the same chapter, the church in Smyrna was told that **"you will have tribulation ten days."** Then, in verse 19 of the same chapter, the church in Thyatira was told, **"I gave her time to repent of her sexual immorality, and she did not repent."** (Revelation 2:21) In these three places a passing of time is not just hinted at, but is distinctly stated. So we have a total of five statements indicating that these letters speak of a passage of time.

There are also other hints that are not stated, as such, but are just as real. One of these is the manifest progression of evil in the sequence of these letters. This clearly, even though not directly, indicates a time sequence. For, contrary to what some imagine, the scriptures very clearly teach that the church will progressively grow more evil. We read, for instance, **"For I know this, that after my departure savage wolves will come in among you, not sparing the flock. Also from among yourselves men will rise up, speaking perverse things, to draw away the disciples after themselves."** (Acts 20:29-30) We also read, **"But know this, that in the last days perilous times will come: For men will be lovers of themselves, lovers of money, boasters, proud, blasphemers, disobedient to parents, unthankful, unholy, unloving, unforgiving, slanderers, without self-control, brutal, despisers of good, traitors, headstrong, haughty, lovers of pleasure** rather than lovers of God, having a form of godliness but denying its power." (2 Timothy 3:1-5a) This warning led to a crescendo eight verses later, where the Holy Spirit declared that **"evil men and impostors will grow worse and worse, deceiving and being deceived."** (2 Timothy 3:13) And finally, our Lord himself asked the rhetorical question, **"when the Son of Man comes, will He really find faith on the earth?"** (Luke 18:8) So the scriptures plainly teach us to expect the evil in the church to become worse and worse, until, when the Lord finally arrives, He will not even find faith in the earth.

Thus, the general progression of evil in these letters is indeed an indication that they represent a passage of time. There were two exceptions to this general progression of evil, one near the beginning and one near the end. But we will deal with these exceptions later.

In the first letter, the only complaint made by the Lord was **"that you have left your first love."** (Revelation 2:4) In the third letter the complaint was that they were tolerating those who held wicked doctrines in their midst. (verse 15) The first group, **"the church of Ephesus,"** hated **"the deeds of the Nicolaitans,"** (verse 6) and in the third group, **"the church in Pergamos,"** there were some that held their evil doctrine. (verse 14) But the fourth group, **"the church in Thyatira,"** not only tolerated those that held these wicked doctrines, they were allowing such persons to teach. (verse 20) Scripture does not tell us what the wicked deeds and doctrines of these **"Nicolaitans"** were. These were clearly stated by various ancient Christian writers. But we will not go into what these writers said, as this is not the point of these letters.

The decline then accelerates in the fifth group, **"the church in Sardis,"** where the Holy Spirit declares, **"you have a name that you are alive, but you are dead."** (Revelation 3:1) And it is finally complete in the last group, **"the church of the Laodiceans,"** Where the Lord is on the outside, knocking on the door. (verse 20) He tells them **"you are neither cold nor hot. I could wish you were cold or hot. So then, because you are lukewarm, and neither cold nor hot, I will vomit you out of My mouth."** (verses 15-16)

Thus we see a gradual progression from everything still being outwardly right, but having lost their first love, to everything being so wrong that the Lord himself is on the outside, not even in the church.

Indeed, the last church is not even called the church of, or in, the city being addressed, but instead of this terminology, which was used for all the other churches in this series, the last one is only called **"the church of the Laodiceans."** (Revelation 3:14) In other words, the Lord was denying that this last church was even his own. He only called it their church, not his church.

Other hints about this time sequence are to be found in a comparison of the details in these seven letters. There are two systematic differences in these seven letters. The most noticeable of these is that the first three letters speak of their times ending, while the later four ones speak distinctly of them still being present at the time of the Lord's coming. We will examine this point in greater detail below.

And finally, there is a systematic difference in the promises to the overcomers in these seven churches. In each of the first three, the promise comes before the words, **"He who has an ear, let him hear what the Spirit says to the churches,"** which are said to all seven. (See chapter 2, verses 7, 11, and 17.) But in each of the last four, the promise comes after these words. (See chapter 2, verses 26-28 and chapter 3, verses 5, 12, and 21.) It has been pointed out that this seems to indicate that in the first three, all are called to heed the exhortation to hear, while in the last four, the overall body is ignored, and this exhortation is only addressed to the overcomers.

So we see that there are a total of six distinct hints, buried within the very wording of the text of these seven letters, that they speak of the whole time between when the Revelation was given and when the Lord will return.

Now this is only interpretation. And *all* interpretations of scripture are subject to error. So we cannot positively insist that "this is what the Bible teaches." But These details most certainly *seem* to indicate that these letters at least speak in some general way of the entire span of time from when the Revelation was given until the time when our Lord will return.

But in addition to these distinctly stated hints in the text of scripture itself, we find a remarkable parallel between the details found in these letters and the historical records of the church.

In verse 5 of chapter 2, the church of Ephesus was told that unless they repented, the Lord would **"come to you quickly and remove your lampstand from its place."** This has indeed happened, as what was once the thriving city of Ephesus has shrunk to a mere village. And that village is now 100% Muslim. There is no longer even one person in Ephesus that even pretends to be a Christian. The candlestick has been removed out of its place. For the glorious light of the gospel of Christ no longer has even a glimmer or a glow in Ephesus.

Again, in verse 10 of chapter 2, the church in Smyrna was told **"you will have tribulation ten days."** And indeed, after its post apostolic state, the church passed through ten periods of persecution. The first of these was under the Roman emperor Nero, beginning around A.D. 67. This was followed by ones under the Roman emperors Domitian, Trajan, Marcus Aurelius Antoninus, Severus, Maximus, Decius, Valerian, Aurelian, and finally Diocletian, ending around A.D. 303.

Some might complain that it does not say ten periods, but ten days. But the word **"day"** is often used in the scriptures to represent a general period of time. We find this, for instance, in the Old Testament in Isaiah 19:18-25, in which a future period of time is called **"that day"** no less than five times. Likewise, in the New Testament, in Luke 6:23 a generic time of persecution is called **"that day,"** and in John 16:23 the future in general is called **"that day."** And finally, the time during which it is possible to be saved is called a **"day"** in 2 Corinthians 6:2, saying, **"Behold, now *is* the accepted time, now *is* the day of salvation."**

But then, in verse 13 of chapter 2, **"the church in Pergamos"** was told, **"I know your works, and where you dwell, where Satan's throne is."** After the final persecution under Diocletian, in A.D. 311 an Edict of Toleration was issued by the Roman Tetrarchy of Galerius, Constantine and Licinius, this was followed about two years later by the Edict of Milan, issued by the Emperors Constantine and Licinius, and a third edict almost fifty years later, issued by Julian the Apostate. The net effect of these three edicts was that Christianity became officially recognized as legal, allowing the church to settle down in the world.

Forgetting that **"our citizenship is in heaven,"** (Philippians 3:20) the church settled down in the world, dwelling **"where Satan's throne is."** But now, being comfortable, they became careless. Writers that had earlier been condemned as heretics began to be studied. And their evil doctrines began to be taught in the very bosom of the church itself. Even the idolatry and sexual immorality of the Nicolaitans become tolerated. And this church was called to **"repent,"** or the Lord Himself would come, and fight against them with the sword of His mouth. And indeed, in time this wickedness was exposed by the preaching of the true word of God.

But then the basic message to the various churches changes. In verses 22 to 25 of chapter 2, Jezebel and her adulterous lovers are told they will be **"cast" "into great tribulation"** unless they repent, but the faithful of Thyatira are told to **"hold fast what you have till I come."** Then, in chapter 3, in verse 3 the church in Sardis was told that unless they repented and watched, **"I will come upon you as a thief, and you will not know what hour I will come upon you."** and in verse 10 the church in Philadelphia was told, **"I also will keep you from the hour of trial which shall come upon the whole world, to test those who dwell on the earth."** the Greek word here translated "from" is *ek*, which literally means "from," but in the sense of "out of." And in verse 16 of chapter 3, the last church, **"the church of the Laodiceans,"** which is a church in name only, is warned that **"I will vomit you out of my mouth."** So we see that in these details, the Holy Spirit was indicating that the first three churches would come to an end, but the next four would continue until He comes.

All this is very convincing evidence that chapters 2 and 3 of the Revelation present the Christian era, and from chapter 4 onward, we find what will come after the end of that era.

But now, examining these seven letters in greater detail, we find that in the immediate post-Apostolic era, all seemed to be going on well in the church as a whole. But it is very revealing to compare the praise received by **"the church of Ephesus,"** saying, **"I know your works, your labor, your patience,"** (Revelation 2:2a) with the praise the same Holy Spirit gave a church during an earlier time, the Apostolic era. Earlier, He had commended the Thessalonians for **"your work of faith, labor of love, and patience of hope."** (1 Thessalonians 1:3) But here, He only speaks of **"your works, your labor, your patience."** (Revelation 2:2a) They still worked. But it was no longer a **"work of faith."** they still labored, but it was no longer a **"labor of**

love." and they still had **"patience"**, but it was no longer a **"patience of hope."** But what was the *basic* problem? **"I have this against you, that you have left your first love."** (Revelation 2:4) This is like the complaint in the old song by Frank Sinatra, "You never seem to want my romancing. The only time you hold me is when we're dancing." Everything in **"the church of Ephesus"** was still outwardly right and proper. But God, who knows all, knew that they no longer loved him with the fervor that had once burned in their hearts. **"The cares of this world, and the deceitfulness of riches"** was choking the word in their hearts. (Matthew 13:22, Mark 4:19, see also Luke 8:14) And this grieved their Savior, who had shed his blood for them.

But even though they had left their first love, we still read, that **"you cannot bear those who are evil. And you have tested those who say they are apostles and are not, and have found them liars; and you have persevered and have patience, and have labored for My name's sake and have not become weary."** (Revelation 2:2b-3) And even **"But this you have, that you hate the deeds of the Nicolaitans, which I also hate."** (Revelation 2:6)

What a warning this should be to all of us. Everything can indeed be outwardly exactly as it ought to be. We can still be faithful, and even reliable. But if the love in our hearts has become dim we will still disappoint our Lord, who loves us so much that He died for us. And how many of us can truthfully say that the love in our hearts has not become dim, that we still love Him with the fervor of our first love? Almost none of us, including myself. So this exhortation is to myself, as much as to anyone else.

We need to remember who this is that is so speaking. **"These things says He who holds the seven stars in His right hand, who walks in the midst of the seven golden lampstands:"** (Revelation 2:1) Our Lord loves us more than His own life, and stands in our midst, holding us in His hand.

Yet, even as He holds us in His holy right hand, He stands in our midst as a judge. And a judge must judge righteously. So He gives this church, where everything was outwardly right and proper, a warning. **"Remember therefore from where you have fallen; repent and do the first works, or else I will come to you quickly and remove your lampstand from its place--unless you repent."** (Revelation 2:5) And as we noted previously, this church did not repent. And its **"lampstand"** has been removed **"from its place."** For today, not even one person in **"Ephesus"** even pretends to be a Christian. It is 100% Muslim.

And this letter ends with a charge and a promise. **"He who has an ear, let him hear what the Spirit says to the churches. To him who overcomes I will give to eat from the tree of life, which is in the midst of the Paradise of God."** (Revelation 2:7) Although the order in which this charge and promise are given is reversed midway in the series, and although the specific promise to the overcomers in each church is different, yet both this charge and this promise are contained in every one of the seven letters. They are all called to hear, that is, heed, **"what the Spirit says to the churches."** But the individual promises given vary with the individual circumstances. And those who overcome in conditions where everything is outwardly right and proper, yet having lost their first love, are promised to be allowed **"to eat from the tree of life, which is in the midst of the Paradise of God."**

But soon widespread persecution arose. There had always been persecutions. But they had mostly been local. But now wave after wave of worldwide persecution against the church rose from the great Roman Empire itself. As we have noted, history tells us that there were a total of ten successive persecutions launched by various Roman Emperors. So **"the church in Smyrna"** was told **"you will have tribulation ten days."** (Revelation 2:10) we have noticed that in the scriptures, the word **"day"** is often used to represent an undefined period of time, as in the oft repeated expression, **"the last days,"** or the Holy Spirit's words, **"now is he day of salvation."** (2 Corinthians 6:2) We should also note here that, as this church was suffering, our Lord had nothing but comfort and encouragement for them.

This does not mean that there was nothing wrong with this church, but only demonstrates our Savior's compassion. When his own are suffering, He does not correct or rebuke them, but only comforts and encourages them.

This church, which was about to enter a period of intense persecution, is neither taught anything nor corrected about anything. Instead, the Lord refers to Himself only as **"the First and the Last, who was dead, and came to life."** (Revelation 2:8) and then He says, **"I know your works, tribulation, and poverty (but you are rich); and I** *know* the blasphemy of those who say they are Jews and *are* not, but are a synagogue of Satan. Do not fear any of those things which you are about to suffer. Indeed, the devil is about to throw *some* of you into prison, that you may be tested..." (Revelation 2:9-10a)

And then come the words we have already noticed, **"and you will have tribulation ten days. Be faithful until death, and I will give you the crown of life."** (Revelation 2:10b) So these suffering saints are given nothing but encouragement. And their letter ends with the same charge and praise given to all the others. **"He who has an ear, let him hear what the Spirit says to the churches. He who overcomes shall not be hurt by the second death."** (Revelation 2:11) And we again see the design of the specific promise to the specific needs of the individuals to whom it was directed. For those saints who were facing physical death were promised that they would not be **"hurt by the second death."**

But sadly, as we have noted, when the persecutions finally ended the church settled down in the world. For it had become comfortable to be a Christian. This is treated in the third of these seven letters, the one to **"the church in Pergamos."** They were told that **"you dwell, where Satan's throne *is*."** This concept of "dwelling" in the Revelation does not simply imply their address, as it were, but the place where their hearts were occupied. We are told of **"those who dwell on the earth"** in Revelation 3:10, 11:10, 13:8, 13:12, 13:14 (twice) 14:6 and 17:8," and always in the light of people who will receive the judgment of God. So their dwelling **"where Satan's throne *is*"** was neither a commendation nor an encouragement, but a criticism.

To this church, the Lord refers to Himself as **"He who has the sharp two-edged sword."** (Revelation 2:12) We remember that **"the word of God is living and powerful, and sharper than any two-edged sword, piercing even to the division of soul and spirit, and of joints and marrow, and is a discerner of the thoughts and intents of the heart."** (Hebrews 4:12) So in referring to Himself as having **"the sharp two-edged sword,"**our Lord was saying that He can discern the deepest secrets of our hearts. These saints, for they were indeed the Lord's own, and not just false pretenders, Were still going on in a way that was outwardly proper. But the decline, which had previously been only that **"you have left your first love,"** had now become **"you dwell,** where Satan's throne *is.*" That is, their hearts were no longer just not fixed on their Lord, who loved them so much He had died for them, but had now become fixed on the world, the place of His enemies.

And which of us would dare to deny that this has become our own sad state? While we all profess our allegiance to the Lord alone, yet in the depths of our hearts, we know that, at least to a large degree, we are actually fixated on this present world. And that nothing will excite us quite as much as any threat to our present comfort and security. In saying this, I am accusing myself, just as much as anyone else.

But there was also a second problem in this church. They not only dwelling **"where Satan's throne *is,*"** but they were tolerating teachers of wicked doctrine in their very midst. For **"you have there those who hold the doctrine of Balaam, who taught Balak to put a stumbling block before the children of Israel, to eat things sacrificed to idols, and to commit sexual immorality."** (verse 14) and, **"you also have those who hold the doctrine of the Nicolaitans, which thing I hate."** (verse 15) And, as we have noted, this is exactly what happened in the church when the persecutions finally ended. The wicked teachers who had previously been cast out, became tolerated in her very bosom. Teachers who had previously been condemned as heretics began to be studied, and their evil opinions began to be openly taught in the church.

This had disastrous results, which we find discussed at length in the fourth letter, the one to **"the church in Thyatira."** And in addressing this church, the Lord styled himself as **"the Son of God, who has eyes like a flame of fire, and His feet like fine brass."** (Revelation 2:18) We will notice the significance of His referring to himself as **"the Son of God"** later. But His **"eyes like a flame of fire"** and His **"feet like fine brass"** indicate that He is acting as a judge.

And the Lord says of this church, **"I know your works, love, service, faith, and your patience; and *as* for your works, the last *are* more than the first."** (Revelation 2:19)

Here the Lord, the righteous judge, commends this church for its **"works, love, service, faith, and your patience."** But then we find a curious statement. **"And *as* for your works, the last *are* more than the first."** This church, which had from the beginning been zealous for good works, instead of becoming less zealous for works, became more so. And indeed, to this day, the church that rose up after the time of Constantine claims that works are necessary for salvation

But the Lord had **"a few things against"** this church. For the wicked teachers that had been tolerated in the last church had now become not only tolerated, but were being allowed to openly teach their wicked doctrines. And this is the first time in this series of letters that we have a long period of time explicitly mentioned. For the Lord said **"I gave her time to repent of her sexual immorality, and she did not repent."** We should note here that the Greek phrase here translated **"did not repent"** translates literally as "not desire to repent." [3] That is, her condemnation was not only that she had failed to repent. but that she had no desire to repent, no intention of repenting. And that is why the Lord says, **"Indeed I will cast her into a sickbed, and those who commit adultery with her into great tribulation, unless they repent of their deeds."** (Revelation 2:22)

In the Greek text, the words here translated **"great tribulation"** are identical to those translated the same way in Matthew 24:21 and similar to those used in Revelation 7:14, except that in Revelation 7 the words are specific, **"the great tribulation."**

All these scriptures are about a future time that has come to be called by the generic name,"the tribulation." This is the last week of Daniel's famous prophecy of seventy weeks. (Daniel 9:24-27) So **"that woman Jezebel, who calls herself a prophetess,"** whom this church has allowed **"to teach, and to seduce"** the Lord's **"servants to commit sexual immorality and to eat things sacrificed to idols,"** rather than being punished in the way earlier churches had been punished, will be cast into the **"great tribulation."** The church that rose up after the time of Constantine has, sadly, become famous for its sexual immorality, and to this day, it still teaches people to worship idols.

But casting her into **"great tribulation"** is not the end of her punishment. For the Lord continues, **"I will kill her children with death, and all the churches shall know that I am He who searches**

---

[3] The actual Greek words used here are "ου θελει μετανοησι," "ou thelei metanonsi" in our alphabet. These words translate literally as "ου = not," "θελει = desire," "μετανοησι = to repent."

the minds and hearts. And I will give to each one of you according to your works." (Revelation 2:23)

But now, even as Thyatira is the first church said to continue to the end times, she is also the first in which a righteous remnant is recognized. For we read: **"Now to you I say, and to the rest in Thyatira, as many as do not have this doctrine, who have not known the depths of Satan, as they say, I will put on you no other burden. But hold fast what you have till I come."** (Revelation 2:24-25)

Here again, as in so many other places in scripture, we see the Lord's compassion for the weak and oppressed among His people. For upon the few that remain faithful to Himself in the midst of this wicked system, He lays **"no other burden. But hold fast what you have."** And how long are they to hold it fast? **"Till I come."** This is another reference to the fact that this church will continue all the way down to the time of the Lord's coming.

And even as the few righteous individuals in the midst of a wicked system are always oppressed, the promise to the overcomers in this church is uniquely designed to comfort the oppressed. For the Lord says, **"And he who overcomes, and keeps My works until the end, to him I will give power over the nations-- 'He shall rule them with a rod of iron; They shall be dashed to pieces like the potter's vessels'-- as I also have received from My Father; and I will give him the morning star."** (Revelation 2:26-28)

Even as those who had faced death for the name of Christ had been promised that they would **"not be hurt by the second death,"** (Revelation 2:11) so these, who have felt the stinging power of the nations that backed their oppressors, are promised to be given **"power over the nations."** But then, they are given a promise far more precious to those who understand it. **"I will give him the morning star."** for we read in Revelation 22:16, **"I, Jesus, have sent My angel to testify to you these things in the churches. I am the Root and the Offspring of David, the Bright and Morning Star."** So in promising to give them **"the morning star,"** our Lord was promising to give Himself to them. That is, He is promising to make Himself their personal possession.

This is a promise beyond comparison. And it is given to the few overcomers in this wicked system. Even as **"no other burden"** is laid upon them than to **"hold fast what you have till I come,"** those who do so are promised that He will reward them with the gift of Himself.

But now we come to a significant change in the format of these seven letters. As we previously noticed, at this point in this series of letters, the location of the call to hear changes. In the three previous letters, the call to hear comes before the promise to the overcomers. But starting with this letter, this call moves to after this promise.

For it is not until verse 29, after the promise to the overcomers in verses 26 to 28, that we read, **"He who has an ear, let him hear what the Spirit says to the churches."** It has been often noticed that this seems to indicate that, as the progression of evil is presented in this series of letters, from this point forward the outward church is seen as hopelessly evil, so evil that there is no hope for it. For she does "not desire to repent," as the Greek text literally states it. So from this point forward, all the way to the end of this entire series of letters, the call to hear is no longer addressed to the church as a whole, but only to the few overcomers in its midst.

The church that rose up after the time of Constantine was basically the entirety of the visible church for about a thousand years. But finally a new movement swept across the body of those professing the name of Christ. In the early 1500s the true gospel began to be preached again by such spiritual giants as Luther, Zwingli, and Calvin.

But problems quickly arose in this new movement. We find the Lord addressing this church, **"the church in Sardis,"** in language even harsher than He used for Thyatira. He says, **"I know your works, that you have a name that you are alive, but you are dead. Be watchful, and strengthen the things which remain, that are ready to die, for I have not found your works perfect before God."** (Revelation 3:1b-2)

In Thyatira, the church was only allowing wicked people to teach and to seduce others. But here, the church itself was living "in name only." And sadly, the church that rose up after the church of the dark ages, has become, for the most part, almost totally apostate. Most of the "mainstream" Protestant churches have given up even the fundamentals of the Christian faith.

So the Lord says, **"Be watchful, and strengthen the things which remain, that are ready to die, for I have not found your works perfect before God."**

The church of the reformation had gone through much persecution and hardship as the truth of the gospel had been restored. So the Lord says to them, **"Remember therefore how you have received and heard; hold fast and repent."** (Revelation 3:3a) But then He adds, **"Therefore if you will not watch, I will come upon you as a thief, and you will not know what hour I will come upon you."** (Revelation 3:3b)

Even as Thyatira's Jezebel had been threatened with being cast **"into great tribulation,"** Sardis is here threatened with the Lord coming **"upon you as a thief."** We need to remember that when He was here the first time, our Lord compared His future coming to the coming of a thief. (Matthew 24:43, Luke 12:39) So we see that, even as **"the church in Thyatira,"** will continue to the time of the **"great tribulation,"** **"the church in Sardis"** will continue to the time when the Lord comes **"as a thief."**

In addressing this church, the Lord styled Himself as **"He who has the seven Spirits of God and the seven stars."** (Revelation 3:1) This expression **"the seven spirits of God"** is also found in Revelation 4:5 and 5:6. But, like **"the seven spirits which are before His throne"** in Revelation 1:4, it is not explained anywhere in scripture. And it is unwise to express opinions on things which our God has not revealed.

But our Lord not only styled Himself as **"He who has the seven Spirits of God,"** but also as **"He who has"** **"the seven stars."** We remember that we were already told that **"The seven stars are the angels of the seven churches."** (Revelation 1:20) And that He held them **"in His right hand."** In the next sentence we see the care for His own expressed in this symbol. **"You have a few names even in Sardis who have not defiled their garments; and they shall walk with Me in white, for they are worthy."** (Revelation 3:4)

But even these words of care for His own faithful ones include a reference to the decadence of Sardis, the church that had **"a name that you are alive, but you are dead."** So the Lord says that **"even in Sardis"** there were **"a few names"** **"who have not defiled their garments."** Again, we need to notice that this condemnation of Sardis is stronger that our Lord's condemnation of Thyatira, the church that was more openly wicked.

But in these words we again see, as we saw in Thyatira, the recognition of a righteous remnant. God saw these **"few names,"** and promised them that **"they shall walk with Me in white, for they are worthy."**

Then, as we saw in Thyatira, the promise to the overcomer comes after the recognition of a righteous remnant. **"He who overcomes shall be clothed in white garments, and I will not blot out his name from the Book of Life; but I will confess his name before My Father and before His angels."** (Revelation 3:5) These ones, whose names had been disparaged as they walked faithfully in a lifeless church are promised that the Lord Himself will **"confess"** their names **"before My Father and before His angels."**

And again, as was done in the letter to **"the church in Thyatira,"** The call to hear comes after the promise to the overcomers. **"He who has an ear, let him hear what the Spirit says to the churches."** (Revelation 3:6)

The next letter is addressed **"to the angel of the church in Philadelphia."** (Revelation 3:7a) In this letter, our Lord styled Himself as **"He who is holy, He who is true, 'He who has the key of David, He who opens and no one shuts, and shuts and no one opens.'"** (Revelation 3:7b)

So in addressing this church, our Lord stressed His holiness, His truth, and His power. The last part of this statement, ***"He who has the key of David, He who opens and no one shuts, and shuts and no one opens,"*** is a direct reference to Isaiah 22:22, where we read of the great promised Messiah, that, **"The key of the house of David I will lay on his shoulder; So he shall open, and no one shall shut; And he shall shut, and no one shall open."**

> This church is told, **"I know your works. See, I have set before you an open door, and no one can shut it; for you have a little strength, have kept My word, and have not denied My name."** (Revelation 3:8)

There is no article in the Greek text to support the addition of the word **"a"** in the expression **"a little strength."** Although it is not conclusive, due to the fact that in the Greek language an indefinite article is not required, the context of this sentence militates against the addition of an article at this place. The context seems to imply that, if we were to add an English word to complete the sense, a better one would have been the word **"*but.*"** For that seems to be what is being said here. That is, the meaning seems to be that this church is commended for its faithful works, in spite of the fact that it only has **"little strength."** So, as we have already noticed, the Lord only encourages them.

Early in the nineteenth century a new movement arose in the church. There began to be a widespread study of the scriptures themselves, as opposed to concentrating on the teachings of respected leaders. Men such as J. N. Darby, D. L. Moody, and the like, began to point Christians back to the Bible itself as the only source of truth. And individual saints of God were encouraged to study the scriptures for themselves. The result was a virtual explosion of scriptural understanding. A quick check of the literature of one of the smaller of these groups (the Plymouth brethren) shows that, although it was so tiny, in the space of its approximately 90 year heyday, its adherents produced over 500 volumes of Christian ministry. To say nothing of the vast array of ministry still available from such sources as Moody Press and Back to the Bible Ministries. But, compared to professing Christendom as a whole, this movement, though it still exists to ths day, is very small. So it indeed has **"little strength."**

This movement was not only notable for its study of the scriptures, but its faithfulness to their teachings. And the result was that the gospel of the grace of God began to be energetically preached throughout the world. And through their preaching thousands came to know the Lord. And it has remained true, that, even as the Lord promised, **"I have set before you an open door, and no one can shut it,"** the opposition, though sometimes severe, has been unable to shut the door held open by **"He who opens and no one shuts, and shuts and no one opens."**

But immediately after this opening statement, the letter **"to the angel of the church in Philadelphia"** contains a perplexing comment. **"Indeed I will make *those* of the synagogue of Satan, who say** they are Jews and are not, but lie--indeed I will make them come and worship before your feet, and to know that I have loved you." (Revelation 3:9)

This entire series of letters is clearly a prophetic outline of the history of the church, from the post apostolic days until the time of the rapture. So why is this statement included here? For there has been no marked attack from Jews at any time during the existence of this movement. This statement differs from a similar one made **"to the angel of the church in Smyrna"** in that at that time, the opposition came from **"those who say they are Jews and are not."** (Revelation 2:9) But nothing is said about the Jews in Smyrna lying. For while both of these groups of false Jews were **"of the synagogue of Satan,"** the enemies in Smyrna, though not Jews by faith because they did not believe their own scriptures, were not actually lying in saying they were Jews. For they were Jews by blood. But the opposition in Philadelphia were lying when they said they were Jews.

One of the major elements of this revival that began in the early nineteenth century was a widespread return to a simple faith in the absolute reliability of the prophecies in the Bible. This simple faith came to be known as Dispensationalism. And one of the chief elements of Dispensationalism is a simple belief of the many Bible prophecies that explicitly state that the ancient nation of Israel will eventually be brought back to its ancient homeland, and once there, will be blessed by God. The enemies of this truth are often very vicious in their attacks upon those who simply believe these prophecies, often calling them "heretics," and even going so far as to falsely claim that this doctrine came out of Satanism.

These resolute enemies of simply believing the prophetic scriptures often claim that they are the true Jews, by wresting such scriptures as **"For he is not a Jew who *is one* outwardly, nor *is* circumcision that which *is* outward in the flesh; but *he is* a Jew who *is one* inwardly; and circumcision *is that* of the heart, in the Spirit, not in the letter; whose praise *is* not from men but from God."** (Romans 2:28-29)

So these implacable enemies of the truth of God, **"say they are Jews and are not, but lie."** And although modern law will not allow the kind of persecution often experienced by the faithful in earlier times, these fierce enemies of the truth continually oppose both the truth of God and those who teach it in many ways, including the type of false accusations that in other times resulted in the deaths of many servants of God.

And what does our God say about this? **"I will make them come and worship before your feet, and to know that I have loved you."**

As a side note, this revival in the nineteenth century of a simple faith in the prophetic scriptures, along with the accompanying belief in the doctrine of the pre-tribulation rapture of the church, was so remarkable that many simply assumed that they both originated at that time. But this was completely incorrect. For both of these concepts had most certainly been taught long before that time. [4]

One of the main elements of Dispensationalism, as well as one of its elements most viciously attacked, is the doctrine we just noticed, the pre-tribulation rapture of the church. Although this concept did not originate with them, this nineteenth century movement preached this doctrine far and wide. So it is significant that the letter to Philadelphia contains one of the strongest statements of this truth in the entire Bible.

For we read, **"Because you have kept My command to persevere, I also will keep you from the hour of trial which shall come upon the whole world, to test those who dwell on the earth."** (Revelation 3:10)

The Greek word translated *from* in this verse means *from*, but in the sense of *away from* or *out of.* [5] Some imagine that this only

---

[4] This is demonstrated at length in my previous book, "Ancient Dispensational Truth," published by Dispensational Publishing House, ISBN #978-1-945774-29-4, where I proved that most of the main concepts of Dispensationalism were taught in the very oldest surviving Christian writings on Bible prophecy, and continued to be taught at least up to the fifth century. Likewise, William C. Watson, in his book "Dispensationalism Before Darby," published by Lampion Press, ISBN #978-1-942614-03-6, proved that the main concepts of Dispensationalism began again to be taught a very short time after the publication of the King James translation first made Bibles available at a price ordinary people could afford.

[5] This Greek word is εχ, *ek* in our alphabet, (word number 1537 in Strong's Greek Dictionary) which means *from*, in the sense of *out of.*

means *out of* the **"hour of trial"** after having been *in* it. But Thayer's Greek-English Lexicon of the New Testament defines *ek*, as it is used in Revelation 3:10, to mean *"to keep one at a distance from."* Indeed, this is obvious when we consider the word **"keep"** in this phrase. [6] So it is clear that the real meaning of this promise is to be *kept out of* **"the hour of trial."**

To really understand this, we need to consider another promise made concerning a part of the same time period. The Lord said to Israel, **"Ask now, and see, Whether a man is ever in labor with child? So why do I see every man *with* his hands on his loins Like a woman in labor, And all faces turned pale? Alas! For that day is great, So that none is like it; And it *is* the time of Jacob's trouble, But he shall be saved out of it."** (Jeremiah 30:6-7) In this case, the Hebrew word translated *saved* means *saved* in the sense of *succor*. [7] We notice this to clearly understand that this Hebrew word carries an entirely different sense from the Greek word *tereo*, that is, *keep*, used in Revelation 3:10.

In Jeremiah 30:7, the Lord promised to *help* some of His own get *through* a time of trouble designed for themselves. But in Revelation 3:10 He promised to *keep* others of His own *out of* a time of testing designed for others,.

But what is this **"the hour of trial"** that they will be *kept out of*? The Greek word translated *hour* in this passage literally means *hour*, but is often used figuratively for a period of time. [8]

But what **hour** are they promised to be *kept out of*? It is not just some general period of time. It is a specific one. It is **"the hour of trial."** It is specifically called **"the hour,"** for the word **"the"** is in the

---

6   This Greek word is τηρησω, *tereso* in our alphabet. (a future form of τηρηω, *tereo* in our alphabet, (word number 5083 in Strong's Greek Dictionary) which literally means *to guard*, but it is translated *keep* more than two-thirds of the times it occurs in the New Testament.

7   This Hebrew word is a form of ישע, "yasha'" in our alphabet. (word number 3467 in Strong's Hebrew Dictionary) In the KJV, this word is rendered *save* 149 times, *deliver* 13 times, *help* 12 times, and *rescue* once.

8   This Greek word is ωρας, a form of ωρα, *hora* in our alphabet, word number 5610 in Strong's Greek Dictionary.

Greek text. [9] For unlike English, in both Biblical Greek and Hebrew, definite articles are normally used only for stress. If the word "the" is in the original text, it means the thing being referred to is something particular, not just something in general. But what **"hour of trial"** is this specific time that they are they promised to be *kept out of*? It is **"the hour of trial which shall come upon the whole world, to test those who dwell on the earth."**

There is a specific **"hour of trial"** coming **"to test those who dwell on the earth."** When we see the reason this hour is coming we understand the term **"hour of trial."** For the Greek word here translated *to test* literally means exactly as it is translated, **"to test."** [10]

So we see that this scripture explicitly tells us that there is a particular time of testing coming, and that the purpose of that time is **"to test those who dwell on the earth."** Its purpose is not **"to test"** the saints of God, but **"to test"** **"those who dwell on the earth."** This is a moral class, those whose hearts are on the earth, rather than in heaven. This moral class is labeled in these words eight times in the Revelation, [11] and always in a negative light.

But we are also explicitly told *where* this time of testing will come. It **"shall come upon the whole world."** The Greek word translated *whole* in this clause literally means *whole*, or *all*, that is, *complete*. [12] That is, there is no part of the world that will be exempted from this time of testing. So there is coming a specific time of testing, and it is coming **"upon the whole world."**

But the Lord's own are promised that they will be *kept out of* that time of testing. Now if this time is coming upon the whole world, but the Lord's own will be *kept out of* it, they cannot be in the world during that time of testing. So we see that Revelation 3:10

---

9   This Greek word is της, a form of o, *ho* in our alphabet, word number 3588 in Strong's Greek Dictionary.

10   This Greek word is πειρασμου, an infinitive form of πειρασμος, *peirasmos* in our alphabet, word number 3985 in Strong's Greek Dictionary.

11   See Revelation 3:10, 11:10, 13:8, 13:12, 13:14 (twice) 14:6 and 17:8. See them also as **"inhabitants of the earth"** in Revelation 12:12.

12   This Greek word is ολης, a form of ολος, *holos* in our alphabet, word number 3650 in Strong's Greek Dictionary.

shows that the Lord's own will be removed from the earth before this time of testing begins.

We see this again in a passage about Noah and Lot. **"For if God did not spare the angels who sinned, but cast them down to hell and delivered them into chains of darkness, to be reserved for judgment; and did not spare the ancient world, but saved Noah, one of eight people, a preacher of righteousness, bringing in the flood on the world of the ungodly; and turning the cities of Sodom and Gomorrah into ashes, condemned them to destruction, making them an example to those who afterward would live ungodly; and delivered righteous Lot, who was oppressed by the filthy conduct of the wicked (for that righteous man, dwelling among them, tormented his righteous soul from day to day by seeing and hearing their lawless deeds)—*then* the Lord knows how to deliver the godly out of temptations and to reserve the unjust under punishment for the day of judgment."** (2 Peter 2:4-9)

Here the Holy Spirit gives us two specific examples, Noah and Lot, both of whom were physically removed from the scene of judgment before it took place. Then, in the context of these two examples, the He said, **"*then* the Lord knows how to deliver the godly out of temptations and to reserve the unjust under punishment for the day of judgment."** (2 Peter 2:9)

Thus the Holy Spirit showed His intention to **"deliver the godly out of temptations"** by physically removing them from the scene **"of temptations"** before they take place, just as He did for Noah and Lot. [13]

But then the Lord says, **"Behold, I am coming quickly! Hold fast what you have, that no one may take your crown."** (Revelation 3:11) In view of the extreme opposition to the truth of the pre-tribulation rapture, it is highly significant that these words are directed **"to**

---

13   The Greek word here translated *out of* is the same *ek* translated as *from* in Revelation 3:10. Which normally means *from* in the sense of *away from* or *out of*. And the Greek word translated *temptations* is *peirasmou*, the same word that was used in Revelation 3:10. There are no accidents in the precise wprding of scripture. The fact that the Holy Spirit used these same two Greek words in these two parallel passages is highly significant.

the angel of the church in Philadelphia." This church is instructed to **"Hold fast what you have,"** because **"I am coming quickly."**

And the promise to the overcomers in this church is uniqualy precious to those who have long felt despised because they are "outside" of the mainstream. **"He who overcomes, I will make him a pillar in the temple of My God, and he shall go out no more. And I will write on him the name of My God and the name of the city of My God, the New Jerusalem, which comes down out of heaven from My God. And *I will write on him* My new name."** (Revelation 3:12) First, after having been cast out as evil, and driven from place to place, they are promised a permanent place in the very temple of the God they love. Then they are promised to be recognized by their God, by having His own name placed upon them, along with the name of His city.

And finally, after the promise to the overcomers, we again find the call, **"He who has an ear, let him hear what the Spirit says to the churches."** (Revelation 3:13)

But, although its seeds had been sown in the nineteenth century, in the twentieth century a horrible movement, which came to be called "modernism," swept over the church. In this movement, the professing church gave up all pretense of continuing to believe the scriptures. Most of the Bible came to be considered a collection of ancient myths, and men began to pick and choose which parts they considered still applicable in "these modern times." This final form of the church is addressed in the letter **"to the angel of the church of the Laodiceans."** We have already noticed that all the other churches were mentioned as either **"in"** or **"of"** a city. But this one is mentioned as **"of"** *the people* of a city. It seems that in so referring to this church, our Lord was denying that it was His church at all. It was only their church.

To this church, our Lord styled Himself as **"the Amen, the Faithful and True Witness, the Beginning of the creation of God."** (Revelation 3:14) As these people were unfaithful He points out that He is faithful. And as they have chosen to deny creation, He calls Himself **"the beginning of the creation of God."**

This it the only church in the entire series about which the Lord says nothing good at all. There is not even a righteous remnant recognized. Instead, there is only unsparing condemnation. Our Lord first says, **"I know your works, that you are neither cold nor hot. I could wish you were cold or hot. So then, because you are lukewarm, and neither cold nor hot, I will vomit you out of My mouth."** (Revelation 3:15-16) Cold drinks are refreshing. And hot drinks are good. But lukewarm drinks are disgusting. The Lord uses this comparison to express His disgust at the fact that these people simply do not care. They consider themselves to be neither His friends nor His enemies. They simply do not care about Him. And Our Lord finds this disgusting. So he says it will make Him vomit.

The one attitude that marks this movement above all others, is its sense of self-sufficiency. They see themselves as so wise and so wealthy, that they already have everything they need. So the Lord says to them. **"Because you say, 'I am rich, have become wealthy, and have need of nothing' --and do not know that you are wretched, miserable, poor, blind, and naked--I counsel you to buy from Me gold refined in the fire, that you may be rich; and white garments, that you may be clothed,** *that* **the shame of your nakedness may not be revealed; and anoint your eyes with eye salve, that you may see."** (Revelation 3:17-18)

While these fools see themselves **"rich," "wealthy,"** and in **"need of nothing,"** the Lord sees them as they actually are, **"wretched, miserable, poor, blind, and naked."** That is, that their wealth is nothing but the fleeting wealth of this world. And their wisdom is actually foolishness. So in regard to the riches that last, they have nothing, they see (understand) nothing, and they have no covering for their sins.

But, even as we are told that **"God so loved the world that He gave His only begotten Son, that whoever believes in Him should not perish but have everlasting life."** (John 3:16) Our God loves even these. So He says, **"As many as I love, I rebuke and chasten. Therefore be zealous and repent."** (Revelation 3:19)

But then comes an astounding statement. Rather than being in this church, our Lord is on the outside, knocking at the door. For He says. **"Behold, I stand at the door and knock. If anyone hears My voice and opens the door, I will come in to him and dine with him, and he with Me."** (Revelation 3:20) The Lord does not even call the group as a whole. He is calling individuals, **"anyone,"** to **"hear** his voice," and "open the door." And for "anyone" who does this, He promises to "come in to him and dine with him, and he with Me."

Those few among them who so open the door to the Lord's knocking become overcomers, so He says, **"To him who overcomes I will grant to sit with Me on My throne, as I also overcame and sat down with My Father on His throne."** (Revelation 3:21) And this is followed by the exhortation given to all, **"He who has an ear, let him hear what the Spirit says to the churches."** (Revelation 3:22)

We have examined these two chapters together, and taken all this time, to see that, while these seven churches did indeed exist at the time the Revelation was given, and these seven letters indeed applied directly to each of these seven churches, still, the basic purpose and intent of these letters goes far beyond being only specific letters to specific churches. To see that they do indeed constitute a hidden prophecy of the entire history of the church, from the post Apostolic days until the Lord's coming.

But this brings up a different question. If God indeed here intended this section as a prophesy of the entire history of the church, why did He hide it? Why did He not just state it in plain words, like so many other prophesies in the Bible?

When we consider this question, the answer becomes obvious. And it lies in a doctrine we call "imminence." The saints of God are plainly taught to expect the Lord's coming at any moment. We find this in many passages, such as:

> **"Let your waist be girded and *your* lamps burning; and you yourselves be like men who wait for their master, when he will return from the wedding, that when he comes and knocks they may open to him immediately. Blessed *are* those servants whom the master, when he comes, will find watching. Assuredly, I say to you that he will gird himself and have them sit down *to eat*, and will come and serve them. And if he should come in the second watch, or come in the third watch, and find *them* so, blessed are those servants." (Luke 12:35-38)**

But our God also wanted us to understand that the things that have happened to us have not "just happened," that they were all parts of His design since the very beginning. Even as He had said so much earlier:

"I have declared the former things from the beginning; They went forth from My mouth, and I caused them to hear it. Suddenly I did *them,* **and they came to pass. Because I knew that you** *were* **obstinate, And your neck** *was* **an iron sinew, And your brow bronze, Even from the beginning I have declared** *it* **to you; Before it came to pass I proclaimed** *it* **to you, Lest you should say, 'My idol has done them, And my carved image and my molded image Have commanded them.' "** (Isaiah 48:3-5)

If our God had simply stated, here is what will happen during the thousands of years that will pass before I return, this would have destroyed the concept of imminence, which is so clearly taught in the scripture we noticed, as well as many others. We indeed are instructed, and clearly instructed, to watch continually, for He might return at any time. And if our God had made this prophecy in plain words, the saints through the ages would have known that it would be a long time before He returned. So He disguised this prophecy in a way that kept it from being understood until the beginning stirrings of the Laodecian age of lukewarmness. For, although that movement became prevalent in the twentieth century, its seeds were sown in the nineteenth century. And there does not appear to be any record of anyone having ever noticed the prophetic character of these seven letters before that time.

REVELATION 4

As we have already noticed, this chapter opens with the words, **"After these things I looked, and behold, a door *standing* open in heaven. And the first voice which I heard *was* like a trumpet speaking with me, saying, 'Come up here, and I will show you things which must take place after this.' "** (Revelation 4:1)

We need to notice several details about this sentence. First, the word **"*was*"** is set in italics, because it is not found in the Greek text. The translators added this word because they assumed that the prophet was saying that, after seeing the **"door *standing* open in heaven,"** the first thing he heard was a **"voice"** which was **"like a trumpet."** But when we compare this statement with Revelation 1:10, we see that this was an error. The Holy Spirit was not telling us that the first thing that John heard was a **"voice"** which was **"like a trumpet,"** But that when John saw the **"door *standing* open in heaven,"** he **"heard" "the first voice,"** that is, the **"voice"** he had previously heard, the one that had been **"like a trumpet."** For the words **"the first voice which I heard," "like a trumpet,"** are a direct reference to John's previous words, **"I heard behind me a loud voice, as of a trumpet."** (Revelation 1:10) Thus we see that this statement is directly tying this vision back to the first vision John had seen.

Why is this important? Because of the second detail of this sentence, which we have already noticed, that the actual Greek wording of its last two words is "after these," not **"after this,"** as our translation reads. As we noticed earlier, Chapters 2 and 3 are sandwiched between the words **"Write the things which you have seen, and the things which are, and the things which will take place after"** [these.] (Revelation 1:19) and the words **"Come up here, and I will show you things which must take place after"** [these.] (Revelation 4:1) So, in the combination of these two statements, we are being told that everything after Revelation 4:1 is about something that will take place after the things that were revealed in Revelation 2 and 3.

And then we have a description of a marvelous vision which reminds us of two previous visions that had been seen by prophets of God, the first by Isaiah (Isaiah 6:1-4), and the second by Ezekiel (Ezekiel 1:4-28.) Both of those visions introduced the calls of those two prophets. And this vision introduces the future portion of the Revelation. All three of these visions depict the majesty and greatness of God. But the first and last of them not only depict, but directly declare, His holiness.

> "And one cried to another and said: 'Holy, holy, holy is the LORD of hosts; The whole earth is full of His glory!' " (Isaiah 6:3) And "*The* four living creatures, each having six wings, were full of eyes around and within. And they do not rest day or night, saying: 'Holy, holy, holy, Lord God Almighty, Who was and is and is to come!' " (Revelation 4:8)

So now, as we examine this vision in detail, we find:

"Immediately I was in the Spirit; and behold, a throne set in heaven, and *One* sat on the throne. And He who sat there was like a jasper and a sardius stone in appearance; and *there was* a rainbow around the throne, in appearance like an emerald." (Revelation 4:2-3)

"Immediately" after having heard **"the first voice,"** calling him to **"Come up here"** and being promised **"I will show you things which must take place after"** [these,] John **"was in the Spirit."** There was no delay. This was immediate.

Isaiah did not describe **"the Lord"** he saw **"sitting on a throne,"** other than in the words **"high and lifted up, and the train of His robe filled the temple."** (Isaiah 6:1) But Ezekiel described in detail the one he saw **"above" "the likeness of a throne,"** (Ezekiel 1:26) saying, **"from the appearance of His waist and upward I saw, as it were, the color of amber with the appearance of fire all around within it; and from the appearance of His waist and downward I saw, as it were, the appearance of fire with brightness all around."** (Ezekiel 1:27) But in the present passage, John saw, sitting on the **"throne set in heaven,"** One who **"was like a jasper and a sardius stone in appearance."**

I am highly dissatisfied with the identifications of the jasper and sardius stones given by various modern writers. For none of them seem to fit Revelation 21:11, where we read that **"Her light *was* like a most precious stone, like a jasper stone, clear as crystal."** Both of these stones were set in the priest's breastplate in Exodus 28:17-20 and 39:10-13. And his garments were designed **"for glory and for beauty."** (Exodus 28:2) And in Ezekiel 28:13, both of these stones were in the **"covering"** of **"the anointed cherub"** (verse 14) who was **"perfect in beauty."** (Verse 12) And finally, both of these stones are among the foundations (Revelation 21:19-21) of the beautiful city which is called **"the bride, the Lamb's wife."** (verse 9) So, whatever these stones actually looked like, it is clear that they both represent the beauty of God.

His beauty is further seen in the **"rainbow around the throne, in appearance like an emerald."** (Revelation 4:3) So also in the vision of Ezekiel. **"Like the appearance of a rainbow in a cloud on a rainy day, so *was* the appearance of the brightness all around it."** (Ezekiel 1:28)

But the rainbow signifies more than beauty. For God told Noah: **"I set My rainbow in the cloud, and it shall be for the sign of the covenant between Me and the earth. It shall be, when I bring a cloud over the earth, that the rainbow shall be seen in the cloud; and I will remember My covenant which *is* between Me and you and every living creature of all flesh; the waters shall never again become a flood to destroy all flesh. The rainbow shall be in the cloud, and I will look on it to remember the everlasting covenant between God and every living creature of all flesh that *is* on the earth."** (Genesis 9:13-16) So the rainbow speaks of our God continually remembering His **"everlasting covenant"** with **"every living creature."**

Many Christians fail to realize the importance our God places on covenants. But we read, **"Now there was a famine in the days of David for three years, year after year; and David inquired of the**

LORD. And the LORD answered, '*It is* because of Saul and *his* bloodthirsty house, because he killed the Gibeonites.' So the king called the Gibeonites and spoke to them. Now the Gibeonites *were* not of the children of Israel, but of the remnant of the Amorites; the children of Israel had sworn protection to them, but Saul had sought to kill them in his zeal for the children of Israel and Judah."** (2 Samuel 21:1-2) Roughly 430 years after Joshua's ill advised covenant with the Gibeonites, (Joshua 9:14-15) God punished Israel for having broken it.

We remember that long before that time, He had commanded, **"If a man makes a vow to the LORD, or swears an oath to bind himself by some agreement, he shall not break his word; he shall do according to all that proceeds out of his mouth."** (Numbers 30:2) If our God requires such of mere mortals, what of His own words?

> "Thus says the LORD: 'If you can break My covenant with the day and My covenant with the night, so that there will not be day and night in their season, then My covenant may also be broken with David My servant, so that he shall not have a son to reign on his throne, and with the Levites, the priests, My ministers. As the host of heaven cannot be numbered, nor the sand of the sea measured, so will I multiply the descendants of David My servant and the Levites who minister to Me.' "(Jeremiah 33:20-22)

So the rainbow about the throne is a memorial of God's covenants, a reminder of the immutability of every one of His promises.

"Around the throne *were* twenty-four thrones, and on the thrones I saw twenty-four elders sitting, clothed in white robes; and they had crowns of gold on their heads." (Revelation 4:4) Numerous commentators have opined that this number twenty-four represents all the saints of God of all times, twelve representing the twelve patriarchs, that is, the Old Testament saints, and twelve representing the twelve Apostles, that is, the New Testament saints. If this is correct, and I believe it is, then this depicts all the saints of God assembled in heaven before the beginning of the judgments revealed in the remaining visions of this most awesome book. That is, that the rest of this book speaks of events that will take place after the rapture. As this is only an interpretation, we cannot insist it is correct. But I firmly believe that this is what our God is revealing here.

"And from the throne proceeded lightnings, thunderings, and voices." (Revelation 4:5a) Even as **"lightnings"** and **"thunderings"** warn us that a storm is about to break, and as **"voices"** announce coming events, these symbols are seen in scripture again and again as portents of impending judgment. (Exodus 9:23-34, 1 Samuel 2:10, 7:10, 12:18, Psalm 77:18, 104:7, Isaiah 29:6)

"Seven lamps of fire *were* burning before the throne, which are the seven Spirits of God." (Revelation 4:5b) What are **"the seven Spirits of God"**? We are not told. Even as we are told both that **"God is one"** (Deuteronomy 6:4) and that He consists of **"the Father, the Son, and the Holy Spirit,"** (Matthew 28:19) we are told here of **"the seven Spirits of God."** and, like the mystery of the Trinity, this is also not explained. But we should notice that the **"four living creatures"** in the next verse are not only **"around the throne,"** but actually **"in midst of the throne."** We are also told in Zechariah 6:5 of **"four spirits of heaven, who go out from *their* station before the Lord of all the earth."** And **"the Father, the Son, and the Holy Spirit"** plus four is seven. All these numbers are interesting, and are obviously intended to reveal various aspects of a God that is simply beyond human comprehension. But we can easily get ourselves into serious trouble if we allow ourselves to speculate about things that our God has not revealed.

"Before the throne *there was* a sea of glass, like crystal." (Revelation 4:6a) The sea was a place for washing. But, as in heaven there is nothing to defile, there is no need for washing. So the sea is **"glass, like crystal."**

We have already noticed the words **"And in the midst of the throne, and around the throne, *were* four living creatures"** But these **"living creatures"** were **"full of eyes in front and in back."** (Revelation 4:6b) So these **"living creatures"** see everything, whether it is in front of them or behind them. But their description continues:

> **"The first living creature *was* like a lion, the second living creature like a calf, the third living creature had a face like**

a man, and the fourth living creature *was* like a flying eagle. *The* **four living creatures, each having six wings, were full of eyes around and within."** (Revelation 4:7-8a)

What do we learn from these similitudes? We read of **"A lion, which *is* mighty among beasts And does not turn away from any."** (Proverbs 30:30) So being **"like a lion"** represents strength. And we read that **"Israel is stubborn Like a stubborn calf."** (Hosea 4:16) So being **"like a calf"** represents stubbornness, that is, being impossible to be deterred from its purpose. Proverbs 30:2 speaks of **"the understanding of a man."** So having **"a face like a man"** indicates fully understanding everything. And finally, we read that **"The LORD will bring a nation against you from afar, from the end of the earth,** *as swift* **as the eagle flies."** (Deuteronomy 28:49) And again, **"Their horses also are swifter than leopards, And more fierce than evening wolves. Their chargers charge ahead; Their cavalry comes from afar; They fly as the eagle** *that* **hastens to eat."** (Habakkuk 1:8) So being **"like a flying eagle"** speaks of swiftness in their actions.

But in addition, the **"living creatures"** are not only **"full of eyes in front and in back,"** but also **"full of eyes around and within."** Eyes are connected with perception in many scriptures, such as **"Open my eyes, that I may see Wondrous things from Your law."** (Psalm 119:18) So their having eyes **"around and within"** would seem to indicate that they have a full comprehension, not only of their surroundings, but also of themselves. They completely comprehend, not only everything around themselves, but even their own internal workings. They do not just know what they are doing, but why they are doing it. That is, they thoroughly understand their own motives.

'And they do not rest day or night, saying: 'Holy, holy, holy, Lord God Almighty, Who was and is and is to come!' " (Revelation 4:8b) Here we see stressed both the holiness and the eternal nature of God, which these **"four living creatures"** continually proclaim.

And **"Whenever the living creatures give glory and honor and thanks to Him who sits on the throne, who lives forever and ever, the twenty-four elders fall down before Him who sits on the throne and worship Him who lives forever and ever, and cast their**

crowns before the throne, saying: 'You are worthy, O Lord, To receive glory and honor and power; For You created all things, And by Your will they exist and were created.' " (Revelation 4:9-11)

The assembled saints all have crowns. But when the worship of God begins, they doff their crowns and cast them at His feet. For in comparison to Him, they are nothing. And they praise Him as not only the creator, but also the sustainer, of the universe.

 **REVELATION 5**

A scroll sealed with seven seals

"**And I saw in the right *hand* of Him who sat on the throne a scroll written inside and on the back, sealed with seven seals.**" (Revelation 5:1) The fact that this scroll was **"written inside and on the back"** would seem to indicate that it was filled with meaning. And indeed, as we study the prophetic scriptures, we realize more and more that there is no detail, no matter how small, that is not significant, that every syllable is pregnant with meaning. Not only is every word important, but even the very spelling of every word. For Jesus said, **"assuredly, I say to you, till heaven and earth pass away, one jot or one tittle will by no means pass from the law till all is fulfilled."** (Matthew 5:18) the **"jot"** and the **"tittle"** were the two smallest marks used in writing the Hebrew language. And our Lord Himself said that every one of them was significant. And this is why it is so important to pay careful attention to the fine details of the wording of everything our God has said. For Jesus himself taught us that it does not contain a single detail that is not important. But this detail that this scroll was not only **"written inside,"** but also **"on the back,"** would also seem to indicate that it contains a hidden meaning that does not appear in a casual reading. That is, that there is a deeper meaning hidden behind the simple words as they are written in this scroll.

But what of the **"seven seals"**? As we have noticed earlier, the number seven seems to represent perfection. But what is this scroll? We remember that a previous book of the Bible had been sealed. For Daniel had been told, **"Go *your way*, Daniel, for the words *are* closed up and sealed till the time of the end."** (Daniel 12:9) And we should remember that **"the last hour"** had already come in John's day. (1 John 2:18)

As we progress through this important book of the Bible, we will see that as the Lamb opens each of the seven seals on this **"scroll written inside and on the back,"** (Revelation 5:1) there comes a vision of destruction on an appalling scale.

This destruction reveals the solution to a great problem in understanding much of Bible prophecy, and particularly of the book of Daniel. For we are explicitly told of many things that will happen to various nations that appear to have ceased to exist. And if they no longer exist, how can the events prophesied about them take place? But as the seals are opened, we realize that the existing world order is going to be completely destroyed.

What happens when the existing world order is destroyed? We have recently seen this take place before out very eyes. When the apparently invincible USSR collapsed, various nations of Eastern Europe collapsed with it. And what happened? As if by magic, the old order of nations suddenly popped up. The ancient ethnic groups were still right there, where they had always been. The modern political realities had glossed over these ethnic identities. But when this artificial political system was destroyed, the old, natural, divisions immediately became apparent.

Even so, a complete destruction of the existing world order will open the way for the ancient (natural) world order to rise again. And this shows how the prophecies of Daniel can still come to pass, even though many of the nations mentioned in them appear to have disappeared.

And after the seals have all been opened, we will see that the prophet was given a vision of a **"little book"** that was **"open."** (Revelation 10:2, 8) Then, in Revelation 10:9, John was told to **"eat"** the book, which he did in verse 10.

Up to that point in this book of Revelation, the symbols used are based on other parts of scripture. But for chapters thereafter, the symbols are based on the book of Daniel.

From this I conclude that the instruction in chapter 10 to **"eat"** the little book means to go back at this point and study the book of Daniel, for it is needed to understand the rest of the book of Revelation. But the book of Daniel could not be understood until its seals were opened in Revelation 6-9. If this interpretation is correct, no part of the Bible is still sealed. All of it has now been opened to the eye of faith.

> **"Then I saw a strong angel proclaiming with a loud voice, 'Who is worthy to open the scroll and to loose its seals?' And no one in heaven or on the earth or under the earth was able to open the scroll, or to look at it. So I wept much, because no one was found worthy to open and read the scroll, or to look at it."** (Revelation 5:2-4)

This indeed shows us that the scroll was the very counsel of God Himself. For **"no one"** was, not only **"worthy,"** but even **"able,"** to open and read the scroll. But not only was **"no one" "able to open and read the scroll,"** but **"no one"** was even **"worthy" "to look at it."**

Few seem to have noticed what an awesome revelation we have here. How often do we hear ignorant men brashly say, of this or that part of the word of God, "I think it means." As some have said, "fools rush in where angels fear to tread." **"No one in heaven or on the earth or under the earth"** was even **"worthy" "to look at it."** But many today exalt themselves to declare their personal opinions of what the various symbols represent. We know the meaning of a symbol in scripture only from scripture itself. And in matters where God is silent, the wise also remain silent.

But, though **"no one was found worthy to open and read the scroll,"** The prophet greatly desired to know its contents. So he **"wept much, because no one was found worthy to open and read the scroll, or to look at it."** And what was the result? Jesus Himself prevailed to loose the seals.

> "But one of the elders said to me, 'Do not weep. Behold, the Lion of the tribe of Judah, the Root of David, has prevailed to open the scroll and to loose its seven seals.' " (Revelation 5:5)

Who could be more worthy **"to open the scroll and to loose its seven seals"** than its very author? For even as **"all scripture *is* given by inspiration of God,"** (1 Timothy 3:16) and **"prophecy never came by the will of man, but holy men of God spoke *as they were* moved by the Holy Spirit."** (2 Peter 1:2) Jesus Himself, being **"the true God,"** (1 John 5:20) is the only one **"worthy to open the scroll and to loose its seals."** For who but God is worthy to open a seal placed at the direct order of God Himself?

> "And I looked, and behold, in the midst of the throne and of the four living creatures, and in the midst of the elders, stood a Lamb as though it had been slain, having seven horns and seven eyes, which are the seven Spirits of God sent out into all the earth. Then He came and took the scroll out of the right hand of Him who sat on the throne." (Revelation 5:6-7)

"The Lion of the tribe of Judah, the Root of David" comes. but when He comes, He appears as **"a Lamb as though it had been slain."** Our claim upon Him rests, in its entirety, on the fact that He was **"slain."** We have no other claim upon Him, than that He, **"Himself bore our sins in his own body on the tree."** (1 Peter 2:24)

But He does not just appear as **"a Lamb as though it had been slain."** He also appears **"having seven horns and seven eyes, which are the seven Spirits of God."** So He appears, not only as the **"slain" "Lamb,"** but as the very fullness of the Godhead itself. The perfect **"seven Spirits of God"** are wrapped up in the **"Lamb as though it had been slain." "For in Him dwells all the fullness of the Godhead bodily."** (Colossians 2:9) So it is God Himself, in all His fullness, that reveals to us the mysteries contained in the **"scroll written inside and on the back, sealed with seven seals."**

And these **"seven Spirits of God"** are **"sent out into all the earth."** We remember that Jesus said **"when the Helper comes, whom I shall send to you from the Father, the Spirit of truth who proceeds from the Father, He will testify of Me."** (John 15:26) **"And when He has come, He will convict the world of sin, and of righteousness, and of judgment."** (John 16:8)

So, taking His authority as **"the fullness of the Godhead,"** the **"Lamb"** acts. **"Then He came and took the scroll out of the right hand of Him who sat on the throne."** (Revelation 5:7) And what is heaven's reaction to this?

"Now when He had taken the scroll, the four living creatures and the twenty-four elders fell down before the Lamb, each having a harp, and golden bowls full of incense, which are the prayers of the saints." (Revelation 5:8) So here we see, not only the assembled **"elders"** around the throne, but even the **"living creatures"** that were **"in the midst of the throne"** itself, fall down before Him. For we remember that our God's ultimate purpose is **"that in the dispensation of the fullness of the times He might gather together in one all things in Christ, both which are in heaven and which are on earth--in Him."** (Ephesians 1:10)

So now, in keeping with that ultimate purpose, all creation joins together in their praise of **"the Lamb,"** and of **"Him who sits on the throne."**

> "And they sang a new song, saying:
> 'You are worthy to take the scroll,
> And to open its seals;
> For You were slain,
> And have redeemed us to God by Your blood
> Out of every tribe and tongue
> and people and nation,
> And have made us kings and priests to our God;
> And we shall reign on the earth.'
> Then I looked, and I heard the voice of many angels around the throne, the living creatures, and the elders; and the number of them was ten thousand times ten thousand, and thousands of thousands, saying with a loud voice:

'Worthy is the Lamb who was slain
To receive power and riches and wisdom,
And strength and honor and glory and blessing!'
And every creature which is in heaven and on the earth and under the earth and such as are in the sea, and all that are in them, I heard saying:
'Blessing and honor and glory and power
Be to Him who sits on the throne,
And to the Lamb, forever and ever!'
Then the four living creatures said, 'Amen!' And the twenty-four elders fell down and worshiped Him who lives forever and ever." (Revelation 5:9-14)

This is one of the many passages of scripture that does not need to be explained. It only needs to be felt. As one said so long ago, "it needs to be felt, not telt."

Revelation 6

As we begin this chapter, we again see details that indicate the meaning of the seals, and of their openings. For as **"the Lamb"** opened each of the first four seals, the prophet was told, **"Come and see."** For the opening of the seals was not the unleashing of the awesome judgments depicted as they were opened, but the unleashing of the secret (in scriptural language, the revealing of the mystery) that these judgments would fall. So the prophet was called to **"Come and see"** what was going to happen.

We should also notice that it was a different one of the **"four living creatures"** which were **"in the midst of the throne"** (Revelation 4:6) that called John to **"Come and see"** each of the first four judgments revealed. And we remember that **"The first living creature *was* like a lion, the second living creature like a calf, the third living creature had a face like a man, and the fourth living creature *was* like a flying eagle."** (Revelation 4:7) We will notice these various details as we examine the openings of these first four seals.

The first seal is opened:

> "Now I saw when the Lamb opened one of the seals; and I heard one of the four living creatures saying with a voice like thunder, 'Come and see.' And I looked, and behold, a white horse. He who sat on it had a bow; and a crown was given to him, and he went out conquering and to conquer." (Revelation 6:1-2)

Although here, we are only told that the **"living creature"** that called John to **"Come and see"** was **"one of the four living creatures,"** all the rest of thr **"living creaatures"** are called by the same numerical designations used in Revelation 4:7. So this was evidently **"the first living creature,"** the one that **"*was* like a lion"** in Revelation 4:7. And he spoke **"with a voice like thunder."** Job said, **"the thunder of His power who can understand?"** (Job 26:14) so this speaks of power, even as this **"living creature"** being **"like a lion"** represents strength.

But what does the prophet see?

> **"And I looked, and behold, a white horse. He who sat on it had a bow; and a crown was given to him, and he went out conquering and to conquer."** (Revelation 6:2)

But what is the significance of the fact that this person comes sitting on **"a white horse"**? We find the significance of the color white in two scriptures, **" 'Come now, and let us reason together,' Says the LORD, 'Though your sins are like scarlet, They shall be as white as snow; Though they are red like crimson, They shall be as wool.' "** (Isaiah 1:18) And again, **"Many shall be purified, made white, and refined."** (Daniel 12:10)

So the fact that this rider sits on **"a white horse"** indicates that he comes professing a righteous cause. But his character is seen in that **"he went out conquering and to conquer."** In view of this clear statement of scripture, I find it nothing short of astounding that many imagine that this ruler will come in peacefully. They say, "it says he had a bow, but no arrows are mentioned." But in saying this, they are ignoring the fact that it explicitly says **"he went out conquering and to conquer."** [14]

---

14   The Greek word here translated **"conquering"** is "νικων," "nikon" in our alphabet. This is a form of word number 3528 in Strong's Greek Dictionary. This word literally means "subduing." And it most certainly does not mean subduing peacefully. For it is derived from the Greek word "νικη," "nike" in our alphabet, word number 3529 in Strong's Greek Dictionary, which is a primary word that literally means "conquest." The same is also true of the Greek word here translated **"to conquer."** For it is "νικηση," "nikese" in our alphabet, which is simply an infinitive of the same word number 3528 in Strong's Greek Dictionary.

This strange notion seems to be based on Daniel 11:21, which speaks of **"a vile person, to whom they will not give the honor of royalty; but he shall come in peaceably, and seize the kingdom by intrigue."** But that verse is part of a very long prophecy in Daniel 11:5-34. That prophecy describes a multi-generational war between the Ptolemies, a dynasty that ruled out of Alexandria in Egypt, which it called **"the king of the south,"** and the Seleucids, a dynasty that ruled out of Antioch in Syria, which it called **"the king of the north."** Every part of this prophecy was literally fulfilled, down to the tiniest detail, so accurately that unbelievers claim that its very accuracy is proof that it could not have been written before these wars took place. And the verse in question, Daniel 11:21, described a particularly evil Selucid ruler named Antiochus Epiphanes.

The point of this prophecy was to identify two rulers who are called by the same titles, **"the king of the south"** and **"the king of the north,"** in a continuation of this prophecy in Daniel 11:36-45. The two sections of this very long prophecy are divided by Daniel 11:35, which describes a condition which it says will continue **"*until* the time of the end; because *it is* still for the appointed time."** While all of Daniel 11:5-34, has been literally fulfilled, exactly as written, no part of Daniel 11:36-45 has been fulfilled, even to this day.

So the opening of this first seal reveals a coming conqueror who will become a king, for he is given a crown. And his coming is revealed by God, acting in strength and power.

> "When He opened the second seal, I heard the second living creature saying, 'Come and see.' Another horse, fiery red, went out. And it was granted to the one who sat on it to take peace from the earth, and that *people* should kill one another; and there was given to him a great sword." (Revelation 6:3-4)

The second **"living creature"** was the one **"like a calf."** (Revelation 4:7) We remember that being **"like a calf"** speaks of stubbornness of purpose, that nothing can turn God aside from what He has determined to accomplish. So the horrible revelation that comes with the opening of this second seal comes with God's revelation that He has purposed this, and that absolutely nothing can deter Him from bringing it to pass.

The horseman revealed in **"the first seal,"** the one on **"a white horse,"** went out **"conquering and to conqueror."** This plainly speaks of war, but of war on a more or less formal manner. That is, it has a distinct purpose, (the fact that the horse is white indicating a profession of a righteous cause) and thus a foreseeable end. But the opening of this **"second seal"** reveals something far worse. Wherever we find the color red, the color of blood, in the scriptures, it always depicts something evil, as we see in the promise:

> " 'Though your sins are like scarlet,
> They shall be as white as snow;
> Though they are red like crimson,
> They shall be as wool.' "
> (Isaiah 1:18)

So the fact that this rider sits on a **"fiery red"** horse indicates no pretense whatsoever of a just cause, but only pure evil. **"And it was granted to the one who sat on the horse."** This was not just a position he took for himself. It was **"granted to"** him, by the God whose stubborn purpose cannot be thwarted. And what was **"granted to"** him? **"to take peace from the earth, and that *people* should kill one another."** This is not merely war, but anarchy.

While war, and particularly war with a professed just cause, is logical, and proceeds to a foreseeable end, anarchy descends rapidly into nothing but senseless destruction and killing. There is no way to predict where it will go, or when it will end. The riots of 2020 in the United States, for instance, were allegedly in protest of white prejudice against blacks. But the vast majority of the crimes committed in those riots, including the vast majority of the murders, were committed against black people.

This anarchy is prophesied to extend throughout **"the earth,"** **"that *people* should kill one another."** And to this end **"there was** given to him a great sword." So in truth, the awful judgment revealed in the opening of **"the second seal"** is even more terrible than that revealed in the opening of **"the first seal."**

But here we need to notice that, in prophetic language, **"the earth,"** does not mean **"the whole world."** For these two terms are distinctly differentiated in Revelation 16:14, where we read of **"spirits of demons, performing signs,** *which* **go out to the kings of the earth and of the whole world."** We note this at this point in our discussion only to understand that this prophecy does not speak of a world wide catastrophe.[15]

> "When He opened the third seal, I heard the third living creature say, 'Come and see.' So I looked, and behold, a black horse, and he who sat on it had a pair of scales in his hand. And I heard a voice in the midst of the four living creatures saying, 'A quart of wheat for a denarius, and three quarts of barley for a denarius; and do not harm the oil and the wine.'" (Revelation 6:5-6)

And the prophet was called to **"Come and see"** this vision by **"the third living creature."** This is the one that **"had a face like a man."** (Revelation 4:7) That is, that God has full understanding of what He is doing here, and of why He is doing it.

But what did John see? **"a black horse, and he who sat on it had a pair of scales in his hand."**

In the scriptures, the color black represents mourning.[16] So the fact that this rider sits on a black horse indicates a time of great sorrow.

---

15 In the same way, in the contrast between verses 1 and 11 of Revelation 13, We see **"the sea"** and **"the earth"** as two distinct habitations of mankind.

16 The Hebrew word קדר, "qadar" in our alphabet, word number 6937 in Strong's Hebrew Dictionary, is often correctly translated "mourn," as in "grieve." But it is also often just as correctly translated "black." Although the Revelation was give us in Greek, rather then Hebrew, we point this out to understand that in the scriptures, black represents mourning.

But what of the scales? Although it is a different prophecy speaking of a different time, we read in Ezekiel 4:16-17, **"surely I will cut off the supply of bread in Jerusalem; they shall eat bread by weight and with anxiety, and shall drink water by measure and with dread, that they may lack bread and water, and be dismayed with one another, and waste away because of their iniquity."** So the scales speak of a scarcity of even basic necessities. And the prices stated are unimaginable.

"A quart of wheat for a denarius, and three quarts of barley for a denarius; and do not harm the oil and the wine." This **"denarius"** is exactly the daily wage agreed upon with the harvest laborers in Matthew 20:2. So enough wheat to make a single loaf of bread would cost a full day's wage. You could get more barley for that, but oil and wine would be too expensive to even consider.

So here we see the natural result of the previous wars and anarchy. Scarcity on a scale unheard of. But this is not just something that will happen, but something planned by the God of heaven. For the declaration of this scarcity comes from **"a voice in the midst of the four living creatures."** and according to Revelation 4:6 these **"living creatures"** themselves are not only **"around the throne,"** but **"in the midst of the throne."** So this scarcity is decreed by God himself.

> "When He opened the fourth seal, I heard the voice of the fourth living creature saying, 'Come and see.' So I looked, and behold, a pale horse. And the name of him who sat on it was Death, and Hades followed with him. And power was given to them over a fourth of the earth, to kill with sword, with hunger, with death, and by the beasts of the earth." (Revelation 6:7-8)

"The fourth living creature" was the one that **"was like a flying eagle."** (Revelation 4:7) And we remember that this speaks of swiftness of action. But what of the **"pale"** color of the horse? [17] An

---

17   The Greek word used here, "χλωρς," "chloros" in our alphabet, word number 5515 in Strong's Greek Dictionary, is used in this sense nowhere else in the New Testament. The word, when taken by itself, literally means green, but many trans-

equivalent Hebrew word, [18] is rendered as "pale" in Jeremiah 30:6-7, where we read:

> "Ask now, and see, Whether a man is ever in labor with child? So why do I see every man *with* his hands on his loins Like a woman in labor, And all faces turned pale? Alas! For that day *is* great, So that none *is* like it; And it *is* the time of Jacob's trouble, But he shall be saved out of it"

So we see that a **"pale"** color represents fear, so the **"pale horse"** represents something to fear. And, as we have already noticed, this being announced by the **"living creature"** that *"was* **like a flying eagle"** represents this fearful calamity coming swiftly. But what was coming?

> "And the name of him who sat on (the pale horse) was Death, and Hades followed with him. And power was given to them over a fourth of the earth, to kill with sword, with hunger, with death, and by the beasts of the earth." (Revelation 6:8)

So now we see widespread death, coming about by violence, (the sword) famine, (hunger) disease, (death) and by the beasts of the earth. But this is not only death, but hell (Hades) following with him. Famine and pestilence indeed are common along with times of war and anarchy, And now even the beasts of the earth join in the carnage. But the scope of this judgment is limited. Rather than falling on the entire earth, it falls upon **"a fourth of the earth."**

---

lators agree that in this context it means "pale." In addition to the translation we are using, the NKJV, this reading is found in the KJV, ASV, DRV, ESV, GWN, ICB, and NCV translations, as well as those by Montgomery, Darby, Wesley, and Young. Other translations render this word as "pale green" or "ashen."

18 This is a form of the Hebrew word ירקון, "yeraqon" in our alphabet, word number 3420 in Strong's Hebrew Dictionary. It literally means "yellowish green," but is rendered as "pale" in the NKJV, KJV, ASV, CWSB, CEV, ESV, GWN, HCSB, NASB, NRSV, MSG, and TEV versions, as well as in the translations by Darby and Young.

This is the last of the judgments announced by the **"four living creatures"** but is not the end of the seals.

> **"When He opened the fifth seal, I saw under the altar the souls of those who had been slain for the word of God and for the testimony which they held. And they cried with a loud voice, saying, 'How long, O Lord, holy and true, until You judge and avenge our blood on those who dwell on the earth?' Then a white robe was given to each of them; and it was said to them that they should rest a little while longer, until both *the number of* their fellow servants and their brethren, who would be killed as they *were*, was completed."** (Revelation 6:9-11)

This seal reveals that there will come a time of persecution. But it reveals far more than that. Who are these persecuted ones? Many imagine that this shows the church still being on the earth at that time. But in truth it shows something entirely different.

What is the attitude of these martyrs? They cry, **"How long, O Lord, holy and true, until You judge and avenge our blood on those who dwell on the earth?"** Such a desire for vengeance is totally contrary to the attitude of a godly Christian. For our Lord Jesus instructed His own to **"Love your enemies, do good to those who hate you, bless those who curse you, and pray for those who spitefully use you."** (Luke 6:27-28) And as He hung on the tree, He prayed, **"Father, forgive them, for they do not know what they do."** (Luke 23:34) As the first Christian martyr, Stephen, died, he prayed, **"Lord, do not charge them with this sin."** (Acts 7:60) And Paul said, **"At my first defense no one stood with me, but all forsook me. May it not be charged against them."** (2 Timothy 4:16)

But, though their attitude is totally contrary to the attitude we are instructed to have, and totally contrary to the examples we have been given, these are spirits in heaven. And, rather than being reproved for their attitude, they are comforted, and not only comforted, but given a reward. For **"a white robe was given to each of them."**

But what are they told as they are comforted? **"That they should rest a little while longer, until both *the number of* their fellow servants and their brethren, who would be killed as they *were*, was completed."** (Revelation 6:11) So the opening of this seal reveals not only that persecution will arise at this time, but that it will continue.

But to return to our question, who are these persecuted ones? We have seen that their attitudes reveal them to not be Christians. But if they are not Christians, who are they? We see this same desire for vengeance in the twice repeated cry, **"Let me see Your vengeance on them."** (Jeremiah 11:20 and 20:12) and in the cry **"take vengeance for me on my persecutors."** (Jeremiah 15:15) And in the blood curdling cry:

> "O daughter of Babylon, who are to be destroyed,
> Happy the one who repays you
> as you have served us!
> Happy the one who takes and dashes
> Your little ones against the rock!"
> (Psalm 137:8-9)

So we see that these people, though indeed saints of God, (for they are in heaven,) are saints of the Old Testament variety, even though they are saints of a future time.

This becomes obvious when we remember that the age of **"the things which are,"** the age of the church, is over, and we are now in the age of **"the things which will take place after this,"** or as more accurately translated, "the things which will take place after these *things*." (Revelation 1:19)

> **"I looked when He opened the sixth seal, and behold, there was a great earthquake; and the sun became black as sackcloth of hair, and the moon became like blood. And the stars of heaven fell to the earth, as a fig tree drops its late figs when it is shaken by a mighty wind. Then the sky receded as a scroll when it is rolled up, and every mountain and island was moved out of its place. And the kings of the earth, the great men, the rich men, the commanders, the mighty men, every slave and every free man, hid themselves in the caves**

and in the rocks of the mountains, and said to the mountains and rocks, 'Fall on us and hide us from the face of Him who sits on the throne and from the wrath of the Lamb! For the great day of His wrath has come, and who is able to stand?' " (Revelation 6:12-17)

In scripture, an earthquake is associated with punishment from God as we see in **"You will be punished by the LORD of hosts With thunder and earthquake and great noise, *With* storm and tempest And the flame of devouring fire."** (Isaiah 29:6) But what of the other symbols here? We find all of them in a passage from Genesis.

"Then he dreamed still another dream and told it to his brothers, and said, 'Look, I have dreamed another dream. And this time, the sun, the moon, and the eleven stars bowed down to me.' So he told it to his father and his brothers; and his father rebuked him and said to him, 'What is this dream that you have dreamed? Shall your mother and I and your brothers indeed come to bow down to the earth before you?' " (Genesis 37:9-10)

In Joseph's dream, his father, who was a prophet of God, (see Genesis 48:3-22) saw the sun as representing Joseph's father, (himself) the moon as representing Joseph's mother, and the stars as representing his brothers. That is, the sun represents the ultimate authority, the moon represents secondary authority, and the stars represent human leaders.

So what we see represented here is that in this great upheaval, **"the sun"** becoming **"black as sackcloth of hair"** speaks of a total breakdown of national governments. And **"the moon"** becoming **"like blood"** speaks of lesser governments restoring order in the only way possible after such a complete upheaval, by a violent (bloody) use of whatever power is at their disposal. And all the great leaders are totally removed from the scene. They all fall **"as a fig tree drops its late figs when it is shaken by a mighty wind."** Remember we are told in another scripture of **"ten kings who have received no kingdom as** yet, but they receive authority for one hour as kings with the beast." (Revelation 17:12)

And next we read:

"Then the sky receded as a scroll when it is rolled up, and every mountain and island was moved out of its place." (Revelation 6:14)

We find the meaning of a mountain in Jeremiah 51:25, where the Lord tells the mighty nation of Babylon, " 'I am against you, O destroying mountain, Who destroys all the earth,' says the LORD. 'And I will stretch out My hand against you, Roll you down from the rocks, And make you a burnt mountain' " So a mountain speaks of a great nation.

We do not find much of a hint about the meaning of an island in the Greek scriptures. But in the Hebrew, the very meaning of the word explains its prophetic significance. For the Hebrew word for island means an island in the sense of being a habitable spot. [19]

So **"every mountain and island"** being **"moved out of its place,"** indicate a dislocation, not only of every great nation, but of every spot suitable for habitation. That is, all nations, great and small. And what is the effect of this disruption?

> "And the kings of the earth, the great men, the rich men, the commanders, the mighty men, every slave and every free man, hid themselves in the caves and in the rocks of the mountains, and said to the mountains and rocks, 'Fall on us and hide us from the face of Him who sits on the throne and from the wrath of the Lamb! For the great day of His wrath has come, and who is able to stand?' " (Revelation 6:15-17)

Here we see all men, from the greatest (**"kings"**) to the least (**"slaves,"**) filled with terror. But it is not just an unnamed terror, but a persuasion that **"the great day of His wrath has come."** We should

---

19 This Hebrew word is אִי, ay in our alphabet, word number 336 in Strong's Hebrew Dictionary.

notice that this is not God saying that **"the great day of His wrath has come,"** But this is the panicked persuasion of mankind in general.

There is, embedded in the heart of mankind, a realization that we have rebelled against God, and that some day He will take action about this rebellion. Whenever there comes a disaster of unusual proportions, men instinctively begin to speak fearfully that it is a sign that "the world is coming to an end." According to historians, this was a common theme when the black death struck Europe in the fourteenth century, and in every major pandemic or disruption since then, including those of 2020.

So it will be with these that at this time cry out, **"the great day of His wrath has come."** These are not prophets of God, or even godly men, that so cry out, for they are seeking to hide from God. They say **"to the mountains and rocks, 'Fall on us and hide us from the face of Him who sits on the throne and from the wrath of the Lamb!' "** So it is not God that is here saying that **"the great day of His wrath has come."** Instead, this is the terrified cry of sinful men.

For when **"the great day of His wrath"** comes **"who is able to stand?"** No one. And they all know it. And that is why they say **"to the mountains and rocks, 'Fall on us and hide us from the face of Him who sits on the throne and from the wrath of the Lamb!' "**

# Revelation 7

The seals are not finished. There is one more, the seventh seal, yet to be opened. But now we come to a parenthesis. The scene suddenly changes, and a new vision begins.

> "After these things I saw four angels standing at the four corners of the earth, holding the four winds of the earth, that the wind should not blow on the earth, on the sea, or on any tree. Then I saw another angel ascending from the east, having the seal of the living God. And he cried with a loud voice to the four angels to whom it was granted to harm the earth and the sea, saying, 'Do not harm the earth, the sea, or the trees till we have sealed the servants of our God on their foreheads.' " (Revelation 7:1-3)

The first thing we need to notice here is that there is more destruction coming. There are **"four angels to whom it was granted to harm the earth and the sea."** And these angels will inflict their harm through the **"winds."**

But then we need to notice that these angels are restrained. They are commanded to wait until something else is finished. And what must be accomplished first? **"The servants of our God"** must be **"sealed," "on their foreheads."**

We remember another time such a thing was done. We read in Ezekiel 9:4-6, **"and the LORD said to him, 'Go through the midst of the city, through the midst of Jerusalem, and put a mark on the** foreheads of the men who sigh and cry over all the abominations that are done within it.' To the others He said in my hearing, 'Go after him through the city and kill; do not let your eye spare, nor have any pity. Utterly slay old and young men, maidens and little children and women; but do not come near anyone on whom *is* the mark.' "

So we understand that this is done to mark **"the servants of God"** for protection during the coming calamities.

But who is sealed?

> "And I heard the number of those who were sealed.
> One hundred *and* forty-four thousand
> of all the tribes of the children of Israel *were* sealed:
> of the tribe of Judah twelve thousand *were* sealed;
> of the tribe of Reuben twelve thousand *were* sealed;
> of the tribe of Gad twelve thousand *were* sealed;
> of the tribe of Asher twelve thousand *were* sealed;
> of the tribe of Naphtali twelve thousand *were* sealed;
> of the tribe of Manasseh twelve thousand *were* sealed;
> of the tribe of Simeon twelve thousand *were* sealed;
> of the tribe of Levi twelve thousand *were* sealed;
> of the tribe of Issachar twelve thousand *were* sealed;
> of the tribe of Zebulun twelve thousand *were* sealed;
> of the tribe of Joseph twelve thousand *were* sealed;
> of the tribe of Benjamin twelve thousand *were* sealed."
> (Revelation 7:4-8)

Many falsely claim that an end time blessing of Israel is not taught in the New Testament. But how could our God have made it more explicit that these **"servants of our God"** who will be so **"sealed"** will be **"of the children of Israel."**

Here we see, as we saw in the last chapter, that **"the servants of God"** at this time are a different group from **"the church."** While there is indeed some excuse for imagining that the scriptures apply the name **"Israel"** to **"the church,"** (although no scripture actually says that,) there is absolutely no excuse, anywhere in the entire Bible, for interpreting the indiviidual names of any of **"the twelve tribes of Israel"** to mean **"the church."** Yet here, we are specifically told of "twelve thousand" being sealed as "servants of God," from each of "the twelve tribes of Israel." This shows, and clearly shows, that at the time spoken of here, our God will have resumed His dealings with the nation of "Israel."

For our purposes it is insignificant whether the numbers of those sealed are symbolical or literal. Either way, this clearly speaks of a very large number of "servants of our God" that are "of the children of Israel." If the number is symbolic, rather than literal, it represents a complete number, multiplied many times over, from each of "the twelve tribes of Israel."

And the impending clamities, of whatever nature they might be, are restrained until these Israelite "servants of our God" have been sealed.

But now the prophet's attention is directed to a completely different group. The last group was composed entirely of descendants of the ancient nation of Israel. And it was on the earth, because work of "the four angels to whom it was granted to harm the earth and the sea" (Revelation 7:2) was restrained until they had been sealed. But this is both a different group of people and in a different place.

> "After these things I looked, and behold, a great multitude which no one could number, of all nations, tribes, peoples, and tongues, standing before the throne and before the Lamb," (Revelation 7:9a)

So, rather than being "of all the tribes of the children of Israel," (Revelation 7:4) as was the previous group, this group is composed "of all nations, tribes, peoples, and tongues." And rather than being a specific number, this group is "a great multitude which no one could number." And instead of being on the earth, this group is "standing before the throne and before the Lamb."

This new group is "Clothed with white robes, with palm branches in their hands." and what are they doing? "crying out with a loud voice, saying, 'Salvation *belongs* to our God who sits on the throne, and to the Lamb!' " (Revelation 7:9b-10)

And what is heaven's response to this?

> "All the angels stood around the throne and the elders and the four living creatures, and fell on their faces before the throne and worshiped God, saying:
> 'Amen!
> Blessing and glory and wisdom,
> Thanksgiving and honor and power and might,
> *Be* to our God forever and ever.
> Amen.' "
> (Revelation 7:9b-12)

But now a question arises, and its answer is given.

> "Then one of the elders answered, saying to me, 'Who are these arrayed in white robes, and where did they come from?' And I said to him, 'Sir, you know.' So he said to me, 'These are the ones who come out of the great tribulation, and washed their robes and made them white in the blood of the Lamb.' " (Revelation 7:13-14)

We need to take a careful look at the Greek words used here, and compare them with a statement in Revelation 3:10 that some imagine is similar.

Here, the Greek words translated **"the ones who come out of the great tribulation"** are "εισιν οι ερχομενοι εκ της θλιψεωςς της μεγαλης." But the Greek words translated **"I also will keep you from the hour of trial"** in Revelation 3:10, are "καγω σε τηρησω εκ της ωρας του πειρασμου." Just by inspection, it is obvious, even to a person who knows no Greek at all, that these two clauses, though their English translations seem similar, are very different in Greek.

But to understand how completely difference these two clauses are, we need to arrange them in two columns, with the literal translation of each Greek word beside it.

REVELATION 7:14		REVELATION 3:10	
εισιν	they	καγω	(I) also
οι	the	σε	you
ερχομενοι	come	τηρησω	will keep
εκ	out of	εκ	out of
της	the	της	the
θλιψεως	tribulation	ωραϛh	our (of)
της	the	του	the
μεγαλης	great	πειρασμου	trial

Arranged this way, we can easily see that the central words **"come out of"** "ερχομενοι εκ" are not only different from **"will keep you out of"** "σε τηρησω εκ," but that the difference is fundamental. That is, that the difference between these statements lies at a basic level. Their meanings are entirely different, even though both use the same Greek word εκ, that is, **"out of."** For the words **"come out of"** indicate having first been in something. But the words **"will keep you out of"** indicate being kept from ever getting into it.

This, of course, is interesting, but what it the point? Why are we even bothering with this close examination of Greek words? Because this shows us that the people seen in Revelation 7:10 are completely different from the people in Revelation 3:10. One group will be *kept* **"out of"** what the other group will *come* **"out of."** To those kept **"out of"** it, it will only be **"the hour of trial"** which will come upon others. But to those who **"come out of"** it, it will be **"the great tribulation,"** because they will have experienced it.

We remember that in Revelation 3:10, the promise to be *kept* **"out of"** the hour of the **"trial"** was given to **"the church,"** as it was manifested **"in Philadelphia."** (Revelation 3:7) So this other group, that *comes* "out of the tribulation the great" has to be a different group, that is people that are not part of **"the church."** For these *come* **"out of"** what the church will be *kept* **"out of."** So, while this is technical, it is another reason for understanding that the rapture will take place before **"the great tribulation."**

But, even though these are not **"the church,"** as was the case in Revelation 3:10, these are saints of God, and are blessed forever in His presence. For the elder went on to say of them:

"Therefore they are before the throne of God, and serve Him day and night in His temple. And He who sits on the throne will dwell among them. They shall neither hunger anymore nor thirst anymore; the sun shall not strike them, nor any heat; for the Lamb who is in the midst of the throne will shepherd them and lead them to living fountains of waters. And God will wipe away every tear from their eyes." (Revelation 7:15-17)

# REVELATION 8

The parenthesis of Revelation 7 now being finished, this chapter begins with the Lamb opening the seventh seal.

And - nothing happens!

> **"When He opened the seventh seal, there was silence in heaven for about half an hour."** (Revelation 8:1)

We often comment about the fact that no detail in the Bible is insignificant, that every detail, no matter how small, has a meaning. And even so, this silence is an exceedingly important detail. We speak of "a pregnant pause" when someone is speaking. By that, we mean that a speaker has suddenly paused his narrative, to call particular attention to what he is about to say. We *could* see this pause as "a pregnant pause," but I am persuaded it indicates more than simply stressing the importance of what is about to be said.

We read in the KJV version of Isaiah 28:21 **"For the LORD shall rise up as *in* mount Perazim, he shall be wroth as *in* the valley of Gibeon, that he may do his work, his strange work; and bring to pass his act, his strange act."** I use the KJV here because the NKJV, which we are using, improperly (in my opinion) changed the first of the two uses of the word **"strange"** to **"awesome,"** and the second one, perhaps more properly, to **"unusual."**

Our God is a God of love, and judgment is His **"strange work,"** His **"unusual act."** But, as He is also the God of justice, the time comes when He must act in judgment. This pause seems to indicate His reluctance to proceed with what must now be done. To realize the total awesomeness of this silence, we have to remember where we are. This is the very control center of the entire universe. The seat of the central government over everything. And all activity suddenly stops. Nothing whatsoever is happening. But God's justice requires action. So, after a pause of about half an hour, The process begins:

"And I saw the seven angels who stand before God, and to them were given seven trumpets. Then another angel, having a golden censer, came and stood at the altar. He was given much incense, that he should offer it with the prayers of all the saints upon the golden altar which was before the throne. And the smoke of the incense, with the prayers of the saints, ascended before God from the angel's hand. Then the angel took the censer, filled it with fire from the altar, and threw *it* **to the earth. And there were noises, thunderings, lightnings, and an earthquake."** (Revelation 8:2-5)

We realize that all these symbols speak of the judgment of God falling upon the wicked when we read:

> **"You will be punished by the LORD of hosts**
> **With thunder and earthquake and great noise,**
> ***With* storm and tempest**
> **And the flame of devouring fire."** (Isaiah 29:6)

And:

> **"The LORD will cause His glorious voice to be heard,**
> **And show the descent of His arm,**
> **With the indignation of** *His* **anger**
> **And the flame of a devouring fire,**
> ***With* scattering, tempest, and hailstones."** (Isaiah 30:30)

And now the action begins:

"So the seven angels who had the seven trumpets prepared themselves to sound." (Revelation 8:6)

But before we begin to examine this series of judgments, we need to consider what is being indicated in the fact that they all fall upon **"a third"** of whatever is being judged. There is not a specific scripture that gives us the significance of a third part of everything. But this clearly indicates that the trumpet judgments are limited in scope. That is, they do not fall upon the entire world, but only upon a part of it. But we cannot escape from the fact that it has become a common expression to speak of "the east, the west, and the third world." That is, in the minds of modern man, the world is divided into basically three divisions: The east, that is the Asiatic world. The west, that is the portion of the world whose culture is derived from the ancient Romans, And the rest of the world. And as many other prophecies make it clear that the Roman world is the major stress of much of Bible prophecy, this would seem to indicate that these judgments fall upon the Roman world. But in realizing this, we need to realize that "the Roman world" is that portion of the world that is called Christendom. So it would seem that these judgments will fall upon the empty shell of the Christian world after all the true Christians have been removed in the rapture.

So we read:

"The first angel sounded: And hail and fire followed, mingled with blood, and they were thrown to the earth. And a third of the trees were burned up, and all green grass was burned up." (Revelation 8:5)

We find the prophetic significance of a tree in Daniel 4, where in verses 10-17 Nebuchadnezzar reported a dream of a great tree that was cut down. And in verses 20-26 Daniel gave the interpretation that the tree was Nebuchadnezzar himself.

So we see that in Bible prophecy, trees represent great men. But what of the grass? We see that in Deuteronomy 11, the Lord promised Israel that, if they obeyed Him, **"I will send grass in your fields for your livestock, that you may eat and be filled."** (Deuteronomy 11:15) So in the scriptures, grass speaks of the ultimate source of food.

So this first trumpet represents the fall of the great men of the earth, And the destruction of the sources of food. But in the context of the rest of this series of judgments, this seems to speak of spiritual food. That is, that the joining of these two symbols represents an apostasy of spiritual leaders, corrupting all sources of spiritual food. In other words, that the leaders of the empty shell of the church abandon all pretense of preaching the truth of God, and begin to openly preach the lies of Satan.

> "Then the second angel sounded: And *something* like a great mountain burning with fire was thrown into the sea, and a third of the sea became blood. And a third of the living creatures in the sea died, and a third of the ships were destroyed." (Revelation 8:8-9)

As we noticed earlier, we find the prophetic significance of a mountain in Jeremiah 51. When the Lord was declaring His coming judgment of the wicked land of Babylon, He said:

> " 'Behold, I *am* against you, O destroying mountain,
> Who destroys all the earth,' says the LORD.
> 'And I will stretch out My hand against you,
> Roll you down from the rocks,
> And make you a burnt mountain.' " (Jeremiah 51:25)

So we see that in Bible prophecy, a mountain speaks of a great nation. But what does the sea speak of? We read:

> "But the wicked *are* like the troubled sea,
> When it cannot rest,
> Whose waters cast up mire and dirt." (Isaiah 57:20)

So the second trumpet represents a great nation collapsing into anarchy. Instead of being something strong and stable, it collapses into the wicked state of mob rule.

> "Then the third angel sounded: And a great star fell from heaven, burning like a torch, and it fell on a third of the rivers and on the springs of water. The name of the star is Wormwood. A third of the waters became wormwood, and many men died from the water, because it was made bitter."
> (Revelation 8:10-11)

We find the spiritual significance of water in the scripture that **"Christ... loved the church and gave Himself for her, that He might sanctify and cleanse her with the washing of water by the word."** (Ephesians 5:25-26) So water speaks of the word of God. And thus, this speaks of all the familiar sources of the words of God, that is all supposedly Christian preachers and teachers, become poisonous. That is, as in the first trumpet, even professedly Christian teachers begin to teach lies that damn men to a lost eternity. [20]

> "Then the fourth angel sounded: And a third of the sun was struck, a third of the moon, and a third of the stars, so that a third of them were darkened. A third of the day did not shine, and likewise the night." (Revelation 8:12)

Here again we see a third of the earth, the empty shell of Christendom, affected. We see the prophetic significance of these symbols in Joseph's second dream.

---

20 But in the case of this trumpet, some have observed that the name of the Russian city Chernobyl, the site of the world's worst nuclear accident, translates into English as **"Wormwood."** And nuclear fallout renders water deadly. If the Holy Spirit's intention in so explicitly naming this star was to refer to the Chernobyl accident, then this fourth trumpet would represent a nuclear attack on a great nation. This interpretation, which is possible, but not necessarily correct, would also avoid the problem of the third trumpet seeming to simply be a repeat of what had just been revealed at the sounding of the first trumpet.
But this line of thought involves two fundamental errors of scriptural interpretation. The first is that we should always interpret scripture on the basis of scripture, and not on the basis of current events. And the second is that we should never speculate about the meaning of scripture.

> "Then he dreamed still another dream and told *it* to his brothers, and said, 'Look, I have dreamed another dream. And this time, the sun, the moon, and the eleven stars bowed down to me.' So he told it to his father and his brothers; and his father rebuked him and said to him, 'What is this dream that you have dreamed? Shall your mother and I and your brothers indeed come to bow down to the earth before you?' And his brothers envied him, but his father kept the matter *in mind.*" (Genesis 37:9-11)

Here we see that the sun represented the primary ruler of the family, Joseph's father. The moon, the secondary ruler of the family, his mother. And the stars, the great men of the family, his older brothers. So the sun represents the supreme authority, the moon the lesser authority, and the stars represent great men. So in the fourth trumpet, all lose their influence. That is, all authority collapses. Throughout Christendom, everything descends into chaos.

And this is followed by a dreadful announcement of three woes:

> **"And I looked, and I heard an angel flying through the midst of heaven, saying with a loud voice, 'Woe, woe, woe to the inhabitants of the earth, because of the remaining blasts of the trumpet of the three angels who are about to sound!' "** (Revelation 8:7-13)

So what is about to come is so much worse that a threefold woe is pronounced upon **"the inhabitants of the earth."** And the reason for this becomes immediately apparent in the next chapter.

REVELATION 9

The first woe

"Then the fifth angel sounded: And I saw a star fallen from heaven to the earth. To him was given the key to the bottomless pit. And he opened the bottomless pit, and smoke arose out of the pit like the smoke of a great furnace. So the sun and the air were darkened because of the smoke of the pit." (Revelation 9:1-2)

Whatever this judgment indicates, the first thing we see is that it represents God allowing the very forces of Satan to be unleashed. For **"the bottomless pit"** is where Satan will be imprisoned, as we read in Revelation 20:1-3. And here, an host of lessor spirits are released. And the immediate effect is to darken **"the sun,"** that is, the supreme authority. But it also darkens **"the air."** and we remember that in Ephesians 2:2, **"the spirit who now works in the sons of disobedience"** is called **"the prince of the power of the air."**

"Then out of the smoke locusts came upon the earth. And to them was given power, as the scorpions of the earth have power." (Revelation 9:3) There is no scripture that states the prophetic significance of a scorpion. But we see in nature that a scorpion is very deceptive in attacking a victim. It distracts the attention of the victim by threatening it with its pinchers, while it hits it from a different direction with the deadly stinger in its tail. Such is the normal practice of teachers of false doctrine. They distract people's attention by expressing widely understood truths, and then, at end of their message, they sneak in deadly lies.

But the power of these liars is limited.

> **"They were commanded not to harm the grass of the earth, or any green thing, or any tree, but only those men who do not have the seal of God on their foreheads."** (Revelation 9:4)

We remember that our Lord said of this time, **"For false christs and false prophets will rise and show great signs and wonders to deceive, if possible, even the elect."** (Matthew 24:24) This clearly implies that it would be impossible **"to deceive" "the elect."** Even so, these evil ones will be forbidden to attack those who **"have the seal of God on their foreheads."** That is, the elect of God.

> **"And they were not given *authority* to kill them, but to torment them for five months. Their torment *was* like the torment of a scorpion when it strikes a man. In those days men will seek death and will not find it; they will desire to die, and death will flee from them."** (Revelation 9:5-6)

This evil doctrine will take away all hope from mankind, even to the point of choosing death over life. But death will not even be an option. They will be forced to continue to live, to experience what is coming.

But now we come to a description of this wicked army.

I find myself greatly distressed when I read such comments as this being a primitive man's attempt to describe helicopters, or that the stingers in their tails were the tail guns found on some airships. All such nonsense is a prime example of an irresponsible and irreverent approach to scripture. To even imply such an idea is to deny that these are the very words of an all wise God who meant everything He said.

Rather than being a "video," as it were, of an end times battle scene, this is a symbolic representation of an evil army. As can be seen in the contradiction involved in locusts shaped like horses, this is not even an attempt to actually describe anything at all.

So let us consider what the meaning of he vision must be. In the first place, the symbolism of the fact that they are represented as locusts is somewhat obvious. Indeed, this is not the first time in scripture that armies were typified as swarms of insects. For we read in Isaiah 7:18-20:

> "And it shall come to pass in that day
> *That* the LORD will whistle for the fly
> That *is* in the farthest part of the rivers of Egypt,
> And for the bee that *is* in the land of Assyria.
> They will come, and all of them will rest
> In the desolate valleys and in the clefts of the rocks,
> And on all thorns and in all pastures.
> In the same day the Lord will shave with a hired razor,
> With those from beyond the River, with the king of Assyria,
> The head and the hair of the legs,
> And will also remove the beard."

The third line from the bottom of this quotation shows that this is speaking of armies, not insects. Likewise, in our current sripture, the depiction of this future horde as a swarm of locusts indicates an army, indicating both their vast numbers and their destructive power. For a plague of locusts destroys everything in its path.

> "The shape of the locusts was like horses prepared for battle. On their heads were crowns of something like gold, and their faces *were* like the faces of men. They had hair like women's hair, and their teeth were like lions' *teeth*. And they had breastplates like breastplates of iron, and the sound of their wings *was* like the sound of chariots with many horses running into battle. They had tails like scorpions, and there were stings in their tails. Their power *was* to hurt men five months." (Revelation 9:7-10)

The fact that these locusts were **"like horses prepared for battle"** again indicates an army. But what of their appearance?

"On their heads were crowns of something like gold." Their crowns were not "of gold," but **"of something like gold."** So they come looking like rulers, but that was false. For **"They had hair like women's hair."** 1 Corinthians 11:3-10 teaches us that a woman's hair is a symbol of the fact that she is under the authority of a man. So the fact that these locusts have hair as the hair of women indicates that, while they pretend to be rulers, they are actually under the rule of others.

The fact that **"their teeth were like lions' *teeth*"** would seem to indicate their ferocity. And the fact that **"they had breastplates like breastplates of iron"** would seem to indicate that their hearts were totally beyond reach. That is, that no appeal to their consciences could even possibly be effective, that they were totally resolute in their commitment to destroy anything and everything in their path. And in this aspect, **"the sound of their wings *was* like the sound of chariots with many horses running into battle."**

And finally, **"they had tails like scorpions, and there were stings in their tails."** We have already noticed that the sting like a scorpion indicates false doctrine. But these are not deceived by their own false doctrine. They understand what they are doing. For **"their faces *were* like the faces of men."**

This becomes plain in the next verse when we read:

"And they had as king over them the angel of the bottomless pit, whose name in Hebrew is Abaddon, but in Greek he has the name Apollyon." (Revelation 9:11)

So this great army, bent on heartless destruction, is ruled by none other that Satan himself. Which is what explains both their heartless destructiveness and their understanding of what they are doing.

And then we come to the chilling words:

"One woe is past. Behold, still two more woes are coming after these things." (Revelation 9:12)

The second woe:

"**Then the sixth angel sounded: And I heard a voice from the four horns of the golden altar which is before God, saying to the sixth angel who had the trumpet, 'Release the four angels who are bound at the great river Euphrates.' So the four angels, who had been prepared for the hour and day and month and year, were released to kill a third of mankind. Now the number of the army of the horsemen *was* two hundred million; I heard the number of them."** (Revelation 9:13-16)

The first thing we notice here is that this is not just revealed as something that will happen, but as something that will happen at the direct command of God himself. These judgments, though they will come through wicked spirits and evil men, will come at the command of **"the Judge of all the earth."** (Genesis 8:25)

The next thing we notice is that this judgment is not just coming sometime. It **"had been prepared for the hour and day and month and year."** That is, that God had planned the exact moment at which He would release this judgment on mankind.

But we need to notice several other details about this army. One is that it comes from beyond the Euphrates River. That is, it comes from the east. Another is that this army is composed of two hundred million men. That is, that it is absolutely huge.

Again, this army is **"released to kill a third of mankind."** And we remember that **"a third of"** is a symbol that speaks of the empty shell of Christendom.

> "**And thus I saw the horses in the vision: those who sat on them had breastplates of fiery red, hyacinth blue, and sulfur yellow; and the heads of the horses *were* like the heads of lions; and out of their mouths came fire, smoke, and brimstone. By these three *plagues* a third of mankind was killed-- by the fire and the smoke and the brimstone which came out of their mouths. For their power is in their mouth and in their tails; for their tails *are* like serpents, having heads; and with them they do harm."** (Revelation 9:17-19)

As we consider the colors of their breastplates, we remember that **"red"** is the color of the great dragon that tries to devour the man child in Revelation 12:3-4. And that **"hyacinth blue"** is similar to the color of the sky. And we remember that Satan is **"the prince of the power of the air."** (Ephesians 2:2) And **"sulfur yellow"** is the color of brimstone. For brimstone was burning sulphur. So all of these colors represent Satanic power.

We see this also in their heads **"like the heads of lions,"** by the fact that **"out of their mouths came fire, smoke, and brimstone,"** and the fact that, like scorpions, **"their tails *are* like serpents, having heads; and with them they do harm."**

And again, we notice where this attack is directed in the fact that **"By these three *plagues* a third of mankind was killed"** So this attack comes to destroy the empty shell of Christendom. It thus appears that this is not speaking of physical death, for the nations involved figure in later prophecies. So they could not have been annihilated at this time. Instead, this speaks of a judgment worse that physical death. It is spiritual death. That is, that everyone that had been falsely professing the name of Christ is now given up to total and open apostasy. They no longer even pretend to be Christians. The time has come when the Lord will do what He said He would do in 2 Thessalonians 2:11-12:

> **"God will send them strong delusion, than they should believe the lie, that they all may be condemned who did not believe the truth but had pleasure in unrighteousness."**

So in this scripture, as in the one before it, God *releases* the wicked messengers that come to deceive the people who had previously rejected His message of salvation. He does not just *allow* them to come. He specifically and explicitly *releases* this deceptive horde of wicked teachers upon the empty shell of Christendom, sending them **"strong delusion."** and why? **"that they all may be condemned who did not believe the truth but had pleasure in unrighteousness."**

Even as I type these words, I am overcome with grief at the horror of this judgement, which is about to fall upon those around us, who live in what is called Christendom. Having heard the truth of

God, they have wilfully rejected it. And God will give them up to the folly they have chosen.

But there is more:

"But the rest of mankind, who were not killed by these plagues, did not repent of the works of their hands, that they should not worship demons, and idols of gold, silver, brass, stone, and wood, which can neither see nor hear nor walk. And they did not repent of their murders or their sorceries or their sexual immorality or their thefts." (Revelation 9:20-21)

Christendom does not consciously worship **"demons."** But much of it indeed worships **"idols"** (they call them icons.) And they do not realize that demons are behind these **"idols of gold, silver, brass, stone, and wood, which can neither see nor hear nor walk."** And they do not repent of this worship. Nor do they **"repent of the works of their hands,"** nor **"of their murders or their sorceries or their sexual immorality or their thefts."**

REVELATION 10

"**I saw still another mighty angel coming down from heaven, clothed with a cloud. And a rainbow *was* on his head, his face *was* like the sun, and his feet like pillars of fire. He had a little book open in his hand. And he set his right foot on the sea and *his* left *foot* on the land.**" (Revelation 10:1-2)

Here we again see an angel presented in an awesome display of power and glory. "**His face was like the sun.**" That is a light unapproachable. "**And his feet like pillars of fire,**" speaking of judgment. But, although he comes in judgment, he has a rainbow about his head, a reminder of God's covenant to never again destroy the earth with a flood. (Genesis 9:12-17) And he is clothed with a cloud, the cloud with which God hid himself on numerous occasions. And he stands on the sea and on the land. We saw in Revelation 7 that the earth speaks of the part of the world that is stable and the sea speaks of the part of the world that has been thrown into confusion

But the angel was holding something. "**He had a little book open in his hand.**" As I noted in the introduction, and again in my comments about Revelation 5, I conclude that this book represents the scroll seen sealed in that chapter. But now that the seals have been opened, it is no longer a Hebrew scroll, but a gentile book, open in the angel's hand. That is, the mysteries of God that had previously been sealed have now been revealed to the eye of faith. And in support of this, we noted that the only previous book of the Bible that had been sealed was the book of Daniel. For Daniel 12:9 says, "**Go *your way*, Daniel, for the words *are* closed up and sealed till the time of the end.**" And "**the last hour**" had already come in John's day. (1 John 2:18)

And the final detail that supports this conclusion is that the book of Daniel, having only twelve chapters, is indeed **"a little book,"** Thus, his conclude that this **"little book open in is hand"** is not only the book that had been **"sealed with seven seals,"** but is also the book of Daniel.

For since the nations involved in the prophecies in Daniel have disappeared long ago, it seems impossible for these prophecies to be fulfilled. But the massive disruptions revealed in the opening of the seven seals show that the existing world order will be completely destroyed, making room for the old (natural) order to rise again. This makes a fulfillment of the prophecies in Daniel no longer seem to be impossible. So what was hidden in Daniel is now revealed.

But now, in speaking of the angel, we are told that he **"cried with a loud voice, as *when* a lion roars. When he cried out, seven thunders uttered their voices. Now when the seven thunders uttered their voices, I was about to write; but I heard a voice from heaven saying to me, 'Seal up the things which the seven thunders uttered, and do not write them.'"** (Revelation 10:3-4)

The **"loud voice"** of this angel was **"as *when* a lion roars."** this, again, speaks of the fact that this is not a message of love, but an announcement of disaster. And it is answered by **"seven thunders."** Everything about this scene is designed to strike terror into the hearts of men. But, even though the sealed book has now been opened, there remain more judgments that God has planned, but He is not going to reveal. For John was told to **"Seal up the things which the seven thunders uttered, and do not write them."**

But now:

"The angel whom I saw standing on the sea and on the land raised up his hand to heaven and swore by Him who lives forever and ever, who created heaven and the things that are in it, the earth and the things that are in it, and the sea and the things that are in it, that there should be delay no longer, [21] **but in the days of the sound-**

---

21 The Greek word that is here correctly translated **"delay,"** was rendered as **"time"** in the KJV, causing many to mistakenly conclude that time itself will cease to exist when the seventh angel sounds. The error of this notion is shown by the fact that in Revelation 20:7 we told, six times over, of a period of one thousand years

ing of the seventh angel, when he is about to sound, the mystery of God would be finished, as He declared to His servants the prophets." (Revelation 10:5-7)

Some have imagined that this announcement sets the time of the rapture, because, they say, the mystery of God is the church. So the time when the church will be finished has to be the time of the rapture. But if they had paid careful attention to the details of the scriptures they are citing, they would not have made this error.

For the first scripture that they are citing says, "... **the mystery of Christ, which in other ages was not made known to the sons of men, as it has now been revealed by the Spirit to His holy apostles and prophets: that the Gentiles should be fellow heirs, of the same body, and partakers of His promise in Christ through the gospel.**" (Ephesians 3:3-6)

And the second scripture they are citing, calls the church, "**... the mystery which has been hidden from ages and from generations, but now has been revealed to His saints. To them God willed to make known what are the riches of the glory of this mystery among the Gentiles: which is Christ in you, the hope of glory.**" (Colossians 1:26-27)

We need to notice that both of these scriptures (and they are the only two that call the church a **"mystery"**) very clearly say that this mystery had not been revealed in the past. The first one phrased it, **"which in other ages was not made known to the sons of men."** And the second one said it **"has been hidden from ages and from generations."**

But **"the mystery of God"** which **"would be finished"** in Revelation 10:7 was **"as He declared to His servants the prophets."** Something that was **"declared to His servants the prophets"** cannot be

---

which will take place after this seventh trumpet sounds. The Greek word in question is "χρονος," "chronos" in our alphabet, (word number 5550 in Strong's Greek Dictionary) although this Greek word indeed means "time," it means time in the sense of "a space of time." And the next Greek word is "ουκετι," "ouketi" in our alphabet. (word number 3765 in Strong's Greek Dictionary) This Greek word means "no more," or "no longer." So the sense of these two words, when taken together, is not that time will cease to exist, but that the allotted space of time will be ended, that is, that there will be no more delay.

what **"in other ages was not made known to the sons of men,"** or what **"has been hidden from ages and from generations."** So the claim that Revelation 10:7 shows the timing of the rapture by saying that at that time **"the mystery of God would be finished"** is clearly erroroneous.

Others, however, interpret the words **"at the last trumpet"** in 1 Corinthians 15:51-52, to be a reference to the seventh trumpet of Revelation. This passage says **"Behold, I tell you a mystery: We shall not all sleep, but we shall all be changed– in a moment, in the twinkling of an eye, at the last trumpet. For the trumpet will sound, and the dead will be raised incorruptible, and we shall be changed."**

The conclusion that this passage refers to the seventh trumpet of Revelation would seem to be strengthened by the fact that we are told that **"the mystery of God," "as He declared it to His servants the prophets," "would be finished" "in the days of the sounding of the seventh angel."**

We have already treated the error of applying the words **"the mystery of God"** to mean "the church." But what of this other interpretation, that "the last trumpet" in 1 Corinthians 15:52 means the last of the seven trumpets of Revelation? If that interpretation were indeed correct, this would conclusively set the timing of the rapture as at the end of the trumpets. But it is by no means conclusive that this interpretation is correct. For **"the last trumpet"** that sounds at the time of the rapture, as is clearly stated in 1 Corinthians 15:51-52, is not the last trumpet of God that will ever be blown. For we are explicitly told of at least two later occasions where a trumpet will be blown.

The first of these is:

> "And it shall come to pass in that day
> *That* the LORD will thresh,
> From the channel of the River to the Brook of Egypt;
> And you will be gathered one by one,
> O you children of Israel.
> So it shall be in that day:

> The great trumpet will be blown;
> They will come, who are about to perish
> in the land of Assyria,
> And they who are outcasts in the land of Egypt,
> And shall worship the LORD in the holy mount
> at Jerusalem." (Isaiah 27:12-13)

And the second one is:

> " 'For I have bent Judah, My *bow*,
> Fitted the bow with Ephraim,
> And raised up your sons, O Zion,
> Against your sons, O Greece,
> And made you like the sword of a mighty man.'
> Then the LORD will be seen over them,
> And His arrow will go forth like lightning.
> The Lord GOD will blow the trumpet,
> And go with whirlwinds from the south.
> The LORD of hosts will defend them;
> They shall devour and subdue with slingstones.
> They shall drink *and* roar as if with wine;
> They shall be filled *with blood* like basins,
> Like the corners of the altar." (Zechariah 9:13-15)

I have quoted so much from each of these passages to show that they are both speaking of times after Messiah has returned and has brought all Israel back to the land.

So each of these passages is clearly about a time that will be after the rapture. But each of these passages clearly speaks of a trumpet being blown. And the second one explicitly says that the one who will blow it will be **"the Lord God."** Why is this important? Because it conclusively proves that, whatever is meant by the words **"at the last trumpet"** in 1 Corinthians 15:52, they do not mean that the trumpet blown at that time will be the last trumpet that will ever be blown. And thus, they do not necessarily mean the seventh trumpet of the Revelation.

If these words were taken by themselves, without other scriptures giving them context, this could indeed be what they mean. But Revelation 3:10, along with 2 Peter 2:4-9, clearly show the timing of the rapture as before the time of testing begins, not after it is finished.

But this is enough about errors in the interpretation of Revelation 10:5-7 What does this passage actually indicate?

The first thing we need to notice about this announcement, is that, in addition to it's being the word of God, as all scripture is, this is confirmed by the strongest oath possible. For the angel **"raised up his hand to heaven and swore by Him who lives forever and ever, who created heaven and the things that are in it, the earth and the things that are in it, and the sea and the things that are in it."** That is, he raised his right hand and swore by God as the creator of everything. Could God have even possibly made any proclamation more absolute? This is something that will most certainly take place.

But what did He swear to? **"That there should be delay no longer."** The time was up. It was all over. But what was over?

"but in the days of the sounding of the seventh angel, when he is about to sound, the mystery of God would be finished." There would be no more secrets. For that is what **"mystery"** means. Everything to come after that was plainly declared, not a **"mystery."** But the **"mystery"** he spoke of was **"as He declared to His servants the prophets."**

God had spoken many things in deep sayings, in symbolic language. But everything to happen after the seventh trumpet was plainly declared, not a **"mystery."**

But after this declaration, a new subject is introduced.

John is told to eat the little book.

> "Then the voice which I heard from heaven spoke to me again and said, 'Go, take the little book which is open in the hand of the angel who stands on the sea and on the earth.' So I went to the angel and said to him, 'Give me the little book.' And he said to me, 'Take and eat it; and it will make your stomach bitter, but it will be as sweet as honey in your

> mouth.' Then I took the little book out of the angel's hand and ate it, and it was as sweet as honey in my mouth. But when I had eaten it, my stomach became bitter. And he said to me, 'You must prophesy again about many peoples, nations, tongues, and kings.' " (Revelation 10:8-11)

The first thing we will notice is that. Although **"the mystery of God"** has now been completely declared, there is still much to prophesy about. So John was told, **"You must prophesy again about many peoples, nations, tongues, and kings."** But before that, there was something important to do. John was instructed to **"eat"** **"the little book,"** now that it had been opened. That is, he was to digest it, to make it part of himself. That is, to study it until he knew it so well that it simply became a part of himself.

But something happened as he obeyed this command. **"The little book"** that was now **"open,"** was **"sweet as honey"** in his mouth. But when he **"had eaten it, it made"** his **"stomach bitter."** That is, it gave him an upset stomach. It made him sick.

And thus it always happens when the prophetic scriptures are sincerely studied. It is unspeakably pleasant as the various pieces begin to come together in the minds of the students, as they see the wondrous wisdom of God in hiding everything from unholy eyes, while declaring it all to His own. But once the message is finally understood, there is nothing pleasant about it. Finally understanding the horror of what is to come will make the student of Bible prophecy sick.

But as this is the point at which John was told to **"eat"** the **"little book,"** we will now do the same. Which is why this book is titled "Revelation And Daniel, Considered Together."

So at this time, before we go on with the rest of the book of Revelation, we will go back and study the book of Daniel, the sealed book that is now open, and which, at this point, the prophet was instructed to **"eat.**

Daniel 1

This very important book of the Bible opens with the ultimate disaster striking the Lord's people. This was a disaster so complete that it would shake the faith of anyone who had never bothered to study and understand the word of God. But He had repeatedly warned them that, unless they repented, this was coming. How solemn is this warning to ourselves, as we observe the increasing evil of all around us, and remember that we have been given a similar warning, that unless we repent, an even worse fate even now hangs over our own heads.

But in Daniel's time, they had not repented, and the blow had fallen.

> **"In the third year of the reign of Jehoiakim king of Judah, Nebuchadnezzar king of Babylon came to Jerusalem and besieged it. And the Lord gave Jehoiakim king of Judah into his hand, with some of the articles of the house of God, which he carried into the land of Shinar to the house of his god; and he brought the articles into the treasure house of his god."** (Daniel 1:1-2)

Not only had the nation and its capital city, Jerusalem, fallen. But even the temple, the Holy Place of the very God of heaven, had been ransacked. All was lost. It had indeed been the ultimate disaster. And then the conqueror did something very wise, by human standards. He selected those that might be tempted to lead a rebellion, and took them to be officials in his own administration. This would give them a vested interest in his security, turning potential enemies into allies.

> "Then the king instructed Ashpenaz, the master of his eunuchs, to bring some of the children of Israel and some of the king's descendants and some of the nobles, young men in whom *there was* no blemish, but good-looking, gifted in all wisdom, possessing knowledge and quick to understand, who *had* ability to serve in the king's palace, and whom they might teach the language and literature of the Chaldeans." (Daniel 1:3-4)

But, although he took them as captives, this king did not want these specially selected individuals to feel like slaves. So:

> "And the king appointed for them a daily provision of the king's delicacies and of the wine which he drank, and three years of training for them, so that at the end of *that time* they might serve before the king." (Daniel 1:5)

The idea was to assimilate them into the Chaldean society, so they would think of themselves as Chaldeans, rather than Jews. And not simply as Chaldeans, but as Chaldeans of the privileged class. The goal was to make them faithful servants of the king.

> "Now from among those of the sons of Judah were Daniel, Hananiah, Mishael, and Azariah. To them the chief of the eunuchs gave names: he gave Daniel the name Belteshazzar; to Hananiah, Shadrach; to Mishael, Meshach; and to Azariah, Abed-Nego." (Daniel 1:5-7)

To complete their assimilation, each of these captives was even given a new name. And it is instructive to note that, in the later chapters of this book, only Daniel continued to be known by his godly name. We understand the reason for this when we notice that Daniel purposed not to defile himself.

> "But Daniel purposed in his heart that he would not defile himself with the portion of the king's delicacies, nor with the wine which he drank." (Daniel 1:8a)

"The king's delicacies" and **"the wine which he drank"** contained many foods that were forbidden under the law of Moses. **"But Daniel purposed in his heart."** His heart was steadfast toward the God of his fathers, the very God of heaven. So he **"purposed in his heart that he would not defile himself."**

We are reminded of the old Sunday School refrain:

> "Dare to be a Daniel.
> Dare to stand alone.
> Dare to have a purpose firm.
> Dare to make it known."

But Daniel, already being a godly man, though he was still young, realized that this disaster had been sent by God. So, although he **"purposed in his heart,"** he was not rebellious in his purpose. Instead of rebelling:

> **"Therefore he requested of the chief of the eunuchs that he might not defile himself."** (Daniel 1:8b)

And what was the result of Daniel accepting the authority he knew had been sent by God, even though it was oppressive? First, we have a short explanation.

> **"Now God had brought Daniel into the favor and goodwill of the chief of the eunuchs."** (Daniel 1:9)

This had not just been something that had happened. It had been brought about by God. We remember the old saying, "God works behind the scenes. But He moves the scenes He is behind." So, as a direct result of an act of God, **"the chief of the eunuchs"** was favorably disposed toward Daniel. But, although he was so favorably disposed, there was a problem.

> "And the chief of the eunuchs said to Daniel, 'I fear my lord the king, who has appointed your food and drink. For why should he see your faces looking worse than the young men who are your age? Then you would endanger my head before the king.'" (Daniel 1:10)

So Daniel, already wise beyond his years, and filled with faith in his God, proposed a test. And relying upon his God, he knew how it would work out.

> "So Daniel said to the steward whom the chief of the eunuchs had set over Daniel, Hananiah, Mishael, and Azariah, 'Please test your servants for ten days, and let them give us vegetables to eat and water to drink. Then let our appearance be examined before you, and the appearance of the young men who eat the portion of the king's delicacies; and as you see fit, *so* deal with your servants.'" (Daniel 1:12-13)

And Daniel was not disappointed in his faith.

> "So he consented with them in this matter, and tested them ten days. And at the end of ten days their features appeared better and fatter in flesh than all the young men who ate the portion of the king's delicacies. Thus the steward took away their portion of delicacies and the wine that they were to drink, and gave them vegetables." (Daniel 1:14-16)

We find an important lesson here. For we are explicitly commanded to **"submit yourselves to every ordinance of man for the Lord's sake, whether to the king as supreme, or to governors, as to those who are sent by him for the punishment of evildoers and *for the* praise of those who do good. For this is the will of God, that by

doing good you may put to silence the ignorance of foolish men-- as free, yet not using liberty as a cloak for vice, but as bondservants of God." (1 Peter 2:13-16)

Many Christians in the United States, fearing we will lose our Constitutionally protected rights, are arming themselves in preparation for rebellion against a potential future oppressive government. And, considering the known intentions of some political entities in this nation, that danger is real. But, even if our God should allow this in our fair land, His command to us remains the same. For we are also told, **"Let every soul be subject to the governing authorities. For there is no authority except from God, and the authorities that exist are appointed by God. Therefore whoever resists the authority resists the ordinance of God, and those who resist will bring judgment on themselves."** (Romans 13:1-2)

If our God allows an oppressive government to exercise oppressive power in our fair land, We are still to submit ourselves, in every case except when they command us to disobey a direct command of God. In that case, we are not authorized to rebel, but instead are instructed to submit ourselves to the higher authority, that of God, and obey Him, rather than the lower authority. For this we have the example of the Apostles themselves, who told the rulers who had forbidden them to teach in the name of Jesus that **"We ought to obey God rather than men."** (Acts 5:29)

And what was the result of the commitment of Daniel and his three friends to follow the Lord?

> "As for these four young men, God gave them knowledge and skill in all literature and wisdom; and Daniel had understanding in all visions and dreams. Now at the end of the days, when the king had said that they should be brought in, the chief of the eunuchs brought them in before Nebuchadnezzar. Then the king interviewed them, and among them all none was found like Daniel, Hananiah, Mishael, and Azariah; therefore they served before the king. And in all matters of wisdom *and* understanding about which the king examined them, he found them ten times

better than all the magicians *and* astrologers who were in all his realm." (Daniel 1:17-20)

God Himself honored those who honored Him. And He **"gave them knowledge and skill in all literature and wisdom."** And to their leader, Daniel, He gave a special gift. For **"Daniel had understanding in all visions and dreams."**

And the result was that **"Thus Daniel continued until the first year of King Cyrus."** (Daniel 1:21)

 **Daniel 2**

Now comes a most interesting story of Nebuchadnezzar's dream.

> "Now in the second year of Nebuchadnezzar's reign, Nebuchadnezzar had dreams; and his spirit was so troubled that his sleep left him. Then the king gave the command to call the magicians, the astrologers, the sorcerers, and the Chaldeans to tell the king his dreams." (Daniel 2:1-2a)

The Lord had given Nebuchadnezzar a message in a dream. And He gave it in such a way that the great ruler realized it had not just been a dream, but had been a very important warning. We are not told how the Lord impressed this upon him. But from the way he acted, this seems to have been more than just ancient superstition. Somehow, he *knew* this was important. So he did the only thing he knew to do. He called **"the magicians, the astrologers, the sorcerers, and the Chaldeans."** These men were supposed to know such things. So he called them. But he was cagy. He had his doubts about thm. So he gave them a test.

In response to his summons, **"they came and stood before the king. And the king said to them, 'I have had a dream, and my spirit is anxious to know the dream.'"** (Daniel 2:2b-3) Startled, they answered **"O king, live forever! Tell your servants the dream, and we will give the interpretation."** (Daniel 2:4) But the cagy monarch replied, **"My decision is firm: if you do not make known the dream** to me, and its interpretation, you shall be cut in pieces, and your houses shall be made an ash heap." (Daniel 2:5)

This was a serious test, and a significant one. If they could really tell the unknowable, they would be able to tell him, not only what his dream meant, but what it was. Some translations make this sound like he had forgotten the dream, only remembering that it had terrified him. But our NKJV rendering gives its true sense. He was testing them. This is shown by the fact that he put teeth in the test. **"if you do not make known the dream to me... you shall be cut in pieces, and your houses shall be made an ash heap."**

But then he tried to sweeten the pot, saying, **"However, if you tell the dream and its interpretation, you shall receive from me gifts, rewards, and great honor. Therefore tell me the dream and its interpretation."** (Daniel 2:6)

Dumbfound, the rascals replied, **"Let the king tell his servants the dream, and we will give its interpretation."** (Daniel 2:7) But he answered them **"I know for certain that you would gain time, because you see that my decision is firm: if you do not make known the dream to me,** *there is only* **one decree for you! For you have agreed to speak lying and corrupt words before me till the time has changed. Therefore tell me the dream, and I shall know that you can give me its interpretation."** (Daniel 2:8-9)

So now the king comes right out and plainly says *why* he is making such an outrageous demand. He had long suspected that they were frauds, and now was his chance to test them. So he says, **"tell me the dream, and I shall know that you can give me its interpretation."**

Now desperate, they answer, **"There is not a man on earth who can tell the king's matter; therefore no king, lord, or ruler has** *ever* **asked such things of any magician, astrologer, or Chaldean.** *It is* **a difficult thing that the king requests, and there is no other who can tell it to the king except the gods, whose dwelling is not with flesh."** (Daniel 2:10-11) And thus the God of heaven tricked these desperate men into the confession He wanted. For truly, only God could reveal such a thing. And God was preparing to do that very thing. But **"For this reason the king was angry and very furious, and gave a command to destroy all the wise men of Babylon."** (Daniel 2:12)

This seemed like an unjustified fit of rage. But it was not. These men had long pretended to have such powers, and now it had been proved that they did not. So a death penalty was decreed upon all of them. **"So the decree went out, and they began killing the wise men; and they sought Daniel and his companions, to kill them."** (Daniel 2:13) There was no trial, no appeal. The killing began immediately. And in very short order, it came to the Hebrew captives. For their reputation as wise men had already been firmly established.

> **"Then with counsel and wisdom Daniel answered Arioch, the captain of the king's guard, who had gone out to kill the wise *men* of Babylon; he answered and said to Arioch the king's captain, 'Why is the decree from the king so urgent?' Then Arioch made the decision known to Daniel. So Daniel went in and asked the king to give him time, that he might tell the king the interpretation."** (Daniel 2:14-16)

Daniel goes directly to the king, and makes a very simple request and an offer. Just give me a little time, and I will give you your answer. Daniel was once again putting his trust in his almighty God. He knew God would reveal this to him, if he asked. So he asked the king to give him a chance.

> **"Then Daniel went to his house, and made the decision known to Hananiah, Mishael, and Azariah, his companions, that they might seek mercies from the God of heaven concerning this secret, so that Daniel and his companions might not perish with the rest of the wise *men* of Babylon."** (Daniel 2:17-18)

Such is always the way of the Godly. When faced with a desperate situation, they seek the face of their God. And He does not disappoint them. For **"Then the secret was revealed to Daniel in a night vision."** (Daniel 2:19a)

And what is the first thing the godly man does? **"So Daniel blessed the God of heaven."** (Daniel 2:19b) And then:

> "Daniel answered and said:
> 'Blessed be the name of God forever and ever,
> For wisdom and might are His.
> And He changes the times and the seasons;
> He removes kings and raises up kings;
> He gives wisdom to the wise
> And knowledge to those who have understanding.
> He reveals deep and secret things;
> He knows what is in the darkness,
> And light dwells with Him.
> 'I thank You and praise You, O God of my fathers;
> You have given me wisdom and might,
> And have now made known to me what we asked of You,
> For You have made known to us the king's demand.' "
> (Daniel 2:20-23)

> "Therefore Daniel went to Arioch, whom the king had appointed to destroy the wise *men* of Babylon. He went and said thus to him: 'Do not destroy the wise *men* of Babylon; take me before the king, and I will tell the king the interpretation.' Then Arioch quickly brought Daniel before the king, and said thus to him, 'I have found a man of the captives of Judah, who will make known to the king the interpretation.' " (Daniel 2:24-25)

Arioch, having found the "kill" order very distasteful, makes haste to bring the king word. And the king gives Daniel the same test he had given the fakers.

"The king answered and said to Daniel, whose name *was* Belteshazzar, 'Are you able to make known to me the dream which I have seen, and its interpretation?' " (Daniel 2:26) And the godly Daniel gives credit where credit is due, answering, **"The secret which the king has demanded, the wise *men*, the astrologers, the magicians, and the soothsayers cannot declare to the king. But there is a God in heaven who reveals secrets, and He has made known to King Nebuchadnezzar what will be in the latter days. Your dream, and the visions of your head upon your bed, were these: As for you, O king, thoughts came *to* your *mind while* on your bed, *about* what**

would come to pass after this; and He who reveals secrets has made known to you what will be. But as for me, this secret has not been revealed to me because I have more wisdom than anyone living, but for *our* sakes who make known the interpretation to the king, and that you may know the thoughts of your heart." (Daniel 2:27-30)

We now realize that God had set all this up to make it exceedingly clear to **"King Nebuchadnezzar"** that this was indeed a message from himself. He is the one that had given the king the idea of this impossible test. For no one but a true prophet of God could even possibly tell him what he had dreamed. But beyond just telling him what he had dreamed, the prophet reinforced the message by even telling him what he was thinking. So now he *really* had the monarch's attention.

> "You, O king, were watching; and behold, a great image! This great image, whose splendor *was* excellent, stood before you; and its form *was* awesome. This image's head *was* of fine gold, its chest and arms of silver, its belly and thighs of bronze, its legs of iron, its feet partly of iron and partly of clay. You watched while a stone was cut out without hands, which struck the image on its feet of iron and clay, and broke them in pieces. Then the iron, the clay, the bronze, the silver, and the gold were crushed together, and became like chaff from the summer threshing floors; the wind carried them away so that no trace of them was found. And the stone that struck the image became a great mountain and filled the whole earth. This *is* the dream. Now we will tell the interpretation of it before the king." (Daniel 2:31-36)

Knowing that this was exactly what he had seen in his dream, the great king listens intently as Daniel continues:

"You, O king, *are* a king of kings. For the God of heaven has given you a kingdom, power, strength, and glory; and wherever the children of men dwell, or the beasts of the field and the birds of the heaven, He has given *them* into your hand, and has made you ruler over them all--you *are* this head of gold. But after you shall arise another kingdom inferior to yours; then another, a third kingdom of bronze, which shall rule over all the earth.

And the fourth kingdom shall be as strong as iron, inasmuch as iron breaks in pieces and shatters everything; and like iron that crushes, *that kingdom* will break in pieces and crush all the others. Whereas you saw the feet and toes, partly of potter's clay and partly of iron, the kingdom shall be divided; yet the strength of the iron shall be in it, just as you saw the iron mixed with ceramic clay. And *as* the toes of the feet *were* partly of iron and partly of clay, *so* the kingdom shall be partly strong and partly fragile. As you saw iron mixed with ceramic clay, they will mingle with the seed of men; but they will not adhere to one another, just as iron does not mix with clay. And in the days of these kings the God of heaven will set up a kingdom which shall never be destroyed; and the kingdom shall not be left to other people; it shall break in pieces and consume all these kingdoms, and it shall stand forever. Inasmuch as you saw that the stone was cut out of the mountain without hands, and that it broke in pieces the iron, the bronze, the clay, the silver, and the gold--the great God has made known to the king what will come to pass after this." (Daniel 2:37-45a)

And then, with the calm assurance of a true prophet of God, Daniel adds, **"The dream is certain, and its interpretation is sure."** (Daniel 4:45b) And the potentate was stunned:

"Then King Nebuchadnezzar fell on his face, prostrate before Daniel, and commanded that they should present an offering and incense to him. The king answered Daniel, and said, 'Truly your God is the God of gods, the Lord of kings, and a revealer of secrets, since you could reveal this secret.' Then the king promoted Daniel and gave him many great gifts; and he made him ruler over the whole province of Babylon, and chief administrator over all the wise *men* of Babylon." (Daniel 2:46-48)

But Daniel did not really want all this, so **"Daniel petitioned the king, and he set Shadrach, Meshach, and Abed-Nego over the affairs of the province of Babylon; but Daniel *sat* in the gate of the king."** (Daniel 2:49)

But now, having finished the story part of this account, since we are trying to **"eat" "the little book,"** we need to go back and carefully consider the fine details of this prophecy, to digest it, to make it a part of ourselves.

The prophet's answer began with the words **"As for you, O king, thoughts came *to* your *mind while* on your bed, *about* what would come to pass after this; and He who reveals secrets has made known to you what will be."** (Daniel 2:29) And it ended with the words **"the great God has made known to the king what will come to pass after this. The dream is certain, and its interpretation is sure."** (Daniel 2:45) So there can be zero doubt that the subject of this message was what was going to come to pass in the future. But how far into the future did it go? It extends to the time when **"in the days of these kings the God of heaven will set up a kingdom which shall never be destroyed; and the kingdom shall not be left to other people; it shall break in pieces and consume all these kingdoms, and it shall stand forever."** (Daniel 2:44)

"The God of heaven" is going to **"set up a kingdom."** And this kingdom **"shall break in pieces and consume all these kingdoms."** Some imagine that this happened in the first century. But we must ask, did **"the kingdom of God,"** as it was set up in the first century **"break in pieces and consume all these"** other **"kingdoms?"** The answer is, of course, clearly no.

All of these kingdoms except the last one involved mainly areas where Christianity is all but non-existent. They are almost 100% Islamic. **"These kingdoms"** have never been broken **"in pieces"** and consumed by **"the kingdom of God,"** as it exists today. This has unquestionably never happened, even to the present day. So this prophecy extends even into our own future.

But what of the dream itself? In that dream the king saw **"a great image... whose splendor *was* excellent... and its form *was* awesome"** (Daniel 2:31) As the description develops we realize that what the king saw was what we would call a statue. A huge statue, in the form of a man. But, unlike an ordinary statue, the various parts of this statue were made from different materials, which were described from the top down.

> **"This image's head *was* of fine gold, its chest and arms of silver, its belly and thighs of bronze, its legs of iron, its feet partly of iron and partly of clay."** (Daniel 2:32)

In the divinely inspired interpretation, the king was told that **"You, O king, *are* a king of kings. For the God of heaven has given you a kingdom, power, strength, and glory; and wherever the children of men dwell, or the beasts of the field and the birds of the heaven, He has given *them* into your hand, and has made you ruler over them all--you *are* this head of gold."** (Daniel 2:37-38)

The kingdom of **Nebuchadnezzar** had not just happened. It had been given to him by **"the God of heaven."** Indeed, we are told in the New Testament that **"there is no authority except from God, and the authorities that exist are appointed by God."** (Romans 13:1) And God had made him ruler of the entire known world. He was **"this head of Gold."**

But below **"this head of Gold,"** the statue's **"chest and arms"** were **"of silver, its belly and thighs of bronze, its legs of iron."** And in the inspired interpretation, the king was told, **"But after you shall arise another kingdom inferior to yours; then another, a third kingdom of bronze, which shall rule over all the earth. And the fourth kingdom shall be as strong as iron, inasmuch as iron breaks in pieces and shatters everything; and like iron that crushes, *that kingdom* will break in pieces and crush all the others."** (Daniel 2:39-40)

We notice two things about this succession. The material that represented each of these succeeding kingdoms was not as valuable as what represented the previous one, but, in every case except the last one, was stronger than what represented the previous one. And so it was in history. The world kingdom of Babylon and the Chaldeans, set up by Nebuchadnezzar, was replaced by the Medo-Persian empire under the leadership of Darius. This, in turn, was replaced by the Greek empire set up by Alexander the great, which was in turn replaced by the Roman Empire. And, just as depicted in the statue, each of these world empires was more powerful, but less noble, than the one before it.

But there was more. In the king's dream, below the statue's **"legs of iron,"** he saw **"its feet partly of iron and partly of clay."** (Daniel 2:33) And the inspired interpretation of this was:

> **"Whereas you saw the feet and toes, partly of potter's clay and partly of iron, the kingdom shall be divided; yet the**

> **strength of the iron shall be in it, just as you saw the iron mixed with ceramic clay. And *as* the toes of the feet *were* partly of iron and partly of clay, *so* the kingdom shall be partly strong and partly fragile. As you saw iron mixed with ceramic clay, they will mingle with the seed of men; but they will not adhere to one another, just as iron does not mix with clay."** (Daniel 2:41-43)

Now we see a condition that has never existed in recorded history. The Roman Empire remained strong until the time of its fall. And its eventual fall did not come about as a result of internal division, but as a result of widespread degradation. The population in general became soft, used to a life of luxury instead of the life of a soldier. In the election of rulers, the cry "bread and the circuses" became the rallying cry. All the people wanted was to be given food without having to work for it, and to be entertained. So when the barbarians attacked, there was no strength to resist. As a song put it some years ago,

> "They were so busy being merry ones,
> That they didn't notice the barbarians." [22]

So this condition, in which the kingdom was **"partly strong and partly fragile,"** has never existed. It is therefore future. So this part of the image represents a revival of the Roman Empire. It has to still be Rome, for it is still made of iron. But in this future condition a weak element is added.

There is today a movement to reunite Europe into a single nation, like the Unites States of America. But there is a serious problem with that effort. Americans think of themselves first as Americans, and then as citizens of whatever state they live in, Ohio, Wyoming, or whatever. But Europeans think of themselves first as citizens of a particular nation, Germany, France, or whatever, and then as Europeans. So a reunited Europe can never have the unified strength of a single nation. **"They will mingle with the seed of men; but they will not adhere to one another, just as iron does not mix with clay."**

---

22 "Up With People - Freedom Isn't Free," by Paul & Ralph Colwell.

So this prophecy states what we now see developing, that the Roman Empire will be revived. And in that revival, there will be a measure of strength. But it will have the inherent weakness that its people will not bond together as a united entity.

Then, as the king watched, **"a stone was cut out without hands, which struck the image on its feet of iron and clay, and broke them in pieces. Then the iron, the clay, the bronze, the silver, and the gold were crushed together, and became like chaff from the summer threshing floors; the wind carried them away so that no trace of them was found. And the stone that struck the image became a great mountain and filled the whole earth."** (Daniel 2:33-35)

The inspired interpretation of ths part of the dream was:

"And in the days of these kings the God of heaven will set up a kingdom which shall never be destroyed; and the kingdom shall not be left to other people; it shall break in pieces and consume all these kingdoms, and it shall stand forever. Inasmuch as you saw that the stone was cut out of the mountain without hands, and that it broke in pieces the iron, the bronze, the clay, the silver, and the gold--the great God has made known to the king what will come to pass after this." (Daniel 2:44-45)

But we need to pay particular attention to what happened when the **"stone cut out without hands"** struck the statue. The first thing we notice is that it **"struck the image on its feet of iron and clay."** That is, it did not strike the image on the part that represented the ancient Roman Empire, that was **"as strong as iron."** nstead, it struck it on the part that represented the future revival of that Empire.

That clearly shows that this stone cannot represent **"the kingdom of God"** as it exists today. For the present **"kingdom of God"** collided with ancient Rome in the days of its strength, the part of the statue that was represented by **"iron."** No, this stone **"struck the image on its feet of iron and clay."** That is, it struck the statue on the part that represents the Roman Empire in its future condition of being partly strong and partly weak.

But there is more. For when the **"stone cut out without hands"** **"struck the image,"** **"Then the iron, the clay, the bronze, the** silver, and the gold were crushed together, and became like chaff from the summer threshing floors."

We have already noticed that **"the kingdom of God,"** as it exists today, has most certainly not crushed the Islamic regions that are the current remnants of the head of Gold, Babylon, the southern part of modern Iraq. And it has most certainly not crushed the chest and arms of silver, the Medo-Persian Empire, modern Iran. So this again makes it very clear that this crushing remains to be accomplished in a day that is still future.

But if **"the stone that was cut out without hands"** is not **"the kingdom of God"** as it exists today, what does it represent? First we notice that **"the stone that struck the image became a great mountain and filled the whole earth."** And the Divinely inspired interpretation of this was:

"And in the days of these kings the God of heaven will set up a kingdom which shall never be destroyed; and the kingdom shall not be left to other people; it shall break in pieces and consume all these kingdoms, and it shall stand forever." (Daniel 2:44)

So **"the stone"** unquestionably represents **"the kingdom of God."** But it represents it in a future state, unlike its present existence on this earth.

Many want to deny that there will be such a future earthly kingdom. But it is very clearly described in many scriptures.

A typical one of these is:

> " 'Behold, *the* days are coming,'" says the LORD,
> 'That I will raise to David a Branch of righteousness;
> A King shall reign and prosper,
> And execute judgment and righteousness in the earth.
> In His days Judah will be saved,
> And Israel will dwell safely;
> Now this is His name by which He will be called:
> THE LORD OUR RIGHTEOUSNESS.
> 'Therefore, behold, *the* days are coming,' says the LORD, 'that they shall no longer say, "As the LORD lives who brought up the children of Israel from the land of Egypt," but, "As

the LORD lives who brought up and led the descendants of the house of Israel from the north country and from all the countries where I had driven them." And they shall dwell in their own land.' " (Jeremiah 23:5-8)

So there can be no question whatsoever that there is coming a time when **"the Kingdom of God"** will exist on this earth in a physical form that all will be able to see. And that is what is represented by the **"stone cut out without hands"** becoming **"a great mountain"** and filling **"the whole earth"** after it has broken **"in pieces"** and consumed **"all these kingdoms." "And it shall stand forever."**

Daniel 3

But, although **Nebuchadnezzar** was deeply impressed by the fact that Daniel had proved to him that his dream had indeed been a message from God. He was, at this point, still nothing but an evil oriental potentate, a man who ruled everything according to the dictates of his own evil heart. He was so impressed by the statue in his dream, that he decided to make one himself. But this was even grander than the one in his dream. For it was made completely of gold. So we read about Nebuchadnezzar's image:

"Nebuchadnezzar the king made an image of gold, whose height *was* sixty cubits *and* its width six cubits. He set it up in the plain of Dura, in the province of Babylon." (Daniel 3:1)

We realize the pretentiousness of this image when we realize that in our measurements, that was 90 feet high and 9 feet wide. That is a huge amount of gold, and its cost was beyond belief. But nothing is too expensive for self aggrandizement. After all, was not he the great Nebuchadnezzar, king of the entire known world? For he had not yet been humbled by **"the God of heaven."** But this potentate's pride caused him to commit a serious crime against **"the God of gods,"** demanding the worship that is due to God alone.

"And King Nebuchadnezzar sent *word* to gather together the satraps, the administrators, the governors, the counselors, the treasurers, the judges, the magistrates, and all the officials of the provinces, to come to the dedication of the image which King Nebuchadnezzar had set up. So the satraps, the

> administrators, the governors, the counselors, the treasurers, the judges, the magistrates, and all the officials of the provinces gathered together for the dedication of the image that King Nebuchadnezzar had set up; and they stood before the image that Nebuchadnezzar had set up. Then a herald cried aloud: 'To you it is commanded, O peoples, nations, and languages, *that* at the time you hear the sound of the horn, flute, harp, lyre, *and* psaltery, in symphony with all kinds of music, you shall fall down and worship the gold image that King Nebuchadnezzar has set up; and whoever does not fall down and worship shall be cast immediately into the midst of a burning fiery furnace.' " (Daniel 3:2-6)

In fear of this dreadful punishment,

> "So at that time, when all the people heard the sound of the horn, flute, harp, *and* lyre, in symphony with all kinds of music, all the people, nations, and languages fell down *and* worshiped the gold image which King Nebuchadnezzar had set up." (Daniel 3:7)

But then the king was informed that some had dared to disobey his order.

> "Therefore at that time certain Chaldeans came forward and accused the Jews. They spoke and said to King Nebuchadnezzar, 'O king, live forever! You, O king, have made a decree that everyone who hears the sound of the horn, flute, harp, lyre, *and* psaltery, in symphony with all kinds of music, shall fall down and worship the gold image; and whoever does not fall down and worship shall be cast into the midst of a burning fiery furnace. There are certain Jews whom you have set over the affairs of the province of Babylon: Shadrach, Meshach, and Abed-Nego; these men, O king, have not paid due regard to you. They do not serve your gods or worship the gold image which you have set up.' " (Daniel 3:8-12)

REVELATION AND DANIEL

In a fit of rage, the despot called these three before him.

> "**Then Nebuchadnezzar, in rage and fury, gave the command to bring Shadrach, Meshach, and Abed-Nego. So they brought these men before the king. Nebuchadnezzar spoke, saying to them, 'Is it true, Shadrach, Meshach, and Abed-Nego,** *that* **you do not serve my gods or worship the gold image which I have set up? Now if you are ready at the time you hear the sound of the horn, flute, harp, lyre,** *and* **psaltery, in symphony with all kinds of music, and you fall down and worship the image which I have made,** *good***! But if you do not worship, you shall be cast immediately Into the midst of a burning fiery furnace.'** " (Daniel 3:13-15a)

And then the foolish monarch made an unfortunate challenge.

"And who *is* **the god who will deliver you from my hands?"** (Daniel 3:15b) It seems from these words that, from his past experiences, perhaps those with Daniel, that he knew that the Jews claimed that their God had power. So he derisively asked them if they really imagined that their God could deliver them from his own power, which he imagined was irresistible.

This was a serious test for these men of God. A test that, until quite recently, most of us here in the United States have never imagined we would ever have to face. But it is now becoming increasingly obvious that such tests may indeed be soon allowed here. We need to seriously consider whether or not we are ready for such a test. But **"Shadrach, Meshach, and Abed-Nego"** passed it. For:

"Shadrach, Meshach, and Abed-Nego answered and said to the king, 'O Nebuchadnezzar, we have no need to answer you in this matter. If that *is the case*, **our God whom we serve is able to deliver us from the burning fiery furnace, and He will deliver** *us* **from your hand, O king. But if not, let it be known to you, O king, that we do not serve your gods, nor will we worship the gold image which you have set up.'** " (Daniel 3:16-18)

Their answer was very simple. And it is the only way we can answer if such a test ever comes to us. "Of course our God is able to deliver us. But even if He does not, we still will not betray Him." The despot's anger now knew no bounds.

> "Then Nebuchadnezzar was full of fury, and the expression on his face changed toward Shadrach, Meshach, and Abed-Nego. He spoke and commanded that they heat the furnace seven times more than it was usually heated. And he commanded certain mighty men of valor who *were* in his army to bind Shadrach, Meshach, and Abed-Nego, *and* cast *them* into the burning fiery furnace." (Daniel 3:19-20)

Many have questioned why Daniel does not appear in this confrontation. But it would seem that the answer lies in Daniel's special office in the government, more of an advisor to the king himself, than one of **"the satraps, the administrators, the governors, the counselors, the treasurers, the judges, the magistrates, and all the officials of the provinces."** So it would appear that Daniel was not among those summoned to the dedication of the image.

But the result of the kings furious order was that:

"Then these men were bound in their coats, their trousers, their turbans, and their other garments, and were cast into the midst of the burning fiery furnace. Therefore, because the king's command was urgent, and the furnace exceedingly hot, the flame of the fire killed those men who took up Shadrach, Meshach, and Abed-Nego. And these three men, Shadrach, Meshach, and Abed-Nego, fell down bound into the midst of the burning fiery furnace." (Daniel 3:21-23)

Our God has not promised to keep us from our problems. But He has promised to be with us in them. And so it was here.

> "Then King Nebuchadnezzar was astonished; and he rose in haste *and* spoke, saying to his counselors, 'Did we not cast three men bound into the midst of the fire?' They answered and said to the king, 'True, O king.' 'Look!' he answered, 'I see four men loose, walking in the midst of the fire; and they

> are not hurt, and the form of the fourth is like the Son of God.' " (Daniel 3:24-25)

Suddenly, the king realizes that **"the Most High God"** had answered his challenge, **"who *is* the god who will deliver you from my hands?"** Instead of doing something trivial like forcibly stopping him from throwing his faithful servants into the fire, their God had gone into the fire with them, and cooled its fury.

The king had just had seen the mightiest men in his army fall dead from the terrible heat of just casting these men into the fire. And now he sees them walking around, not harmed in the slightest, and when they come out, not even smelling like smoke. Both he and all his counselors were stunned. The king was defeated. And they all knew it.

> **"Then Nebuchadnezzar went near the mouth of the burning fiery furnace *and* spoke, saying, 'Shadrach, Meshach, and Abed-Nego, servants of the Most High God, come out, and come *here*.' Then Shadrach, Meshach, and Abed-Nego came from the midst of the fire. And the satraps, administrators, governors, and the king's counselors gathered together, and they saw these men on whose bodies the fire had no power; the hair of their head was not singed nor were their garments affected, and the smell of fire was not on them."** (Daniel 3:26-27)

But, still a pagan at heart, though stunned by the power of the Almighty God, the king now makes a decree that is similar to his previous one, even though it is now directed in the opposite direction from the last one.

> **"Nebuchadnezzar spoke, saying, "Blessed be the God of Shadrach, Meshach, and Abed-Nego, who sent His Angel and delivered His servants who trusted in Him, and they have frustrated the king's word, and yielded their bodies, that they should not serve nor worship any god except their own God! Therefore I make a decree that any people, nation,**

or language which speaks anything amiss against the God of Shadrach, Meshach, and Abed-Nego shall be cut in pieces, and their houses shall be made an ash heap; because there is no other God who can deliver like this.' " (Daniel 3:28-29)

The lesson we see here is that, although God will not always keep His own out of troubles, He will always be with them in the troubles He allows. And the long term result was:

"Then the king promoted Shadrach, Meshach, and Abed-Nego in the province of Babylon." (Daniel 3:30)

Daniel 4

We now come to a unique part of scripture, not even written in the Hebrew or Greek language. For it was penned by none other than the great Nebuchadnezzar himself.

Although he had now been twice awestruck by the power of **"the Most High God,"** Nebuchadnezzar had continued to be nothing but a despotic pagan, an oriental potentate whose pride knew no bounds. But God always finishes whatever He begins. And He was working on the proud monarch. This is the story of Nebuchadnezzar's conversion.

So Nebuchadnezzar began his story, **"Nebuchadnezzar the king, To all peoples, nations, and languages that dwell in all the earth: Peace be multiplied to you. I thought it good to declare the signs and wonders that the Most High God has worked for me. How great *are* His signs, And how mighty His wonders! His kingdom is an everlasting kingdom, And His dominion is from generation to generation."** (Daniel 4:1-3)

And his story ends with the words, **"Now I, Nebuchadnezzar, praise and extol and honor the King of heaven, all of whose works *are* truth, and His ways justice. And those who walk in pride He is able to put down."** (Daniel 4:37)

So we know that the pride of this evil monarch, who was represented as a wild beast later on in this book, was finally subdued by **"the Most High God,"** as was further symbolized by his being **"lifted up"** and given **"a man's heart."** (Daniel 7:4)

The account begins in a way similar to the account in the second chapter of this book, with the one difference that the king does not demand the outrageous test he made at that time, For Daniel had already proven himself to him.

> "I, Nebuchadnezzar, was at rest in my house, and flourishing in my palace. I saw a dream which made me afraid, and the thoughts on my bed and the visions of my head troubled me. Therefore I issued a decree to bring in all the wise *men* of Babylon before me, that they might make known to me the interpretation of the dream. Then the magicians, the astrologers, the Chaleans, and the soothsayers came in, and I told them the dream; but they did not make known to me its interpretation. But at last Daniel came before me (his name is Belteshazzar, according to the name of my god; in him is the Spirit of the Holy God), and I told the dream before him, *saying*: 'Belteshazzar, chief of the magicians, because I know that the Spirit of the Holy God is in you, and no secret troubles you, explain to me the visions of my dream that I have seen, and its interpretation.' " (Daniel 4:4-9)

The first thing we notice is that, having finally been humbled by the power of God, Nebuchadnezzar recognizes the prophet of God, first by calling him by his Hebrew name, and then by flatly saying that **"in him is the Spirit of the Holy God."**

Then he describes his dream:

> "These were the visions of my head *while* on my bed:
> 'I was looking, and behold,
> A tree in the midst of the earth,
> And its height was great.
> The tree grew and became strong;
> Its height reached to the heavens,
> And it could be seen to the ends of all the earth.
> Its leaves *were* lovely,
> Its fruit abundant,
> And in it *was* food for all.
> The beasts of the field found shade under it,

> The birds of the heavens dwelt in its branches,
> And all flesh was fed from it.
> 'I saw in the visions of my head *while* on my bed, and there was a watcher, a holy one, coming down from heaven. He cried aloud and said thus:
> "Chop down the tree and cut off its branches,
> Strip off its leaves and scatter its fruit.
> Let the beasts get out from under it,
> And the birds from its branches.
> Nevertheless leave the stump and roots in the earth,
> *Bound* with a band of iron and bronze,
> In the tender grass of the field.
> Let it be wet with the dew of heaven,
> And let him graze with the beasts
> On the grass of the earth.
> Let his heart be changed from *that of* a man,
> Let him be given the heart of a beast,
> And let seven times pass over him.
> "This decision is by the decree of the watchers,
> And the sentence by the word of the holy ones,
> In order that the living may know
> That the Most High rules in the kingdom of men,
> Gives it to whomever He will,
> And sets over it the lowest of men." ' " (Daniel 4:10-17)

Having thus described the dream, Nebuchadnezzar said.

> "This dream I, King Nebuchadnezzar, have seen. Now you, Belteshazzar, declare its interpretation, since all the wise *men* of my kingdom are not able to make known to me the interpretation; but you are able, for the Spirit of the Holy God is in you." (Daniel 4:18)

He had told Daniel that he knew that **"no secret troubles you."** But he was wrong. This secret certainly troubled Daniel. For we read that **"Then Daniel, whose name was Belteshazzar, was astonished for a time, and his thoughts troubled him."** (Daniel 4:19a)

> "So the king spoke, and said, 'Belteshazzar, do not let the dream or its interpretation trouble you.' Belteshazzar answered and said, 'My lord, *may* the dream concern those who hate you, and its interpretation concern your enemies!' " (Daniel 4:19b)

I believe that the version we are using, the NKJV, fails to capture the true thrust of Daniel's answer, and why it so troubled him. I believe the true sense is captured by the KJV rendering of his answer, **"My lord, the dream be to them that hate thee, and the interpretation thereof to thine enemies."** (Daniel 4:19b KJV) That is, Daniel was not wishing for the dream to apply to the king's enemies, but instead was declaring that it benefitted those enemies. And that shows why it so distressed Daniel. When someone even dared to give such a king a message that could even be interpreted as a threat, he would be putting his own life in dire peril. And this could possibly explain why none of the other wise men could answer the king.

Even if they understood the dream, they would have been afraid to tell him what it meant. But for Daniel, godliness prevailed over fear. So he told the interpretation.

> "The tree that you saw, which grew and became strong, whose height reached to the heavens and which *could be seen* by all the earth, whose leaves *were* lovely and its fruit abundant, in which *was* food for all, under which the beasts of the field dwelt, and in whose branches the birds of the heaven had their home-- it *is* you, O king, who have grown and become strong; for your greatness has grown and reaches to the heavens, and your dominion to the end of the earth. And inasmuch as the king saw a watcher, a holy one, coming down from heaven and saying, 'Chop down the tree and destroy it, but leave its stump and roots in the earth, *bound* with a band of iron and bronze in the tender grass of the field; let it be wet with the dew of heaven, and let him graze with the beasts of the field, till seven times pass over him'; this is the interpretation, O king, and this is the decree of the Most High, which has come upon my lord the king: They shall drive you from men, your dwelling shall be with the

beasts of the field, and they shall make you eat grass like oxen. They shall wet you with the dew of heaven, and seven times shall pass over you, till you know that the Most High rules in the kingdom of men, and gives it to whomever He chooses. And inasmuch as they gave the command to leave the stump *and* roots of the tree, your kingdom shall be assured to you, after you come to know that Heaven rules." (Daniel 4:20-26)

And after giving this interpretation, Daniel moves from the "foreteller" function of a prophet, to the "preacher" function, saying: **"Therefore, O king, let my advice be acceptable to you; break off your sins by *being* righteous, and your iniquities by showing mercy *to the* poor. Perhaps there may be a lengthening of your prosperity."** (Daniel 4:27)

We should notice here that Daniel did not even suggest that this horrible event could be prevented. He only suggested that it could be delayed. So it is with Christians of the present day who see the conditions of Bible prophecy beginning to develop all around us. We know the time for these horrible events will indeed come, and that it cannot be prevented. But we often pray that it might be delayed.

Nebuchadnezzar did not report what his initial reaction was, But only that he had not heeded the warning. For he said,

"All this came upon King Nebuchadnezzar. At the end of the twelve months he was walking about the royal palace of Babylon. The king spoke, saying, 'Is not this great Babylon, that I have built for a royal dwelling by my mighty power and for the honor of my majesty?'" (Daniel 4:28-30) So, after a full twelve months, he was still walking in his pride. But as soon as he had said this, **"While the word was *still* in the king's mouth, a voice fell from heaven: 'King Nebuch adnezzar, to you it is spoken: the kingdom has departed from you! And they shall drive you from men, and your dwelling *shall be* with the beasts of the field. They shall make you eat grass like oxen; and seven times shall pass over you, until you know that the Most High rules in the kingdom of men, and gives it to whomever He chooses'"** (Daniel 4:31-32) And **"That very hour the word was fulfilled concerning Nebuchadnezzar; he**

was driven from men and ate grass like oxen; his body was wet with the dew of heaven till his hair had grown like eagles' *feathers* and his nails like birds' *claws*." (Daniel 4:33)

Here we see that there is no excusing of himself, no glossing over what had happened. The great monarch, now thoroughly humbled before God, tells in plain words exactly what had happened. And is not this the typical testimony of a sinner that has been truly converted to a true and living faith in God? They do not even pretend that there had been anything good in their previous life, they tell it like it was, in all its awfulness. But then they tell what God has done for them. So the king continues:

> "And at the end of the time I, Nebuchadnezzar, lifted my eyes to heaven, and my understanding returned to me; and I blessed the Most High and praised and honored Him who lives forever:
> For His dominion is an everlasting dominion,
> And His kingdom *is* from generation to generation.
> All the inhabitants of the earth are reputed as nothing;
> He does according to His will in the army of heaven
> And *among* the inhabitants of the earth.
> No one can restrain His hand
> Or say to Him, 'What have You done?'
> At the same time my reason returned to me, and for the glory of my kingdom, my honor and splendor returned to me. My counselors and nobles resorted to me, I was restored to my kingdom, and excellent majesty was added to me. Now I, Nebuchadnezzar, praise and extol and honor the King of heaven, all of whose works *are* truth, and His ways justice. And those who walk in pride He is able to put down." (Daniel 4:34-37)

The point of this chapter is so plainly stated here that further comment is neither necessary nor even appropriate. The proud potentate had learned that his power had not come about as a result of his own strength or wisdom, or even his own effort. But it had been given to him by **"the King of heaven,"** who:

> "rules in the kingdom of men,
> Gives it to whomever He will,
> And sets over it the lowest of men."

In this last line, the proud Nebuchadnezzar, now thoroughly humbled, classes himself as among **"the lowest of men."** And such is always the result of a thorough humbling done by the power of the almighty God. Every person so humbled no longer thinks of himself (or herself) as anything to be admired in any way at all, but only as a product of the grace of God.

Daniel 5

But now the other side of this message is given. In the last chapter, the king's pride was replaced by repentance. And restoration followed the discipline. But here, there is only brash disrespect to **"the Lord of heaven,"** with no repentance, and the result is unsparing judgment of Belshazzar's impious feast.

> "Belshazzar the king made a great feast for a thousand of his lords, and drank wine in the presence of the thousand. While he tasted the wine, Belshazzar gave the command to bring the gold and silver vessels which his father Nebuchadnezzar had taken from the temple which *had been* in Jerusalem, that the king and his lords, his wives, and his concubines might drink from them. Then they brought the gold vessels that *had been* taken from the temple of the house of God which had been in Jerusalem; and the king and his lords, his wives, and his concubines drank from them. They drank wine, and praised the gods of gold and silver, bronze and iron, wood and stone." (Daniel 5:1-4)

The vessels which had been made for, and dedicated to, **"the Lord of heaven,"** were being sacrilegiously desecrated by using them in a drunken celebration. But Belshazzar's impiety was rebuked by the very God he had so mocked.

> "In the same hour the fingers of a man's hand appeared and wrote opposite the lampstand on the plaster of the wall of the king's palace; and the king saw the part of the hand that wrote. Then the king's countenance changed, and his thoughts troubled him, so that the joints of his hips were loosened and his knees knocked against each other." (Daniel 5:5-6)

Anyone would have to agree that a sudden appearance of just a part of a man's hand, writing on the wall, would startle just about anyone. But this king's reaction went far beyond merely being startled. He was literally so frightened that **"his knees knocked against each other."** And why was he so frightened? We see that further down the chapter, when, after reviewing what God had dealt with his father, Daniel said, **"But you his son, Belshazzar, have not humbled your heart, although you knew all this. And you have lifted yourself up against the Lord of heaven."** (Daniel 5:22-23a) So the reason for Belshazzar's extreme fear was that he was aware that he had defied **"the Lord of heaven."** And thus, before he learned the meaning of the message, he already realized that the all powerful **"Lord of heaven"** had responded to his defiance.

So "The king cried aloud to bring in the astrologers, the Chaldeans, and the soothsayers. The king spoke, saying to the wise *men* of Babylon, 'Whoever reads this writing, and tells me its interpretation, shall be clothed with purple and *have* a chain of gold around his neck; and he shall be the third ruler in the kingdom.' Now all the king's wise *men* came, but they could not read the writing, or make known to the king its interpretation. Then King Belshazzar was greatly troubled, his countenance was changed, and his lords were astonished." (Daniel 5:7-9)

But "The queen, because of the words of the king and his lords, came to the banquet hall. The queen spoke, saying, 'O king, live forever! Do not let your thoughts trouble you, nor let your countenance change. There is a man in your kingdom in whom *is* the Spirit of the Holy God. And in the days of your father, light and understanding and wisdom, like the wisdom of the gods, were found in him; and King Nebuchadnezzar your father--your father the king--made him chief of the magicians, astrologers, Chaldeans, *and* soothsayers. Inasmuch as an excellent spirit, knowledge, understanding, interpreting dreams, solving riddles, and explaining enigmas were found in this Daniel, whom the king named Belteshazzar, now let Daniel be called, and he will give the interpretation.' " (Daniel 5:10-12)

> "Then Daniel was brought in before the king. The king spoke, and said to Daniel, "'Are you that Daniel who is one of the captives from Judah, whom my father the king brought from Judah? I have heard of you, that the Spirit of God is in you, and *that* light and understanding and excellent wisdom are found in you. Now the wise *men*, the astrologers, have been brought in before me, that they should read this writing and make known to me its interpretation, but they could not give the interpretation of the thing. And I have heard of you, that you can give interpretations and explain enigmas. Now if you can read the writing and make known to me its interpretation, you shall be clothed with purple and *have* a chain of gold around your neck, and shall be the third ruler in the kingdom.' " (Daniel 5:13-16)

But Daniel knew what the writing said, and what it meant. So the king's promises meant nothing to him. So **"Daniel answered, and said before the king, 'Let your gifts be for yourself, and give your rewards to another; yet I will read the writing to the king, and make known to him the interpretation.'** " (Daniel 5:17)

Unlike the similar occasion with his father Nebuchadnezzar, This time Daniel did not even plead with the king to repent. All he did was to deliver a stern announcement that the time for judgment had come. So he said:

"O king, the Most High God gave Nebuchadnezzar your father a kingdom and majesty, glory and honor. And because of the majesty that He gave him, all peoples, nations, and languages trembled and feared before him. Whomever he wished, he executed; whomever he wished, he kept alive; whomever he wished, he set up; and whomever he wished, he put down. But when his heart was lifted up, and his spirit was hardened in pride, he was deposed from his kingly throne, and they took his glory from him. Then he was driven from the sons of men, his heart was made like the beasts, and his dwelling *was* with the wild donkeys. They fed him with grass like oxen, and his body was wet with the dew of heaven, till he knew that the Most High God rules in the kingdom of men, and appoints over it whomever He chooses. But you his son, Belshazzar, have not humbled your heart, although you knew all this. And you have lifted yourself up against the Lord of heaven. They have brought the vessels of His house before you, and you and your lords, your wives and your concubines, have drunk wine from them. And you have praised the gods of silver and gold, bronze and iron, wood and stone, which do not see or hear or know; and the God who *holds* your breath in His hand and owns all your ways, you have not glorified. Then the fingers of the hand were sent from Him, and this writing was written" (Daniel 5:18-24)

And after this stern rebuke, the Prophet interprets the message.

"And this is the inscription that was written:
MENE, MENE, TEKEL, UPHARSIN.
This is the interpretation of each word. MENE: God has numbered your kingdom, and finished it; TEKEL: You have been weighed in the balances, and found wanting; PERES: Your kingdom has been divided, and given to the Medes and Persians." (Daniel 5:24-28)

True to his word, **"Then Belshazzar gave the command, and they clothed Daniel with purple and *put* a chain of gold around his neck, and made a proclamation concerning him that he should be the third ruler in the kingdom."** (Daniel 5:29)

But it was vain, for:

"That very night Belshazzar, king of the Chaldeans, was slain. And Darius the Mede received the kingdom, *being* **about sixty-two years old."** (Daniel 5:30-31)

Even as the message of the fourth chapter had been that **"the Most High rules in the kingdom of men, and gives it to whomev-**

er He chooses." (Daniel 4:25) The message here is that **"the Lord of heaven"** cannot be despised with impunity. For Belshazzar's open disrespect to **"the Lord of heaven"** cost him, not only his throne, but also his life.

Daniel 6

Daniel 6 has a similar message, but directed toward lower level rulers instead of just kings. For the men that conspired against the prophet of God, paid for it with their lives.

First, we are given the background facts:

"It pleased Darius to set over the kingdom one hundred and twenty satraps, to be over the whole kingdom; and over these, three governors, of whom Daniel *was* one, that the satraps might give account to them, so that the king would suffer no loss. Then this Daniel distinguished himself above the governors and satraps, because an excellent spirit was in him; and the king gave thought to setting him over the whole realm." (Daniel 6:1-3)

This is the kind of situation that should be true of any servant of God, regardless of where they serve, that they would demonstrate such an **"excellent spirit"** that their employer values them above all others. But this will often result in envy and resentment from others. And in Daniel's case, it led to a conspiracy.

"So the governors and satraps sought to find *some* charge against Daniel concerning the kingdom; but they could find no charge or fault, because he *was* faithful; nor was there any error or fault found in him. Then these men said, 'We shall not find any charge against this Daniel unless we find it against him concerning the law of his God.'" (Daniel 6:4-5)

This led to an evil and deceptive plan. They appealed to the king's vanity, to his over-inflated ego:

"**So these governors and satraps thronged before the king, and said thus to him: 'King Darius, live forever! All the governors of the kingdom, the administrators and satraps, the counselors and advisors, have consulted together to establish a royal statute and to make a firm decree, that whoever petitions any god or man for thirty days, except you, O king, shall be cast into the den of lions. Now, O king, establish the decree and sign the writing, so that it cannot be changed, according to the law of the Medes and Persians, which does not alter.'**" (Daniel 6:6-8)

They relied upon a detail of their law, that once an edict had been reduced to writing and signed by the king, it could not be altered. Not even by the king himself. So, appealing to the king's vanity, they tricked him into signing an edict that they knew Daniel could not obey. And so, failing to detect the wicked subterfuge, and betrayed by his own evil pride, **"King Darius signed the written decree."** (Daniel 6:9)

Now the trap was set, and they watched Daniel. For they knew what would happen.

> "**Now when Daniel knew that the writing was signed, he went home. And in his upper room, with his windows open toward Jerusalem, he knelt down on his knees three times that day, and prayed and gave thanks before his God, as was his custom since early days.**" (Daniel 6:10)

The servant of the most high God did not flinch. And he did not continue in secret. Instead, he continued to openly pray to the LORD his God three times a day, as he had always done.

When we consider this, we realize it was not a trap for Daniel. They knew ahead of time what Daniel would do. It was a trap for the king. So now they sprang the trap, forcing the king to order Daniel cast into the den of lions.

"Then these men assembled and found Daniel praying and making supplication before his God. And they went before the king, and spoke concerning the king's decree: 'Have you not signed a decree that every man who petitions any god or man within thirty days, except you, O king, shall be cast into the den of lions?' The king answered and said, 'The thing is true, according to the law of the Medes and Persians, which does not alter.' So they answered and said before the king, 'That Daniel, who is one of the captives from Judah, does not show due regard for you, O king, or for the decree that you have signed, but makes his petition three times a day.' " (Daniel 6:11-13)

The king was caught! Now, according to their inalterable law, the decree that in his ego he had foolishly signed, *forces* him to execute the one servant he values above all the others.

Suddenly realizing the error of his prideful command, **"the king, when he heard *these* words, was greatly displeased with himself, and set *his* heart on Daniel to deliver him; and he labored till the going down of the sun to deliver him. Then these men approached the king, and said to the king, 'Know, O king, that *it is* the law of the Medes and Persians that no decree or statute which the king establishes may be changed.' "** (Daniel 6:14-15)

Knowing he was trapped, **"the king gave the command, and they brought Daniel and cast *him* into the den of lions. *But* the king spoke, saying to Daniel, 'Your God, whom you serve continually, He will deliver you.' Then a stone was brought and laid on the mouth of the den, and the king sealed it with his own signet ring and with the signets of his lords, that the purpose concerning Daniel might not be changed."** (Daniel 6:16-17)

Having been forced to commit this dreadful crime, **"the king went to his palace and spent the night fasting; and no musicians were brought before him. Also his sleep went from him. Then the king arose very early in the morning and went in haste to the den of lions. And when he came to the den, he cried out with a lamenting voice to Daniel. The king spoke, saying to Daniel, 'Daniel, servant of the living God, has your God, whom you serve continually, been able to deliver you from the lions?' " (Daniel 6:18-20)

But God could do what the king could not do. **"Then Daniel said to the king, 'O king, live forever! My God sent His angel and shut the lions' mouths, so that they have not hurt me, because I was found innocent before Him; and also, O king, I have done no wrong before you.' Then the king was exceedingly glad for him, and commanded that they should take Daniel up out of the den. So Daniel was taken up out of the den, and no injury whatever was found on him, because he believed in his God."** (Daniel 6:21-23)

But it has never been a good idea to force the hand of an all powerful monarch. And this was no exception to such a hard and fast rule. It was time for the conspirators to pay for their crimes. But not only they had to pay, but also their children and wives. **"And the king gave the command, and they brought those men who had accused Daniel, and they cast *them* into the den of lions--them, their children, and their wives; and the lions overpowered them, and broke all their bones in pieces before they ever came to the bottom of the den."** (Daniel 6:24)

The ferocity of the lions knew no bounds. As the men, women, and children fell down into the den, they were all killed before they even reached the bottom.

But now, as had Nebuchadnezzar before him,

"**King Darius wrote:**

To all peoples, nations, and languages
that dwell in all the earth:
Peace be multiplied to you.
I make a decree that in every dominion of my kingdom men
must tremble and fear before the God of Daniel.
For He is the living God,
And steadfast forever;
His kingdom is the one which shall not be destroyed,
And His dominion shall endure to the end.
He delivers and rescues,
And He works signs and wonders

> In heaven and on earth.
> Who has delivered Daniel from the power of the lions."
> (Daniel 6:25-27)

Darius did not go so far as to say, like Nebuchadnezzar, that **"I praise and extol and honor the king of heaven."** but he praised **"the God of Daniel, For He is the living God."** And he commanded all his people to do the same.

But God is faithful to His servants, **"So this Daniel prospered in the reign of Darius and in the reign of Cyrus the Persian."** (Daniel 6:28)

We have now finished the part of Daniel that teaches by historical examples. The rest of this book deals with the future. But before we leave this part of the book, let us review what we have learned.

> In chapter 1, we saw that God honors those that honor
> Him.
>
> In chapter 2, we saw that God is a revealer of secrets,
> along with a pre-written history of the world.
> In chapter 3, we saw that God will protect
> those who are faithful to Himself.
>
> In chapter 4, we saw that **"the most High"**
> rules in the kingdoms of men,
> and sets over then whomever He wills.
>
> In chapter 5, we learned that even kings
> who despise Him will be punished.
>
> And in this chapter 6, we learned the same of lessor rulers.

Daniel 7

The rest of this **"little book"** which we are now "eating" is prophecy, in the sense of foretelling the future, and much of it is apocalyptic, that is, it is presented in signs and symbols. But, unlike other apocalyptic books, in Daniel the meanings of the signs and symbols are clearly explained.

So first, we need to ask, why bother with signs and symbols, and then give the meanings of these same signs and symbols. Why not just state everything clearly in the first place?

We need to realize that there is a reason for everything God does, and for everything He says. When God gave us this **"little book,"** He had already planned to tell John to **"eat"** it. For God had already planned to use these same signs and symbols in the Revelation, even though He did not plan to give us that book until many hundreds of years later. So the keys needed to understand the book of Revelation are given here in this **"little book"** which we are now "eating." But when this **"little book"** was given, it was **"sealed."** For at the end of the book, Daniel had more questions, but was **"Go *your way,* Daniel, for the words *are* closed up and sealed till the time of the end."** (Daniel 12:9) And it was not until the Revelation was given that its **"seven seals"** were opened in chapters 6-8 of that book.

So now we must ask, why would God bother to tell is these things, but at the same time make them so difficult to understand? Actually, He told us why He did this. And He said it in plain words, more than just once.

First, at the very place where He told Daniel that **"the words are closed up and sealed,"** He went on to say, **"Many shall be purified, made white, and refined, but the wicked shall do wickedly; and none of the wicked shall understand, but the wise shall understand."** (Daniel 12:10) And again, when the disciples asked Jesus **" 'Why do You speak to them in parables?' He answered and said to them, 'Because it has been given to you to know the mysteries of the kingdom of heaven, but to them it has not been given. For whoever has, to him more will be given, and he will have abundance; but whoever does not have, even what he has will be taken away from him.' "** (Matthew 13:10-12)

So our God has clearly told us that, although he desires to reveal His plans to us, He has no intention of revealing them to the wicked. So He designed His word in such a way that those who submit to His teaching through the Holy Spirit can understand it. But the wicked, lacking that Holy Spirit to teach them, will never be able to understand it.

And sadly, this includes even real Christians who value their own *interpretations* of the *meanings* some parts of God's word above what He *actually said* in other parts of that same word. For the scriptures tell us of some who **"having strayed, have turned aside to idle talk,"** desire **"to be teachers of the law, understanding neither what they say nor the things which they affirm."** (1 Timothy 1:6-7)

But to consider what we find in Daniel 7, **"In the first year of Belshazzar king of Babylon, Daniel had a dream and visions of his head *while* on his bed. Then he wrote down the dream, telling the main facts."** (Daniel 7:1)

We are told both that this was revealed in a dream and that it came **"in the first year of Belshassar."** That dates this revelation as having come after the time of the dreams of Nebuchadnezzar. So all the information God had given in those dreams was already known to the prophet, even as it is now known to us.

"Daniel spoke, saying, 'I saw in my vision by night, and behold, the four winds of heaven were stirring up the Great Sea. And four great beasts came up from the sea, each different from the other.' " (Daniel 7:2-3)

The great image seen by Nebuchadnezzar had represented four coming kingdoms. And now he sees **"four great beasts"** rising out of **"the Great Sea," "stirred up"** by **"the four winds of heaven."** In John 3:8, the Spirit of God is compared to a wind. So we understand that **"the four winds of heaven"** speak of four spirits, which are stirring up **"the Great Sea."** That is, that, whatever these **"great beasts"** represent, they had not just come, but were raised up by spiritual powers. But we also remember that Satan is **"the prince of the power of the air."** (Ephesians 2:2) So these spiritual powers were not necessarily good spirits. And these beasts were not the same, for **"each"** was **"different from the other."**

And in the inspired interpretation, Daniel was told, **"Those great beasts, which are four, are four kings *which* arise out of the earth."** (Daniel 7:17) So, like the four parts of the great Image in Nebuchadnezzar's dream these four **"great beasts"** represent **"four kings *which* arise out of the earth."**

But here we also notice that prophetic dreams and visions are not just "videos," as it were, that is, "movies," of things that will happen. For in this dream, the four beasts **"came up from the sea,"** but in the interpretation, they **"arise out of the earth."**

Unless the scriptures reveal the meaning of a prophetic symbol, we should be very cautious about saying what it means. But in this case, we read that **"the wicked *are* like the troubled sea, When it cannot rest, Whose waters cast up mire and dirt."** (Isaiah 57:20) So coming **"up from the Great Sea"** would indicate coming from the confusion of wickedness.

But then we read that **"The first *was* like a lion, and had eagle's wings. I watched till its wings were plucked off; and it was lifted up from the earth and made to stand on two feet like a man, and a man's heart was given to it."** (Daniel 7:2-4)

We remember that, in the beginning, Nebuchadnezzar, like a typical middle eastern potentate, walked in his pride, and **"Whomever he wished, he executed; whomever he wished, he kept alive."** But the **"King of heaven"** had humbled him until he wrote, **"Now I, Nebuchadnezzar, praise and extol and honor the King of heaven, all of whose works *are* truth, and His ways justice. And those who** walk in pride He is able to put down." (Daniel 4:37) so the beast **"was lifted up from the earth and made to stand on two feet like a man, and a man's heart was given to it."**

But then we read, **"And suddenly another beast, a second, like a bear. It was raised up on one side, and *had* three ribs in its mouth between its teeth. And they said thus to it: 'Arise, devour much flesh!' "** (Daniel 7:5) Like the head of Gold changing into the chest and arms of silver in the image of Nebuchadnezzar's dream, the lion is replaced by a bear. And, even as silver is less precious than gold, a bear is smaller than a lion.

But the bear appeared **"suddenly."** And we remember that in chapter five, we learned that Belshazzar was feasting with a thousand of his lords, when his kingdom suddenly fell to **"Darius the Mede."** (Daniel 5:31)

But Daniel continued into **"the reign of Cyrus the Persian."** And we are not told of any wars or conquests involved in this change from being ruled by a **"Mede"** and being ruled by a **"Persian."** History tells us that these were the same kingdom, which it calls the "Medo-Persian Empire." For it was formed by a union between the Medes and the Persians. But the Persians were far more powerful than the Medes, so in the end, they ruled the empire. This uneven power distribution was represented by the detail that the bear **"was raised up on one side."** This united force conquered the Babylonian Empire in three significant campaigns, represented by the three ribs between its teeth. And it was particularly noted for the bloodiness of its conquests, as represented by the words said to it, **"Arise, devour much flesh!"**

But then, **"After this I looked, and there was another, like a leopard, which had on its back four wings of a bird. The beast also had four heads, and dominion was given to it."** (Daniel 7:6) Even as the bear was smaller than a lion, now we see **"a leopard,"** a beast smaller than a bear. This, again, continues the pattern of the image seen by Nebuchadnezzar. For, as the head of gold changed into the chest and arms of silver, followed by the belly and thighs of bronze. So the third beast, the leopard, is smaller than the bear. But, although it is smaller than a bear, a leopard is noted for its speed. But this leopard was particularly swift, for it **"had on its back four wings of a bird."**

The third world kingdom of ancient times was the kingdom of Greece, set up by Alexander the great. And the one great distinguishing feature of the Greek empire was how quickly it moved. In a matter of only a few short years, Alexander conquered the entire known world, aided in this conquest by his four generals. These four generals were represented by the four wings on the beast. But they were also represented by its four heads. For Alexander died while he was still young, and his four generals split the kingdom four ways.

But there was one more beast. **"After this I saw in the night visions, and behold, a fourth beast, dreadful and terrible, exceedingly strong. It had huge iron teeth; it was devouring, breaking in pieces, and trampling the residue with its feet. It *was* different from all the beasts that *were* before it, and it had ten horns."** (Daniel 7:7)

There is no one that is even slightly acquainted with ancient history that does not know that the fourth ancient world kingdom was that of Rome. [23] This kingdom was first described as **"dreadful and terrible, exceedingly strong."** And indeed, in the ancient world, Rome was greatly to be feared. Its power was irresistible, as represented by its **"huge iron teeth."** and it devoured everything before it. But it was not only **"devouring,"** but also **"breaking in pieces, and trampling the residue with its feet."**

The Roman Empire was notable for its particularly spiteful treatment of conquered peoples. It not only enslaved them, as all ancient conquerors did, but went so far as to use them as victims for mass murders, staged purely to entertain the Roman population.

But two other details were given in this initial description. **"It *was* different from all the beasts that *were* before it, and it had ten horns."** The first detail, that **"It *was* different from all the beasts that *were* before it,"** was repeated in the inspired interpretation, as were the words about it **"devouring,"** and **"breaking in pieces."**

---

[23] We should note that the terms "world kingdom" and "known world" are related terms. As the peoples of Bible lands gradually became more aware of other parts of the world, the "known world" expanded, and thus the "word kingdoms" became physically larger. But each of these succeeding kingdoms covered the entire "known world" of its day.

For Daniel was told:

> "The fourth beast shall be
> A fourth kingdom on earth,
> Which shall be different from all *other* kingdoms,
> And shall devour the whole earth,
> Trample it and break it in pieces." (Daniel 7:23)

And indeed, Rome was **"different from all *other* kingdoms"** in that its laws were made by an elected Senate, rather than merely by a king.

But in the explanation, Daniel was explicitly told what the ten horns represented:

> "The ten horns *are* ten kings
> *Who* shall arise from this kingdom." (Daniel 7:24a)

So the scriptures tell us that **"ten kings"** **"shall arise from"** this last **"kingdom."** This is not some wild interpretation. Instead, the scriptures explicitly state this in plain words.

But the account of the dream goes on, saying:

"I was considering the horns, and there was another horn, a little one, coming up among them, before whom three of the first horns were plucked out by the roots. And there, in this horn, *were* eyes like the eyes of a man, and a mouth speaking pompous words." (Daniel 7:8)

And again, we are not left to ourselves to guess the meaning of these details. For in the explanation, After being told, as we have seen, that **"The ten horns are ten kings *Who* shall arise from this kingdom,"** Daniel was told:

> "And another shall rise after them;
> He shall be different from the first ones,
> And shall subdue three kings.

> **He shall speak *pompous* words against the Most High."**
> (Daniel 7:24b-25a)

So we are explicitly told that **"ten kings" "shall rise from"** the fourth kingdom, which was unquestionably the Roman Empire. And that then another king **"shall rise after them."** We are not explicitly told that this eleventh king will rise out of the fourth kingdom, but this is clearly indicated by the two facts that it was seen **"coming up among them"** and that it was seen **"coming up"** on the fourth beast. Then we are explicitly told three things about this eleventh king. **"He shall be different from the first ones, And shall subdue three kings. He shall speak *pompous* words against the Most High."**

And in the symbols we are told one other thing about him. **"in this horn, *were* eyes like the eyes of a man."** The eyes being what we use to see what is about us, this seems to indicate that this eleventh king will have unusual powers of perception. But the fact that **"He shall speak *pompous* words against the Most High."** shows that this is only human perception. He will not perceive the things of God.

And as a side note here, since many irresponsible and unbelieving "teachers" pretend that, even though this is what the scriptures clearly say, Christians never believed it before the nineteenth century, we will turn aside for a moment to notice what Jerome wrote about this passage (Daniel 7:8) early in the fifth century.

"We should therefore concur with the traditional interpretation of all the commentators of the Christian Church, that at the end of the world, when the Roman Empire is to be destroyed, there shall be ten kings who will partition the Roman world amongst themselves. Then an insignificant eleventh king will arise, who will overcome three of the ten kings... Then after they have been slain, the seven other kings will bow their necks to the victor." [24]

So, the concept of interpreting Bible prophecy literally, that is, as meaning exactly what it so plainly says, is not only *not* a nineteenth century innovation, but, at least according to the very famous late fourth and early fifth century scholar Jerome, who produced the

---

[24] "Jerome's Commentary on Daniel," by Jerome, pg. 77, translated by Gleason L. Archer, Jr., pub. by Baker Book House, Grand Rapids, 1958.

Vulgate translation of the Bible into Latin, this was not only believed by some, but was, at least up to his time, "the traditional interpretation of all the commentators of the Christian Church."

But to return to the scriptures themselves, which is the only thing that even counts, Daniel continued:

> "I watched till thrones were put in place,
> And the Ancient of Days *was* seated;
> His garment was white as snow,
> And the hair of His head *was* like pure wool.
> His throne *was* a fiery flame, Its wheels a burning fire;
> A fiery stream issued And came forth from before Him.
> A thousand thousands ministered to Him;
> Ten thousand times ten thousand stood before Him.
> The court was seated, And the books were opened.
> "I watched then because of the sound of the pompous words which the horn was speaking; I watched till the beast was slain, and its body destroyed and given to the burning flame." (Daniel 7:9-11)

A judge has just as much power when he is sitting in his office or eating his dinner. But when he is making a formal investigation or an official pronouncement, he does it in a very intimidating setting. And this vision was designed to strike terror into the heart of anyone who might even think about resisting.

And in the explanation, Daniel was told,

> "But the court shall be seated,
> And they shall take away his dominion,
> **To consume and destroy it forever.**" (Daniel 7:26)

But then, almost as if it were a side detail, (but there are no "side details" in scripture - every word is important) it says:

"As for the rest of the beasts, they had their dominion taken away, yet their lives were prolonged for a season and a time." (Daniel 7:12)

We must ask, why is this so casually tucked in here, almost as if it were not important? The answer is really quite simple. This detail is not significant to the rest of this particular prophecy. But it is very important to understanding other prophecies in this **"little book."** And for that reason we will reserve comment on it until we come to those prophecies (in chapters 8 and 11.)

But then we read:

> "I was watching in the night visions,
> And behold, *One* like the Son of Man,
> Coming with the clouds of heaven!
> He came to the Ancient of Days,
> And they brought Him near before Him.
> Then to Him was given dominion and glory and a kingdom,
> That all peoples, nations, and languages should serve Him.
> His dominion is an everlasting dominion,
> Which shall not pass away,
> And His kingdom *the one*
> Which shall not be destroyed." (Daniel 7:13-14)

We need to take notice of the order of events in this vision. Those who deny that this speaks of the future imagine that this speaks of Christ in His first coming, who, having set up a kingdom, that kingdom conquered the Roman Empire. But that is not what this vision indicates. Rather, it indicates that, *after* the Roman Empire has been destroyed, *then* Christ will come and set up His eternal kingdom.

Then we read, **"I, Daniel, was grieved in my spirit within my body, and the visions of my head troubled me. I came near to one of those who stood by, and asked him the truth of all this. So he told me and made known to me the interpretation of these things:"** (Daniel 7:15-16)

As we have already noticed, the first thing Daniel was told was:

"Those great beasts, which are four, *are* four kings *which* arise out of the earth." (Daniel 7:17) But then he was told:

> "But the saints of the Most High shall receive the kingdom, and possess the kingdom forever, even forever and ever." (Daniel 7:18)

Although it does not explicitly state this, the form of speech used, even in this part of the account, implies that it represents events that will take place in the order stated. That is, that the saints receive the kingdom upon the expiration of the last of these four kingdoms.

But then Daniel continued, asking more questions and was given more details about the vision. And these details removed all doubt about the continuous nature of this vision.

> "Then I wished to know the truth about the fourth beast, which was different from all the others, exceedingly dreadful, *with* its teeth of iron and its nails of bronze, *which* devoured, broke in pieces, and trampled the residue with its feet; and the ten horns that were on its head, and the other horn *which* came up, before which three fell, namely, that *horn* which had eyes and a mouth which spoke pompous words, whose appearance *was* greater than his fellows. I was watching; and the same horn was making war against the saints, and prevailing against them, until the Ancient of Days came, and a judgment was made *in favor* of the saints of the Most High, and the time came for the saints to possess the kingdom." (Daniel 7:19-22)

Historistists try to pretend that this is speaking of the rise of Popery after the Roman empire was broken up. But they neglect the fact that Popery rose before the Roman Empire was defeated. They also neglect the fact that, in prophetic symbolism, a horn always represents an individual ruler, while a dynasty is represented by either a beast or a head. We see this again and agin in the inspired explanations of various visions.

The error of this interpretation becomes even more evident when we consider the explanation Daniel was given:

> "Thus he said:
> 'The fourth beast shall be
> A fourth kingdom on earth,
> Which shall be different from all *other* kingdoms,
> And shall devour the whole earth,
> Trample it and break it in pieces.
> The ten horns *are* ten kings
> *Who* shall arise from this kingdom.
> And another shall rise after them;
> He shall be different from the first *ones*
> And shall subdue three kings.
> He shall speak *pompous* words against the Most High,
> Shall persecute the saints of the Most High,
> And shall intend to change times and law.
> Then the *saints* shall be given into his hand
> For a time and times and half a time.' " (Daniel 7:23-25)

We have already considered parts of this Divinely inspired explanation. But now, in considering the falsehood of the notion that this represents the rise of Popery, we need to consider this explanation in its entirety. We have already seen that the **"fourth kingdom"** is very plainly the Roman Empire. But now we need to consider the horns. First, **"the ten horns are ten kings *Who* shall arise from this kingdom. And another shall rise after them."** this is a clear statement that the **"little horn" "shall rise after"** the other ten horns, and we have already noticed that Popery rose before, not after, The fall of Rome, which was to take place before the rise of **"the ten kings."** But that is not all we notice about this.

First, Popery as evil as it is, has never spoken **"*pompous* words against the Most High."** although it has blasphemed both His people and the use of His word, it has never actually blasphemed God Himself.

Popery has indeed persecuted **"the saints of the Most High."** And may have indeed intended **"to change times and law."** But the saints were never **"given into his hand For a time and times and half a time."** In the first place, Popery cannot even reasonably be called "him." For it is an evil system, not an individual. And second, Popery was allowed to persecute **"the *saints*"** for very much longer than **"a

time and times and half a time," which is a commonly used prophetic expression meaning a period of three and a half years.

So this clearly speaks of a time that is still in our own future, even today, over two and a half thousand years after this prophecy was given.

But the explanation coninued:

> " 'But the court shall be seated,
> And they shall take away his dominion,
> To consume and destroy *it* forever.
> Then the kingdom and dominion,
> And the greatness of the kingdoms under the whole heaven,
> Shall be given to the people, the saints of the Most High.
> His kingdom *is* an everlasting kingdom,
> And all dominions shall serve and obey Him.'
> "This is the end of the account." (Daniel 7:26-28a)

The words, **"the court shall be seated"** indicate a formal judgment before a throne. And this is exactly what Jesus said would take place when he came, saying: **"When the Son of Man comes in His glory, and all the holy angels with Him, then He will sit on the throne of His glory. All the nations will be gathered before Him, and He will separate them one from another, as a shepherd divides *his* sheep from the goats."** (Matthew 25:31-32) And Jesus went on to say of the evil at that time, **"And these will go away into everlasting punishment, but the righteous into eternal life."** (Matthew 25:46) This reflects the words in the explanation of Daniel's dream, **"they shall take away his dominion, To consume and destroy *it* forever."**

But the fact that this is not the final judgment is shown by the words we have already noticed in the description of the dream, that **"As for the rest of the beasts, they had their dominion taken away, yet their lives were prolonged for a season and a time."** (Daniel 7:12)

But there is more here that we need to notice. For Amillennialists and Post Millennialists love to claim that no scripture indicates a future kingdom on this earth. But here we distinctly read, **"And they shall take away his dominion, To consume and destroy** *it* **forever. Then the kingdom and dominion, And the greatness of the kingdoms under the whole heaven, Shall be given to the people, the saints of the Most High."** Here we see the final destruction of the Roman Empire, which was most certainly an earthly kingdom, followed by its being replaced by **"the greatness of the kingdoms under the whole heaven."** Not "of the whole heaven," but **"under the whole heaven,"** that is, on the earth, being **"given to the people, the saints of the Most High."**

And what was the effect of this wonderful dream upon the prophet who saw it? **"As for me, Daniel, my thoughts greatly troubled me, and my countenance changed; but I kept the matter in my heart."** (Daniel 7:28b) That is, this dream greatly distressed him. But for a time, he told no one about it.

Daniel 8

The dream in the last chapter had come **"In the first year of Belshazzar king of Babylon."** (Daniel 7:1) But now, **"In the third year of the reign of King Belshazzar a vision appeared *to* me--to me, Daniel--after the one that appeared to me the first time."** (Daniel 8:1)

There are no accidents in scripture, no casual details that have no significance. Everything we are told, we are told for a reason. And thus, we see that the Holy Spirit, who inspired these words, is making a point of the fact that this is a different prophecy from the first one. In chapter 7. That one had been distinctly stated to have been **"a dream and visions of his head while on his bed."** (Daniel 7:1) But this time, it is called only **"a vision."** This again points out the difference between this vision and the previous one. The Holy Spirit is now revealing something completely different from what He had revealed in chapter 7. He stressed this because this vision reveals the end time activity of a different kingdom, the third kingdom of the previous vision, rather than that of the fourth kingdom, as He had revealed in chapter 7. Sadly, many, even many serious students of Bible prophecy, have failed to notice this, causing much confusion and error.

The vision of the ram and the male goat described in this chapter was in several parts, and in these parts Daniel observed a distinct time sequence. The first part of the vision was:

"Then I lifted my eyes and saw, and there, standing beside the river, was a ram which had two horns, and the two horns *were* high; but one *was* higher than the other, and the higher *one* came

up last. I saw the ram pushing westward, northward, and southward, so that no animal could withstand him; nor *was there any that could deliver from his hand, but he did according to his will and became great.*" (Daniel 8:3-4)

Then, after the passage of an undefined period of time, set forth by the words, **"And as I was considering,"** and the words **"had seen,"** the next part of the vision was:

"And as I was considering, suddenly a male goat came from the west, across the surface of the whole earth, without touching the ground; and the goat *had* **a notable horn between his eyes. Then he came to the ram that had two horns, which I had seen standing beside the river, and ran at him with furious power. And I saw him confronting the ram; he was moved with rage against him, attacked the ram, and broke his two horns. There was no power in the ram to withstand him, but he cast him down to the ground and trampled him; and there was no one that could deliver the ram from his hand. Therefore the male goat grew very great; but when he became strong, the large horn was broken, and in place of it four notable ones came up toward the four winds of heaven."** (Daniel 8:5-8)

At the end of this account, we again we see a distinct passage of time, in the words **"but when he became strong, the large horn was broken, and in place of it four notable ones came up."** But although these words again specifically mention a passage of time, this is actually a part of the second section of the vision.

But then the vision revealed that, after the passage of an additional undefined period of time, designated by the words **"And out of one of them came a little horn,"** there would be further events that would take place

"And out of one of them came a little horn which grew exceedingly great toward the south, toward the east, and toward the Glorious *Land*. And it grew up to the host of heaven; and it cast down *some* of the host and *some* of the stars to the ground, and trampled them. He even exalted *himself* as high as the Prince of the host; and by him the daily *sacrifices* were taken away, and the place of His sanctuary was cast down.

> Because of transgression, an army was given over *to the horn* to oppose the daily *sacrifices*; and he cast truth down to the ground. He did *all this* and prospered." (Daniel 8:9-12)

So all this is presented as one continuous account, with the fact that it involves different periods of time buried right in the original vision, before anything about its meaning is revealed. But the fact that the third part of ths vision spoke of a time, not only after the second part of the vison, but long after that part, is revealed in the divinely inspired explanation.

For Daniel was told two things about the times referred to in the vision. First, **"that the vision *refers* to the time of the end."** (Daniel 8:17) And then, that the last part of the vision refers to a time **"in the latter time of their kingdom, When the transgressors have reached their fullness."** (Daniel 8:23) These two statements eliminate all possibility of rational debate about the fact that this is an end time prophecy.

But then a distinct time period is explicitly defined.

> "Then I heard a holy one speaking; and *another* holy one said to that certain *one* who was speaking, 'How long *will* the vision *be, concerning* the daily *sacrifices* and the transgression of desolation, the giving of both the sanctuary and the host to be trampled under foot?' And he said to me, 'For two thousand three hundred days; then the sanctuary shall be cleansed.' " (Daniel 8:13-14)

So the vision contained three distinct revelations about passages of time, followed by a fourth distinctly specified period of time. And as a period of time contains two ends, the vision speaks of this kingdom at five different times.

But now we need to examine the vision in detail. First, we need to notice the observation point of this vision. **"I saw in the vision, and it so happened while I was looking, that I was in Shushan, the citadel, which is in the province of Elam; and I saw in the vision that I was by the River Ulai."** (Daniel 8:2) So the observation point (not the place where Daniel was located when He saw the vision, but the place from which the vision had him observing the action) was first, generally, **"in Shushan, the citadel, which is in the province of Elam,"** and then, in particular, **"I was by the River Ulai."**

To understand the significance of this point of observation, we need to consider the locations of these specified places. The great city of Babylon was far from the land of Israel. But **"Shushan, the citadel,"** was even farther away, on the far side of **"the province of Elam."** And the **"River Ulai"** was on the far side of **"Shushan"**. So, although many prophetic visions, such as the one beginning in Ezekiel 40:2, are seen from within **"the land of Israel,"** this one was seen, not only from outside the land, but from very far from the land of Israel. This seems to indicate that this vision is about not only an end time power, but one located far from the land of Israel.

Then the identification of this power begins, not with the power which is the subject of the vision, but with a different power which is not indicated to be an end time power.

> **"Then I lifted my eyes and saw, and there, standing beside the river, was a ram which had two horns, and the two horns *were* high; but one *was* higher than the other, and the higher *one* came up last."** (Daniel 8:3-4)

We need to notice that this power is first seen **"standing beside the river."** that is **"the River Ulai,"** which had just been mentioned. And then, in the explanation, Daniel was explicitly told that the ram's two horns are **"Media and Persia"**, saying, **"The ram which you saw, having the two horns--*they are* the kings of Media and Persia."** (Daniel 8:20) We remember that when Babylon had fallen in Daniel 5:30-31, **"Darius the Mede received the kingdom."**

The Medo-Persian kingdom was a collation of two powers, the Medes and the Persians. That is why **"the ram had two horns."** For in prophetic imagery, although an animal represents a kingdom, a horn represents an individual king. But **"the two horns *were* high; but one *was* higher than the other, and the higher *one* came up last."** And although **"Darius the Mede"** was indeed a great ruler, his successor,

"Cyrus the Persian" (Daniel 6:28) was far greater. And the next verse describes the growth of this kingdom. For Daniel **"saw the ram pushing westward, northward, and southward, so that no animal could withstand him; nor *was there any* that could deliver from his hand, but he did according to his will and became great."** (Daniel 8:4) So the Medo-Persian kingdom grew to be a great empire which covered all of the world that was known to the peoples of the Middle East.

But then, after a time, as we have noticed, a different power appeared. **"And as I was considering, suddenly a male goat came from the west, across the surface of the whole earth, without touching the ground; and the goat *had* a notable horn between his eyes."** We are not left to our imaginations to know what ths **"male goat"** represented. For in the explanation, Daniel was explicitly told, **"And the male goat is the kingdom of Greece. The large horn that is between its eyes *is* the first king."** (Daniel 8:21) And we remember that the first great king to come out of Greece was Alexander the Great.

We should note here that, although history records Alexander as "the Macedonian," Macedonia was a part of Greece. So referring to him as a king of Greece was precisely correct, as is everything in the entire Bible, as God originally gave it.

We need to notice the details we are told about this **"male goat."** First, it appeared **"suddenly."** And then, it **"came from the west."** And it came **"across the surface of the whole earth, without touching the ground." "And the goat *had* a notable horn between his eyes."** All of these details perfectly fit the campaign of Alexander the Great. For he arose to prominence **"suddenly."** There had been no past experience of a threat from Greece, no reason to even expect a threat from that direction. He was just **"suddenly"** there. And then he came **"from the west,"** although Greece was north of ancient Babylon. It was more **"from the west"** than from the north. But the two next details are most interesting. It came **"across the surface of the whole earth."** That is, it conquered all of the known world. And it came **"without touching the ground."** This would seem to indicate the amazing speed with which Alexander conquered the known world. And finally, **"the goat *had* a notable horn between his eyes."**

And here, we must take note of the fact that this was not so much as a conquest by the Greek kingdom, as one specifically by

Alexander the Great himself. That is, he did not conquer in the name of "the Greeks," or of "the Macedonians," but in his own name.

And then Alexander's victory over the Medo-Persian Empire is described. **"Then he came to the ram that had two horns, which I had seen standing beside the river, and ran at him with furious power. And I saw him confronting the ram; he was moved with rage against him, attacked the ram, and broke his two horns. There was no power in the ram to withstand him, but he cast him down to the ground and trampled him; and there was no one that could deliver the ram from his hand. Therefore the male goat grew very great."** (Daniel 8:6-8a)

History tells us that Alexander and his people felt a particular animosity toward the Medo-Persian Empire. This was a spite that went beyond a simple desire for conquest. And their victory was so decisive that there was no way that anyone could withstand the advance of this new arrival on the international scene. So the Greek (Macedonian) kingdom **"suddenly"** became very great, accomplishing its conquests in only a few years.

But then something drastic was to happen. In the vision, **"but when he became strong, the large horn was broken, and in place of it four notable ones came up toward the four winds of heaven."** (Daniel 8:8b) and in the explanation we are explicitly told that **"As for the broken *horn* and the four that stood up in its place, four kingdoms shall arise out of that nation, but not with its power."** (Daniel 8:22) History tells us that, while Alexander was still young, he fell during a drunken party, suffering a deadly injury. And his four generals divided his kingdom four ways, exactly as God had prophesied, so long before that time.

But none of this was even the point of this prophecy. All of the vision up to this point was only introductory material to identify the end time individual that was the real subject of this prophecy. For in the vision, **"out of one of them came a little horn which grew exceedingly great toward the south, toward the east, and toward the Glorious *Land*."** (Daniel 8:9)

Here we need to notice a widespread misconception about this prophecy. Many simply assume that the end time king represented by the **"little horn which grew exceedingly great"** is the same end time king as the one in chapter 7, which is **"another horn, a little one"** that came up among the ten horns on the beast of that chapter. And as the ten horned beast is a well known symbol of an end time revival of the Roman Empire, they simply assume that this chapter reveals further details about what the end time Roman ruler will do.

But that is a serious error. For we are clearly told from where this **"little horn"** will arise. The description of the vision explicitly stated that this **"little horn" "came" "out of one of"** the four horns that **"came up"** on the **"male goat"** after its **"large born was broken."** And the explanation of the vision explicitly says that **"the male goat *is* the kingdom of Greece. The large horn that *is* between its eyes *is* the first king. As for the broken *horn* and the four that stood up in its place, four kingdoms shall arise out of that nation, but not with its power."** (Daniel 8:21-22)

So there can be zero doubt that the four horns represent the four kingdoms that resulted from the breakup of the empire of Alexander the Great. And this end time **"little horn"** will come **"out of one of"** these four kingdoms. But none of these four kingdoms included Rome. So this **"little horn"** most certainly cannot represent the end time Roman ruler. We need to also notice that, as none of these four kingdoms ever included any part of Russia, this **"little horn"** also cannot represent the end time ruler of Russia. So this **"little horn"** must, of necessity, be a compltely different end time individual, one that has been neglected by almost every well known commentator of the last 100 years, although he was indeed noticed, and commented upon in detail, by numerous writers of the nineteenth century.

But the misunderstanding about this prophecy does not end there. Many others want to make this out to be a reference to something that happened in ancient times. But the details of the prophecy make this physically impossible. For the explanation given to Daniel began with the words, **"Understand, son of man, that the vision *refers* to the time of the end."** (Daniel 8:17b)

There are two possible interpretations of the words **"the time of the end."** Although this is clearly a reference to a time that it still future, many imagine that this phrase only meant the time of the end of the Old Testament system. And thus, they want to make this to mean the time when ancient Jerusalem was destroyed in about 70 A.D. But the power that destroyed the Old Testament system did not come **"out of one of"** the four horns that represented the breakup of Alexander's kingdom.

Others want to make this out to be a reference to the ancient Greek invader Antiochus Epiphanes. But there is no way to even pretend that his invasion took place at **"the time of the end."** And again, we are explicitly told that this evil attacker **"shall be broken without *human* means."** (Daniel 8:25) And Antiochus Epiphanes was unquestionably not **"broken without *human* means."** So we see that this prophecy speaks of a time that is still in our own future, **"the time of the end"** of our own age. The period leading up to the time when our God will come in power and glory to judge the wicked and to make all things right.

But in addition to being told, both that **"the vision *refers* to the time of the end"** and that this **"little horn" "came" "out of one of"** the four horns that represented the breakup of Alexander's kingdom, in the explanation of the vision we are also clearly told:

> "And in the latter time of their kingdom,
> When the transgressors have reached their fullness,
> A king shall arise,
> Having fierce features,
> Who understands sinister schemes.
> His power shall be mighty, but not by his own power;
> He shall destroy fearfully,
> And shall prosper and thrive;
> **He shall destroy the mighty, and also the holy people."**
> (Daniel 8:23-24)

So we are not only told that **"the vision *refers* to the time of the end,"** but that it refers to **"the latter time of their kingdom, When the transgressors have reached their fullness."** And what will happen at that time? **"A king shall arise,"** who **"shall destroy the mighty, and also the holy people."**

But who is this end time king? We have already seen that he can be neither the end time Roman ruler nor the end time Russian one. We find an end time attacker called **"the Assyrian"** in a surprisingly large number of explicitly stated prophecies. [25] In the last century these prophecies have been largely neglected because many have simply assumed that they were only speaking of the ancient attack on Hezekiah by the Assyrian king Sennacherib. [26] But the prophecies about **"the Assyrian"** contain many details which were unquestionably not fulfilled by Sennacherib, or, for that matter, by any other ancient invader. Nahum 1:11 tells us he will come forth out of Nineveh, whose modern name is Mosul, and Isaiah 7:18-20 tells us in typical language that he will attack at the same time as the Egyptian king, **"the king of the south"** of Daniel 11.

It thus becomes clear that the **"little horn"** is this **"Assyrian."** For Nineveh, whose modern name is Mosul, is within the area of the Selucid Empire, which was one of the four kingdoms **"out of one of"** which the **"little horn"** came. He will have **"fierce features."** He will understand **"sinister schemes."** and **"His power shall be mighty, but not by his own power."** This seems to indicate that not only will he be both fierce and cunning, but that he will be backed by some power greater than himself.

And:

> "Through his cunning
> He shall cause deceit to prosper under his rule;
> And he shall exalt *himself* in his heart.
> He shall destroy many in *their* prosperity.
> He shall even rise against the Prince of princes;
> But he shall be broken without *human* means."
> (Daniel 8:25)

So this evil conqueror will not only be cunning and deceitful, and **"shall destroy many in *their* prosperity,"** but **"He shall even rise against the Prince of princes."** This, of course, will be his fatal mistake, with the result that **"he shall be broken without *human* means."**

---

25 This end time attacker is described in Psalm 83:2-8, Isaiah 10:5-34, 14:24-30, 30:30-31, and 31:8-9, and Micah 5:5-6. All of these explicitly mention either **"Assyria"** or **"the Assyrian."**

26 Sennacherib's attack on king Hezekiah is described in detail in 2 Kings 18:13-19:37, 2 Chronicles 32:1-22, and Isaiah 36:1-37:38.

That is, **"the Prince of princes"** himself, the very God of Heaven, will personally destroy him.

We are also given specific details about what this **"little horn."** will do. First we read of the vision itself, **"And out of one of them came a little horn which grew exceedingly great toward the south, toward the east, and toward the Glorious** *Land*. **And it grew up to the host of heaven; and it cast down** *some* **of the host and** *some* **of the stars to the ground, and trampled them. He even exalted** *himself* **as high as the Prince of the host; and by him the daily** *sacrifices* **were taken away, and the place of His sanctuary was cast down. Because of transgression, an army was given over** *to the horn* **to oppose the daily** *sacrifices***; and he cast truth down to the ground. He did** *all this* **and prospered."** (Daniel 8:9-12)

The vision first indicated that this **"little horn"** will grow **"exceedingly great toward the south, toward the east, and toward the Glorious** *Land*." Here we see a distinct progression. As the king represented by this **"little horn"** becomes **"exceeding great,"** he will first grow **"toward the south"** and then **"toward the east"** and then **"toward the Glorious** *Land*."

Although it is looking ahead in the book of Daniel, we remember that in Daniel 11 there is another reference to kings that come from the breakup of Alexander's kingdom. And there, the greatest of the invaders is called **"the king of the north."** So here, this evil king begins by expanding **"toward the south."** We noticed that this evil end time king is also called **"the Assyrian."** The kingdom of Assyria was the northern part of today's Iraq. And the kingdom of Babylon was the southern part of this same modern nation. And as we are told that he will arise out of Nineveh (today's Mosul,) we see that he first expands his kingdom over the rest of today's Iraq, and then expands to the east, which would be into today's Iran. Iran's ancient name was Elam, and it is named among the attackers of Israel in Isaiah 22:5-7. This has to refer to the future, for in ancient times Elam never invaded Israel.

When we realize that after these two expansions have been completed, this evil king will have at his disposal all the resources of both modern day Iraq and of modern day Iran, we realize that, by the time he is ready to invade **"the Glorious** *Land*,**"** his power will be very great. The awesome speed of this attack is detailed in Isaiah 10:28-32, which describes a defeat of ten cities of Judea in only three days.

But then it tells us of this **"little horn which grew exceedingly great,"** that **"it grew up to the host of heaven; and it cast down *some* of the host and *some* of the stars to the ground, and trampled them."** we are not told who these are that are so described. But **"the host of heaven"** would seem to indicate those that claimed to represent God, even as **"stars"** in scripture often represent great men. (We see this in Joseph's dream in Genesis 37:9-10, where Joseph's brothers were seen as stars.)

We have already noticed that **"He even exalted *himself* as high as the Prince of the host."** But now we need to notice that **"by him the daily *sacrifices* were taken away, and the place of His sanctuary was cast down. Because of transgression, an army was given over *to the horn* to oppose the daily *sacrifices*."** (Daniel 8:11b-12a)

It has been widely accepted, as if the Bible actually said it, that the Roman ruler, whom most commentators call "the Antichrist" will be the one that attacks Jerusalem and destroys the temple. But here we are explicitly told that this will be done, not by **"the beast,"** the end time Roman ruler, but by this **"little horn which grew exceedingly great,"** which **"came"** **"out of one of"** the four horns which represented the breakup of Alexander's kingdom.

And we need to notice whose **"sanctuary was cast down."** it refers to the owner of this **"sanctuary"** as **"His."** This word **"His"** cannot mean **"the little horn,"** because he is the one that will cast it down. And he would not destroy his own sanctuary. So it has to refer to **"the Prince of the host,"** that is, Messiah himself. And this is why the translators of the NKJV captalized both the words **"Prince"** and **"His."**

But then there is one more detail about this evil king's activities. Verse 12 ends with the words **"He did *all this* and prospered."** This seems to indicate that this conquest would not be the end of his evil career, but that he would continue to prosper, even after **"by him the daily *sacrifices* were taken away, and the place of His sanctuary was cast down."**

And indeed, Daniel 11 which, as we have already noticed, calls this evil end time ruler **"the king of the north"** has him, in verses 43-

45, continuing down into Egypt, subduing Lybia and Ethiopia, and then returning to **"between the seas and the glorious holy mountain"** before coming to **"his end."**

But the description of the vision continues, saying, **"Then I heard a holy one speaking; and *another* holy one said to that certain *one* who was speaking, 'How long *will* the vision *be, concerning* the daily *sacrifices* and the transgression of desolation, the giving of both the sanctuary and the host to be trampled under foot?' And he said to me, 'For two thousand three hundred days; then the sanctuary shall be cleansed.'"** (Daniel 8:13-14)

First, under the so-called "year-day theory," which some imagine is taught in scripture, many try to make this out to refer to a passage of two thousand and three hundred years. But there is no excuse for such wresting of scripture.

This vision distinctly says that **"by him the daily *sacrifices* were taken away, and the place of His sanctuary was cast down."** This clearly shows that before he comes, the offering of the **"daily *sacrifices*"** will have been resumed, and the **"sanctuary"** will have been re-built. Additionally, we read in Zechariah 6:12-13:

> "Behold, the Man whose name is the BRANCH!
> From His place He shall branch out,
> And He shall build the temple of the LORD;
> Yes, He shall build the temple of the LORD."

And Ezekiel 40:5-43:5 gives us a highly detailed description of a temple unlike anything that has ever been built, and then it says, **"Then I heard *Him* speaking to me from the temple, while a man stood beside me. And He said to me, 'Son of man, *this is* the place of My throne and the place of the soles of My feet, where I will dwell in the midst of the children of Israel forever.'"** (Ezekiel 43:6-7)

So this prophecy tells us that it will be **"two thousand three hundred days"** from **"the transgression of desolation, the giving of both the sanctuary and the host to be trampled under foot"** until this new temple's **"sanctuary will be cleansed."** And, when we remember that it is **"in the middle of the week"** that **"He shall bring an** end to sacrifice and offering." (Daniel 9:27) and that half of a Hebrew (Biblical) week was 1260 days, that means that the sanctuary of the new temple will be cleansed 1040 days, or just 40 days less than three Biblical years, after the end of the seventieth week. We will examine this final week in more detail when we get to the end of Daniel 9.

The explanation of the vision ended with the words:

> "And the vision of the evenings and mornings
> Which was told is true;
> Therefore seal up the vision,
> For *it refers* to many days *in the future*." (Daniel 8:26)

So here again, for this vision, as we have already noticed in Daniel 12:4 for the entire book of Daniel, the prophet was told to **"seal up the vision."** and why? **"For *it refers* to many days *in the future*."**

And what was the effect of this vision on Daniel? **"And I, Daniel, fainted and was sick for days; afterward I arose and went about the king's business. I was astonished by the vision, but no one understood it."** (Daniel 8:2)

Now why would Daniel faint, and be **"sick for days"**? He had just seen a vision of new troubles for his beloved nation, in their distant future, even long after they would be restored to their homeland. And it was more than he could bear. But the ending of this chapter shows us more than that.

There is an alleged "principle of interpretation" that is taught by many as critical to understanding the scriptures. And although it is stated in various ways, this false "principle" is that we should always interpret the scriptures in the light of how they would have been understood by the original hearers. But here, we are explicitly told that, not only Daniel himself but **"no one understood" "the vision."** So it is clear that Daniel shared this vision with his godly peers. But not even one of them understood what it meant. And why? Because it was sealed, **"For *it refers* to many days *in the future*."**

But later, in Revelation 6:1-8:1, the seven seals were opened. So now it is possible for the saints of God to understand this **"little book"** of Daniel if we approach it reverently, as it really is, the very words, not just of an ancient prophet, holy as he might be, but of the Holy Spirit who inspired him to write this **"little book"** which we are "eating."

Daniel 9

We now come to an exceedingly important part of scripture. But before we take this up, we need to understand just who this Daniel was, that wrote this book, and whose words fill most of this chapter. We remember that in Daniel 6:4-5 we read, **"So the governors and satraps sought to find *some* charge against Daniel concerning the kingdom; but they could find no charge or fault, because he *was* faithful; nor was there any error or fault found in him. Then these men said, 'We shall not find any charge against this Daniel unless we find *it* against him concerning the law of his God.'** " At first, we might dismiss this as mere boasting by the man who penned these words. But we must remember that these are not simply the words of Daniel, but the words the Holy Spirit inspired Daniel to write. And that is not all He had to say about Daniel. For we read in Ezekiel 14:14-20, that the land of Israel was so evil that: " **'Even if these three men, Noah, Daniel, and Job, were in it, they would deliver only themselves by their righteousness,' says the Lord GOD.** 'If I cause wild beasts to pass through the land, and they empty it, and make it so desolate that no man may pass through because of the beasts, even *though* these three men *were* in it, *as* I live,' says the Lord GOD, 'they would deliver neither sons nor daughters; only they would be delivered, and the land would be desolate. Or *if* I bring a sword on that land, and say, "Sword, go through the land," and I cut off man and beast from it, even *though* these three men *were* in it, *as* I live," says the Lord GOD, 'they would deliver neither sons nor daughters, but only they themselves would be delivered. 'Or *if* I send a pestilence into that land and pour out My fury on it in blood, and cut off from it man and beast, even t*hough* Noah,

Daniel, and Job *were* in it, *as* I live,' says the Lord GOD, 'they would deliver neither son nor daughter; they would deliver *only* themselves by their righteousness.'"

So we see that Daniel was actually so righteous a man that, *while he still lived*, God compared him to Noah and Job. It is one thing to say such things about someone after he had died, as God called, *"**David**, the **son** of Jesse, a man after My own heart."* (**Acts 13:22**) But God said this of Daniel while he was still alive. That is, God knew that Daniel was so righteous that he would not be puffed up with pride at hearing God himself compare him to Noah and to Job.

But what was this righteous man doing? He was studying the scriptures. For we read that **"In the first year of Darius the son of Ahasuerus, of the lineage of the Medes, who was made king over the realm of the Chaldeans--in the first year of his reign I, Daniel, understood by the books the number of the years** *specified* **by the word of the LORD through Jeremiah the prophet, that He would accomplish seventy years in the desolations of Jerusalem."** (Daniel 9:1-2)

This had been said in Jeremiah 25:11. And when Daniel realized it, his response was, **"Then I set my face toward the Lord God to make request by prayer and supplications, with fasting, sackcloth, and ashes. And I prayed to the LORD my God, and made confession, and said..."** (Daniel 9:3-4a)

It is exceedingly instructive to read this prayer by one of **"these three men, Noah, Daniel, and Job."** What we need to notice here is that even though Daniel was personally so righteous that God compared him to Noah and Job, he identified himself with the guilt of his people. For in his confession, he did not say, THEY have sinned, but WE have sinned. And in quoting this very long prayer, I have stressed the many places where he said this by capitalizing them. Daniel's prayer of confession was:

"O Lord, great and awesome God, who keeps His covenant and mercy with those who love Him, and with those who keep His commandments, WE have sinned and committed iniquity, WE have done wickedly and rebelled, even by departing from Your precepts and Your judgments. Neither have WE heeded Your servants the prophets, who spoke in Your name to OUR kings and OUR princes,

to OUR fathers and ALL THE PEOPLE of the land. O Lord, righteousness *belongs* to You, but to US shame of face, as *it is* this day–to the men of Judah, to the inhabitants of Jerusalem and ALL ISRAEL, those near and those far off in all the countries to which You have driven them, because of the unfaithfulness which they have committed against You. O Lord, to US *belongs* shame of face, to OUR kings, OUR princes, and OUR fathers, because WE have sinned against You. To the Lord our God *belong* mercy and forgiveness, though WE have rebelled against Him. WE have not obeyed the voice of the LORD our God, to walk in His laws, which He set before US by His servants the prophets. Yes, ALL ISRAEL has transgressed Your law, and has departed so as not to obey Your voice; therefore the curse and the oath written in the Law of Moses the servant of God have been poured out on US, because WE have sinned against Him. And He has confirmed His words, which He spoke against US and against OUR judges who judged us, by bringing upon us a great disaster; for under the whole heaven such has never been done as what has been done to Jerusalem. As *it is* written in the Law of Moses, all this disaster has come upon US; yet WE have not made our prayer before the LORD our God, that WE might turn from our iniquities and understand Your truth. Therefore the LORD has kept the disaster in mind, and brought it upon US; for the LORD our God *is* righteous in all the works which He does, though WE have not obeyed His voice. And now, O Lord our God, who brought Your people out of the land of Egypt with a mighty hand, and made Yourself a name, as *it is* this day – WE have sinned, WE have done wickedly!" (Daniel 9:4-15)

When we realize that *this* prayer, confessing *our* sins, was prayed by one of **"these three men, Noah, Daniel, and Job,"** we realize that this is OUR place of power. Here is the prayer that our God will *always* hear. When we, like our great Savior, confess our corporate sins as OUR OWN, our God will *always* hear, and respond.

We see a very similar prayer in Nehemiah 1:5-7. His confession was **"I pray, LORD God of heaven, O great and awesome God, *You* who keep *Your* covenant and mercy with those who love You and observe Your commandments, please let Your ear be attentive and Your eyes open, that You may hear the prayer of Your servant which I pray before You now, day and night, for the children of Israel Your servants, and confess the sins of the children of Israel which WE have sinned against You. BOTH MY FATHER'S HOUSE AND I have sinned. WE have acted very corruptly against You, and have not kept the commandments, the statutes, nor the ordinances which You commanded Your servant Moses."

Here Nehemiah went beyond what Daniel said, saying something Daniel evidently could not personally say, **"both my father's house and I have sinned."** But both of them cried out to God in repentance for the sins of their nation.

And then, after the confessions, came Daniel's supplications:

"O Lord, according to all Your righteousness, I pray, let Your anger and Your fury be turned away from Your city Jerusalem, Your holy mountain; because for OUR sins, and for the iniquities of OUR FATHERS, Jerusalem and Your people *are* a reproach to all *those* around us. Now therefore, our God, hear the prayer of Your servant, and his supplications, and for the Lord's sake cause Your face to shine on Your sanctuary, which is desolate. O my God, incline Your ear and hear; open Your eyes and see our desolations, and the city which is called by Your name; for we do not present our supplications before You because of our righteous deeds, but because of Your great mercies. O Lord, hear! O Lord, forgive! O Lord, listen and act! Do not delay for Your own sake, my God, for Your city and Your people are called by Your name." (Daniel 9:16-19)

Likewise, after his confession, Nehemiah continued:

"Remember, I pray, the word that You commanded Your servant Moses, saying, 'If you are unfaithful, I will scatter you among the nations; but *if* you return to Me, and keep My commandments and do them, though some of you were cast out to the farthest part of the heavens, *yet* I will gather them from there, and bring them to the place which I have chosen as a dwelling for My name.' Now these *are* Your servants and Your people, whom You have redeemed by Your great power, and by Your strong hand. O Lord, I pray, please let Your ear be attentive to the prayer of Your servant, and to the prayer of Your servants who desire to fear Your name; and let Your servant prosper this day, I pray, and grant him mercy in the sight of this man." (Nehemiah 1:8-11)

And even as these two prayer warriors had been alike in confessing corporate guilt as their own, they were again alike in basing their supplications upon the heart of God.

Daniel prayed, **"we do not present our supplications before You because of our righteous deeds, but because of Your great mercies."** And Nehemiah said, **"these *are* Your servants and Your people, whom You have redeemed by Your great power, and by Your strong hand."**

And what was the result Of their prayers? Nehemiah was commissioned to rebuild the city of Jerusalem. And Daniel was given the great prophecy which is the key to all of end time prophecy. Without an understanding of the prophetic portion of Daniel 9, it would remain basically impossible to even begin to understand the time periods so clearly laid out in Bible prophecy.

So we read next in Daniel 9, **"Now while I *was* speaking, praying, and confessing my sin and the sin of my people Israel, and presenting my supplication before the LORD my God for the holy mountain of my God, yes, while I *was* speaking in prayer, the man Gabriel, whom I had seen in the vision at the beginning, being caused to fly swiftly, reached me about the time of the evening offering. And he informed *me*, and talked with me, and said, 'O Daniel, I have now come forth to give you skill to understand. At the beginning of your supplications the command went out, and I have come to tell *you*, for you *are* greatly beloved; therefore consider the matter, and understand the vision:' "** (Daniel 9:20-23)

Aside from the obvious fact that Gabriel called Daniel by name, telling him he was greatly beloved, and that he told Daniel that he had been sent to give Daniel **"skill to understand,"** there are two great points we need to notice about this message. The first one is that it came **"while I *was* speaking, praying, and confessing MY sin and the sin of my people Israel, and presenting my supplication before the LORD my God."** and the second is that Gabriel told him that **"at the beginning of your supplications the command went out."** That is, we need to realize that, even as Daniel began to confess the sin of his people as his own sin, God answered him while he was yet speaking, taking action immediately.

But now it is time to begin to consider the great prophecy of the seventy weeks given to Daniel, the one designed to give him (and to give us) **"skill to understand."**

> **"Seventy weeks are determined**
> **For your people and for your holy city,**
> **To finish the transgression,**
> **To make an end of sins,**
> **To make reconciliation for iniquity,**
> **To bring in everlasting righteousness,**
> **To seal up vision and prophecy,**
> **And to anoint the Most Holy."** (Daniel 9:24)

First, we see that **"seventy weeks are determined."** Many want to insist that this means that a period of time hat would last seventy weeks is determined. But that is not what it says. And in understanding Bible prophecy, as in the rest of scripture, we need to understand that when God speaks, He speaks precisely, saying exactly what He means. He means what He says. He means *exactly* what He says, and He does not mean *anything* He does *not* say. That is, if a detail is omitted that *we think* should have been there, we need to realize that it was omitted for a reason.

And here we also need to notice another detail. And that is that the Hebrew word that is here translated **"weeks"** did not mean a period of seven days. [27] For the concept of weeks was used in the Bible, not only for periods of seven days, but also for periods of seven years, as we see in the following:

---

27 The Hebrew word used here is שׁבעים, "shabuaym" in our alphabet, which is the plural form of שׁבע, "*shabua*" in our alphabet. (word number 7620 in Srong's Hebrew Dictionary) This Hebrew word literally means a "seven." that is, the Hebrew text actually says, "seventy sevens are determined." But the word itself neither means nor implies the thought of specifically either seven days or seven years.

"And the LORD spoke to Moses on Mount Sinai, saying, 'Speak to the children of Israel, and say to them: 'When you come into the land which I give you, then the land shall keep a sabbath to the LORD. Six years you shall sow your field, and six years you shall prune your vineyard, and gather its fruit; but in the seventh year there shall be a sabbath of solemn rest for the land, a sabbath to the LORD. You shall neither sow your field nor prune your vineyard. What grows of its own accord of your harvest you shall not reap, nor gather the grapes of your untended vine, *for* it is a year of rest for the land.' " (Leviticus 25:1-5)

So interpreting the **"seventy weeks"** to mean seventy periods of seven years is not an application of the false "year-day theory," but is a fully legitimate, literal interpretation of the text of Daniel 9:24-27.

But next we need to notice for whom these **"seventy weeks"** were **"determined."** they were **"determined"** **"For your people and for your holy city."** Daniel's **"people"** were the Jews, and Daniel's **"holy city"** was Jerusalem. So these **"seventy weeks are determined"** for the Jews and for Jerusalem. Understanding this is critical. These **"seventy weeks"** are not **"determined"** for the whole world, nor are they **"determined"** for the church. They are **"determined"** for the Jews and for Jerusalem.

But what is their purpose?

> "**To finish the transgression,**
> **To make an end of sins,**
> **To make reconciliation for iniquity,**
> **To bring in everlasting righteousness,**
> **To seal up vision and prophecy,**
> **And to anoint the Most Holy."**

"Reconciliation for iniquity" was clearly made at Calvary nearly two thousand years ago. But what about the rest of this program? Has **"the transgression"** of Daniel's **"people"** and of Daniel's **"holy city"** been finished? The answer is obviously, no. Indeed, we know from scripture that their worst transgression, other than when they crucified their Messiah, is yet to come, when they will allow **"the**

man of sin," "the son of perdition," to sit **"as God, in the temple of God, showing himself that he is God."** (2 Thessalonians 2:3-4)

Again, are the sins of the Jews and Jerusalem ended? No. For they are still in rebellion, having, even to this day, not yet been cleansed by the blood of Christ. For to this day, they still reject Him as their Messiah, still looking for another.

Thus also, **"everlasting righteousness"** has not yet been brought in for the Jews and for Jerusalem. And vision and prophecy concerning the Jews and Jerusalem remains unfulfilled, not yet sealed up.

This leaves only the purpose, **"to anoint the Most Holy."** The term **"Most Holy"** is the Hebrew words קֹדֶשׁ קָדָשִׁים:, qodesh qodesh, that is, the Hebrew word qodesh, which means holy, doubled. (This is word number 6944 in Strong's Hebrew dictionary.) This is not, as many have supposed, a reference to the Lord Jesus, but to the place behind the veil, first of the tabernacle, as we read in Exodus 26:33-34, **"you shall hang the veil from the clasps. Then you shall bring the ark of the Testimony in there, behind the veil. The veil shall be a divider for you between the holy place and the Most Holy. You shall put the mercy seat upon the ark of the Testimony in the Most Holy."** And then of the temple built by Solomon, as we read in 1 Kings 6:16, **"Then he built the twenty-cubit room at the rear of the temple, from from floor to ceiling, with cedar boards; he built it inside as the inner sanctuary, as the Most Holy *Place*."** It is further used of this room of Solomon's temple in 1 Kings 7:50 and 8:6, 2 Chronicles 4:22, 5:7 and 11, and of the same room in the future temple as described in Ezekiel 41:4, 44:13, and 45:3.

This is distinguished from generic places that were holy, by calling those **"a holy place,"** using the Hebrew words קֹדֶשׁ בְּמָקוֹם, *quadosh maqom* in our alphabet, (words number 6918 and 4725 in Strong's Hebrew dictionary.) This expression can be found in Leviticus 7:6 and 10:17.

The term **"most holy"** is also used of the **"altar of the burnt offering"** in Exodus 29:37 and 40:10, and of the offerings in Exodus 30:10 and 36, Leviticus 2:3 and 10, 6:17, 25, and 29, 7:1, 6, 10:12 and 17, 14:13, 21:22, 24:9, and 27:28, Numbers 18:9, Ezra 2:63, Nehemiah 7:65, and Ezekiel 42:13.

The Greek equivalent of this Hebrew term, *qodesh qodesh*, is the Greek term ἅγια ἅγιον, *agia agion* in our alphabet. Like *qodesh qodesh*, this is simply the word for holy, doubled. It is found only in Hebrews 9:3, where its application to the same room in **"the tabernacle"** is explicitly stated in the words, **"and behind the second veil, the part of the tabernacle which is called the Holiest of All."** [28]

So in the entire rest of the Bible, this term, **"the Most Holy"** is never, even once, used of God himself. Therefore **"the Most Holy"** that was to be anointed in Daniel 9:24 cannot refer to the Lord Jesus. It has to refer to the **"Most Holy"** place in the temple of the seventieth week, which we read about as the **"sanctuary"** of **"the Prince of the host"** in Daniel 8:11: **"He even exalted *himself* as high as the Prince of the host; and by him the daily *sacrifices* were taken away, and the place of His sanctuary was cast down."**

So we see that, although part of this program for the **"seventy weeks"** has indeed been accomplished, most of it remains unfulfilled, even to this day.

The announcement continued, but this time the wording was different. Although the declaration of the **"seventy weeks"** contained no word indicating that they would be continuous, we now find a distinct statement of **"from"** and **"until,"** that is, this part of the prophecy was distinctly stated to be continuous, as opposed to a distinct lack of any such statement concerning the entire **"seventy weeks."**

> "Know therefore and understand,
> *That* from the going forth of the command
> To restore and build Jerusalem
> Until Messiah the Prince,
> *There shall be* seven weeks and sixty-two weeks;
> The street shall be built again, and the wall,

---

[28] The term **"most holy"** is also found in English translations of Jude 20, saying **"your most holy faith."** But here, it is a rendition of the Greek word ἅγιος, *aigios* in our alphabet, (word number 40 in Strong's Greek Dictionary.) As this word simply means holy, its meaning is similar to the Hebrew word *qodesh*. But here it is not intensified in a way similar to any of the Hebrew terms translated **"Most Holy."** And although this Greek word is used well over 200 times in the New Testament, this is the only place where the translators have rendered it as **"most holy."**

Even in troublesome times." Daniel 9:25

There were to be two periods of time, the first lasting seven weeks and the second lasting sixty-two weeks. And this period was to be **"from the going forth of the command To restore and build Jerusalem Until Messiah the Prince."**

Seven plus sixty-two is sixty-nine. And sixty-nine times seven is four hundred and eighty-three. And history tells us that it was indeed four hundred and eighty-three Hebrew years **"from the going forth of the command To restore and build Jerusalem Until Messiah the Prince."** Some contend that this was accurate to the very day, from the day the command was issued until the day of the triumphal entry. And this may indeed be correct. But concluding that it was accurate to the very day requires making assumptions that I am not prepared to make.

Our translation, like others, renders the final words of this section as **"The street shall be built again, and the wall, Even in troublesome times."** But the Hebrew word here rendered **"troublesome"** actually means "strait," that is, narrow. [29] So it would appear that what the Holy Spirit was actually saying here was that **"The street shall be built again, and the wall,"** in he smaller of the two times. And indeed, this is what actually happened. The street and the wall were built again in the forty-nine years, that is, **"seven weeks,"** after **"the command"** went **"forth" "to restore and build Jerusalem."**

Next comes a statement that is critical to understanding this prophecy.

> **"And after the sixty-two weeks**
> **Messiah shall be cut off, but not for Himself;**
> **And the people of the prince who is to come**
> **Shall destroy the city and the sanctuary.**
> **The end of it** *shall be* **with a flood,**

---

29 This Hebrew word is a form of צוּקָה, *suqa* in our alphabet. (word number 6695 in Strong's Hebrew Dictionary) While this word is usually translated with some word meaning distress or anguish, that is a only a figurative usage of this Hebrew word, whose literal meaning is *strait*, in the sense of *narrow*.

> And till the end of the war desolations are determined."
> (Daniel 9:26)

Here, we are explicitly told of three specific things that were to happen **"after the sixty-two weeks."**

> First: **"Messiah shall be cut off, but not for Himself."**
>
> Second: **"the people of the prince who is to come Shall destroy the city."**
>
> Third **"the people of the prince who is to come**
>
> **Shall destroy" "the sanctuary."**

It is critical to understand that the second and third items in this list did not occur within seven years (one **"week"**) after the first one. While exact dates of ancient history are usually impossible to establish with certainty, we know of a certainty that the second and third events in this sequence took place around 70 AD, while the first one took place approximately 41 years earlier. The problem being that we do not know the exact year our Lord was born. Most historians have concluded that our calendars are wrong by four years, making our Lord's birth take place in 4 BC, which would place His death in 29 AD. But that number is not certain. The only thing we know of a certainty is that it was somewhere around 41 years between the events prophesied in Daniel 9:26.

Then we have two details added about the events previously prophesied. **"The end of it *shall be* with a flood, And till the end of the war desolations are determined."** The overwhelming attack on Jerusalem by the Roman armies is here called **"a flood."** And the desolations that accompanied this war are almost too horrible to repeat.

But now we come to the seventieth week.

> "Then he shall confirm a covenant with many for one week;
> But in the middle of the week
> He shall bring an end to sacrifice and offering.

> And on the wing of abominations shall be one
> who makes desolate,
>
> Even until the consummation, which is determined,
> Is poured out on the desolate." (Daniel 9:27)

There are a number of details about this week that we need to understand. The first is that it is not even mentioned until after the three events which were to take place **"after the sixty-two weeks."** And a second is that the only reason we know this is the seventieth week is that the other sixty-nine weeks had already been used up. There was only one week left, and now a covenant is established **"for one week."**

But who is the **"he"** that **"shall confirm a covenant with many for one week"**? Here, we need to rely upon a standard rule of grammar that exists in all languages. This rule is that whenever the word **"he"** is used without any introduction, it is speaking of whatever male is the subject of the discussion, which is usually the last man mentioned. And who is the last man mentioned here? **"The prince that shall come."** the one whose **"people"** would **"destroy the city and the sanctuary."**

And what **"people"** destroyed **"the city and the sanctuary"**? It is a well known fact of history that this was done by the Romans. But here we need to notice that it does not say that **"the prince that shall come"** is the one who **"shall destroy the city and the sanctuary."** Instead, it says that this shall be done by **"the people of the prince that shall come."** As **"the people"** who destroyed **"the city and the sanctuary"** were the Romans, this identifies **"the prince that shall come"** as a Roman. And it says that this would be done by his **"people,"** rather than by himself, because, even to the present day, this **"prince"** has still not come.

How do we know that this **"prince"** has still not come? Because, even to this day, there has been never been a **"prince"** that has confirmed a covenant **"for one week."** The concept of a temporary treaty "to allow things to stabilize" has only recently been introduced into modern politics.

But this **"prince"** will not only **"confirm a covenant with many for one week." "But in the middle of the week He shall bring** an end to sacrifice and offering." That is, half way through the **"week"** of this **"covenant,"** this **"prince"** will do something that **"shall bring an end to sacrifice and offering."** (The word **"He"** is not here captalized to indicate that this would be done by God, but because it is the first word in a line of poetry.) This prophecy does not tell us what this **"prince"** will do to **"bring an end to sacrifice and offering."** It only says he will do it. But other prophecies give us more details about this.

But now we need to stop and ask, why was this made so complicated? Why was it given in such little pieces? We are told the reason in other places:

> "Whom will he teach knowledge?
> And whom will he make to understand the message?
> **Those *just* weaned from milk?**
> **Those *just* drawn from the breasts?**
> **For precept *must* be upon precept, precept upon precept,**
> **Line upon line, line upon line,**
> **Here a little, there a little."** (Isaiah 28:9-10)

So we see that God intentionally did this, but why? Why did God make His words so hard to understand? We are told why in Matthew 13:11-12, where Jesus said, **"it has been given to you to know the mysteries of the kingdom of heaven, but to them it has not been given. For whoever has, to him more will be given, and he will have abundance; but whoever does not have, even what he has will be taken away from him."**

So we see that our Lord plainly told us that He intentionally gave us His word in such a way as to hide its meaning from those who would choose to not believe it.

That is why we see so many and such serious wrestings of the prophecies in the Bible, including this particular passage. It would not be profitable to go into these in detail here. But we will take the time to consider one widely circulated lie about this passage. And that is the claim that the concept of an end time fulfillment of "Daniel's seventieth week" was only invented in the 1800s to defend Dispensationalism. The truth is that this was very clearly taught in the very oldest surviving Christian commentary on scripture, which was a commentary on the book of Daniel written by Hippolytus. This is thought to have been written between the years 202 and 211 A.D., and said:

"As also it was announced to Daniel: 'And one week shall confirm a covenant with many; and in the midst of the week it shall be that the sacrifice and oblation shall be removed" —that the one week might be shown to be divided into two. The two witnesses, then, shall preach three years and a half; and Antichrist shall make war upon the saints during the rest of the week, and desolate the world, that what is written may be fulfilled: "And they shall make the abomination of desolation for a thousand two hundred and ninety days.' " [30]

And even earlier than that, the very oldest surviving Christian commentary on Bible prophecy of any significant length, the last twelve chapters of the very famous work by Irenaeus titled "Against Heresies," which is thought to have been written between the years 186 and 188 A.D., said:

> "And then he points out the time that his tyranny shall last, during which the saints shall be put to flight, they who offer a pure sacrifice unto God: 'And in the midst of the week,' he says, 'the sacrifice and the libation shall be taken away, and the abomination of desolation [shall be brought] into the temple: even unto the consummation of the time shall the desolation be complete.' Now three years and six months constitute the half-week. [31]

---

30 "The interpretation by Hippolytus, (bishop) of Rome, of the visions of Daniel and Nebuchadnezzar, taken in conjunction," by Hippolytus, paragraph 39, from paragraph 2 of "On Daniel," in "The Early Church Fathers: Ante-Nicene Fathers," vol. 5, edited by Alexander Roberts and James Donaldson.

31 "Against Heresies", by Irenaeus, book 5, chapter 25, paragraph 4. From Volume 1 of "The Early Church Fathers: Ante-Nicene Fathers," edited by Alexander Roberts and James Donaldson.

So we see that, instead of having only been invented in the 1800s "to defend Dispensationalism," this concept goes all the way back to the very beginnings of Christian teaching about Bible prophecy. [32]

But, returning now to our chapter, what will happen when **"the prince that shall come"** brings **"an end to sacrifice and offering"**? It says that **"On the wing of abominations shall be one who makes desolate."**

We need to notice here that the actor changes in this statement. Up to this point, the actor is **"he,"** which points back to **"the prince that shall come."** But here, the actor suddenly changes from **"he"** to **"one."** That is, the **"one who makes desolate"** is not the same end time individual as **"the prince that shall come."** This important detail has been overlooked by many.

Rather than being **"the prince that shall come,"** this **"one who makes desolate"** is the one called **"the Assyrian"** in Isaiah 10:5-34, 14:24-30, 30:30-31, and 31:8-9, and also in Micah 5:5-6. He is also the future **"king of the north"** whose actions are described in Daniel 11:40-45. But we will delay further discussion of him until we come to that chapter.

The coming of this **"one who makes desolate"** begins a time which will last **"Even until the consummation, which is determined, Is poured out on the desolate."**

And so ends the prophecy in Daniel 9. This does not sound like a hopeful ending, and it is not intended to be hopeful. For the last part of this prophecy is about the chastening that God will use to finally bring this ancient and rebellious nation to repentance. And **"no chastening seems to be joyful for the present, but painful; nevertheless, afterward it yields the peaceable fruit of righteousness to those who have been trained by it."** (Hebrews 12:11) So, although the end will be blessed, the chastening process will be very painful.

Much detail is omitted in this prophecy. For its purpose was not to give detail, but to present a general overview of the process that

---

32 These ancient statements are not presented with even the slightest implication that their antiquity lends any authority whatsoever to what they say. They are only quoted here to conclusively disprove the lie that this concept was never taught before the early 1800s.

God will use to finally generate repentance in Daniel's **"people,"** the Jews, and Daniel's **"holy city,"** Jerusalem. And to reveal the key to understanding everything the Bible tells us about the period the scriptures call **"the time of the end."** (Daniel 11:40, 12:4, and 12:9)

Daniel 10

Much of the detail that is omitted in Daniel 9 is revealed in Daniel 11 and 12. And this chapter 10 of Daniel is actually a rather long introduction to these two chapters. So Daniel 10 is really the beginning of filling in the details of the general overview of end time prophecy given in Daniel 9.

"In the third year of Cyrus king of Persia a message was revealed to Daniel, whose name was called Belteshazzar." (Daniel 10:1a) As Cyrus came after Darius, this vision was given well after the vision of Daniel 9.

We remember that Daniel 8 had ended with the words, **"I was astonished by the vision, but no one understood it."** (Daniel 8:27b) But this vision was different. For we read:

"The message *was* true, but the appointed time *was* long; and he understood the message, and had understanding of the vision." (Daniel 10:1b)

Then we read:

"In those days I, Daniel, was mourning three full weeks. I ate no pleasant food, no meat or wine came into my mouth, nor did I anoint myself at all, till three whole weeks were fulfilled." (Daniel 10:2-3)

When we consider this, we realize that, even as we are told, **"The secret of the LORD is with those who fear Him,"** (Psalm 25:14) the Lord reveals His mind to those that truly set their hearts upon Himself, to those who *earnestly* seek Him.

> **"Now on the twenty-fourth day of the first month, as I was by the side of the great river, that is, the Tigris, I lifted my eyes and looked, and behold, a certain man clothed in linen, whose waist *was* girded with gold of Uphaz! His body *was* like beryl, his face like the appearance of lightning, his eyes like torches of fire, his arms and feet like burnished bronze in color, and the sound of his words like the voice of a multitude."** (Daniel 10:4-6)

First, we are told exactly when and where Daniel had seen this vision. This was not just some kind of a general impression, but a specific vision, seen at a particular time and place. But we should note here, that the words **"as I was by the side of the great river, that is, the Tigris"** do not indicate where he saw himself in the vision, as had been the case in Daniel 8:2, but the place where he was when he **"lifted up"** his **"eyes"** and saw this marvelous vision. And what did he see? An angelic messenger. **"A certain man clothed in linen, whose waist *was* girded with gold of Uphaz! His body *was* like beryl, his face like the appearance of lightning, his eyes like torches of fire, his arms and feet like burnished bronze in color."**

As he came to bring understanding, **"his body was like beryl."** Beryl is a colorless gemstone. You can see through it. So there is nothing hidden about his message. But he is **"clothed in linen,"** and we remember that we are told in Revelation 19:8 that **"fine linen"** represents **"the righteous acts of the saints."** And his **"waist *was* girded with gold of Uphaz."** we are not explicitly told what gold indicates. But from all the places it is used in scripture, it seems to represent the righteousness of God.

But his face! It was **"like the appearance of lightening."** While this is indeed an awesome appearance, yet the brightness of his face, the brightest light known to ancient man, again indicates that he has come to reveal. The light of his countenance reveals all. And likewise his eyes burned **"like torches of fire."** That is, they could burn through anything. Nothing could be hidden from his gaze. And finally, his feet were **"like burnished bronze in color."** Again, although we are not explicitly told what bronze represents, from its many uses in scripture it seems to indicate judgment, in the sense of punishment. So this would seem to indicate that he had come to reveal the coming judgments of God.

But in addition to what Daniel saw, when this man spoke, it sounded **"like the voice of a multitude."** As if this were the combined voices of many witnesses, attesting to the truth of his words.

> **And I, Daniel, alone saw the vision, for the men who were with me did not see the vision; but a great terror fell upon them, so that they fled to hide themselves. Therefore I was left alone when I saw this great vision."** (Daniel 10:7-8a)

The men around Daniel had seen nothing, but such **"a great terror"** struck them **"that they fled to hide themselves."** So, although the men around Daniel saw nothing, they all knew something awesome had taken place.

And what was the effect of this vision on Daniel? **"No strength remained in me; for my vigor was turned to frailty in me, and I retained no strength. Yet I heard the sound of his words; and while I heard the sound of his words I was in a deep sleep on my face, with my face to the ground."** (Daniel 10:8b-9)

We remember that when John saw the vision of the Lord Jesus as the judge, he **"fell at His feet as dead."** (Revelation 1:17a) And the result in both cases was the same. When John so reacted, The Lord **"laid His right hand on"** him, saying, **"Do not be afraid."** (Revelation 1:17b) And here, **"Suddenly, a hand touched me, which made me tremble on my knees and *on* the palms of my hands. And he said to me, 'O Daniel, man greatly beloved, understand the words that I speak to you, and stand upright, for I have now been sent to you.' While he was speaking this word to me, I stood trembling. Then he said to me, 'Do not fear, Daniel.' "** (Daniel 10:10-12a)

But the angel explained that a demon had resisted him for 21 days, **"for from the first day that you set your heart to understand, and to humble yourself before your God, your words were heard; and I have come because of your words. But the prince of the kingdom of Persia withstood me twenty-one days; and behold, Michael,** one of the chief princes, came to help me, for I had been left alone there with the kings of Persia." (Daniel 10:12b-13)

This should greatly impress any saint of God. We remember that this account had begun with words we skimmed over rather quickly. "**In those days I, Daniel, was mourning three full weeks. I ate no pleasant food, no meat or wine came into my mouth, nor did I anoint myself at all, till three whole weeks were fulfilled.**" (Daniel 10:2-3)

So Daniel had been mourning "**three full weeks,**" and fasting "**till three whole weeks were fulfilled.**" And "**from the first day that**" he had set his "**heart to understand, and to humble**" himself before his God, his "**words were heard.**" but there had been a reason for the delay in answering him, that had nothing to do with Daniel. For "**the prince of the kingdom of Persia withstood me twenty-one days.**"

We remember that Paul wrote to the Thessalonians that "**we wanted to come to you--even I, Paul, time and again--but Satan hindered us.**" (1 Thessalonians 2:18) And in a vision Zechariah was shown "**Joshua the high priest standing before the Angel of the LORD, and Satan standing at his right hand to oppose him.**" (Zechariah 3:1) So we are repeatedly told in the scriptures about Satan resisting the acts of God. And indeed, at times the evil one is allowed to so resist for a while. But only when such delay fits God's long term purpose. And in this case, when "**three whole weeks were fulfilled,**" "**Michael, one of the chief princes, came to help**" the messenger that had been sent to Daniel. So, while the saint of God was mourning and fasting, a great battle had been going on far above, as the messenger that had been sent was being resisted by the forces of evil. But when the delay had fulfilled God's purposes, He sent help. In this case, it was in the person of "**Michael, one of the chief princes.**" In Daniel 12:1, we are told that "**Michael**" is "**the great prince who stands watch over the sons of your people.**" So "**the great prince**" that is responsible for the children of Daniel's people was sent to help the messenger get through to the seeking saint.

But now we need to notice the occasion of Daniel's fast. It had not been stated at the beginning of the chapter. But it is stated here. It was not only that Daniel had set his heart "**to humble himself before**" his "**God,**" but that he had set his heart "**to understand.**" We remember that "**the prophets**" "**inquired and searched carefully,**" "**searching what, or what manner of time, the Spirit of Christ who was in them was indicating." (1 Peter 1:10-11) And we also remember that Daniel himself had ended the account of his vision of the ram and the male goat with the words, **"I was astonished by the vision, but no one understood it."** (Daniel 8:27)

So now, Daniel had set his heart **"to understand."** But how did he seek understanding? By diligent study? Yes, for we read that **"I, Daniel, understood by the books the number of the years *specified* by the word of the LORD through Jeremiah the prophet."** (Daniel 9:2) But it was not only by diligent study, but by humbling himself before his God, even to the point of fasting. This is the secret to learning from God. And if our knowledge does not come from God himself, what good is it? Mere knowledge is indeed useful in the things of this world. But it is useless in spiritual matters. There, we need revelation from God himself. And we cannot receive such revelation without humbling ourselves before Him.

And what was the result of Daniel so humbling himself? The messenger said, **"Now I have come to make you understand what will happen to your people in the latter days, for the vision *refers to many* days yet *to come*."** (Daniel 10:14) So Daniel's quest **"to understand"** had been rewarded with a vision, sent directly from God himself, about what would happen to his people **"in the latter days."**

Many have made much of the amazing accuracy of the part of this vision that referred to events that took place in later years, but still in ancient times. But *that* part of the vision was not even what this vision was *about*. It's subject is **"what will happen to your people in the latter days."** And **"the latter days"** have not yet begin, even to this day.

The effect, even of only this introductory vision, was simply too much for the prophet. For **"When he had spoken such words to me, I turned my face toward the ground and became speechless. And suddenly, *one* having the likeness of the sons of men touched my lips; then I opened my mouth and spoke, saying to him who stood before me, 'My lord, because of the vision my sorrows have overwhelmed me, and I have retained no strength. For how can this servant of my lord talk with you, my lord? As for me, no strength remains in me now, nor is any breath left in me.' "** (Daniel 10:15-17)

But God's response to Daniel's reaction was, **"Then again, *the one* having the likeness of a man touched me and strengthened me. And he said, 'O man greatly beloved, fear not! Peace be to you; be strong, yes, be strong!' So when he spoke to me I was strengthened, and said, 'Let my lord speak, for you have strengthened me.'"** (Daniel 10:18-19)

Now that Daniel had been given supernatural strength, The message began:

"Then he said, 'Do you know why I have come to you? And now I must return to fight with the prince of Persia; and when I have gone forth, indeed the prince of Greece will come. But I will tell you what is noted in the Scripture of Truth. (No one upholds me against these, except Michael your prince.'" (Daniel 10:20-21)

The messenger first reminded Daniel of what he had already told him about why he had come. It was **"to make you understand what will happen to your people in the latter days."** so now he adds, **"But I will tell you what is noted in the Scripture of Truth."**

This was not something new. It was already written down. But it had not yet been revealed to mankind. So the messenger was going to tell Daniel the plans that God had written down earlier. How much earlier, we are not told here. But in other places we are told that God's plans for His people had been made **"before the world,"** (1 Corinthians 2:7) **"before the foundation of the world,"** (Ephesians 1:4) and **"before the world began."** (Titus 1:2)

But then the messenger revealsd a few details about his own work. **"And now I must return to fight with the prince of Persia; and when I have gone forth, indeed the prince of Greece will come."** And afterward he added, **"No one upholds me against these, except Michael your prince."** These seem to be included, not just as matters of possible interest, but so we realize that, while we may imagine that the efforts of men are controlling the things that are taking place, there are far greater powers that, working out of the sight of mere mortals, are controlling everything. [33]

---

33 We should also notice that, in this message, both angels and demons were called "princes."

Daniel 11

Here the Holy Spirit began a highly detailed account of a long series of events that were going take place in Daniel's future. The first part of this account is so highly detailed and so precisely accurate that unbelievers claim its very precision is the proof that it could not have been written before these events had actually taken place. But a simple faith in the power of God removes all such imaginary problems.

But before we begin to examine this account, we need to notice a few things. The first of these is that there is a distinct break in this account. In verse 35 we read, **"And *some* of those of understanding shall fall, to refine them, purify *them*, and make *them* white, *until* the time of the end; because *it is* still for the appointed time."** (Daniel 11:35) we need to particularly notice the words *"until* **the time of the end."** Every detail of every statement in this entire account, up to these words, was literally filled, exactly as it was written, in ancient times. But from these words to the end of the account, none of the rest of this has ever taken place, even to this day. So the break in verse 35 is a jump from ancient times to **"the time of the end,"** which has not yet begun. But after that jump the account then goes on, describing other events which will take place in **"the time of the end."**

But in addition to this very obvious break in this account, we also need to notice an often overlooked significance of the high detail of this account. For this detail disproves two false, but very widely taught, systems of interpreting Bible prophecy.

These two systems of interpretation are called, respectively, Historicism, which was invented during the reformation to bolster the false notion that Popery is "the Antichrist" of Bible prophecy, and Preterism, which was invented during the counter-reformation to oppose Historicism.

The name Historicism is derived from the word history, and refers to the false claim that the events prophesied in the Revelation were fulfilled during the history of the early and medieval church. And the name Preterism is derived from the Latin word preterit, which is the Latin grammatical term for the past perfect tense. So this name refers to the equally false claim that all (or, in the case of what its adherents call Partial Preterism, most) of the events in Bible prophecy were fulfilled in ancient times. Both of these systems of interpretation are necessarily false because they take prophecies which plainly refer to **"the time of the end,"** and pretend that they refer to events which took place long ago.

The adherents of both of these opposing, but equally false, systems of interpretation pour endlessly through historical records, vainly searching for proof that various prophecied events have taken place. And they have found many such records which they claim prove that various prophecies have already been fulfilled. But I have personally examined many of these claims, and have found a consistent rule that runs through essentially all of them. That rule is that when the prophecy they claim to have been fulfilled is compared to the historical record they cite, there is almost no agreement in the details. Typically, only something on the order of ten to fifteen percent of the details in the prophecy in question agree with the details in the historical record that they cite as its fulfillment.

When this almost complete lack of agreement in even the basic details is compared with the agreement between the details of Daniel 11:2-35 and the historical records of the period covered by this prophecy, the difference is astounding. For we find that, in this case, the agreement is *total*. That is, *every* detail of these 34 verses *exactly* matches the details of the historical records about the period covered by this prophecy.

We see the same in the prophecies about the first coming of our Lord. Although in some cases figures of speech were used, we find that every prophesy about the first coming of our Lord was fulfilled literally, down to the tiniest detail, just as was done in this section of Daniel 11. So the hard truth is that, rather than being only stated in broad generalities, the explicitly stated prophecies in the Bible are highly detailed, and mean *exactly* what they say, down to the tiniest detail.

So, as we examine this account, we first find the comment, **"Also in the first year of Darius the Mede, I, *even* I, stood up to confirm and strengthen him."** (Daniel 11:1) The word **"also"** at the beginning of this statement ties it into the last chapter, which is why our translation (the NKJV) punctuates it as the last part of a parenthesis, finishing the statement from Daniel 10:21 that **"No one upholds me against these, except Michael your prince."** (Daniel 10:21b) We remember that the chapter and verse divisions are made by man, rather than inspired by God, so they are sometimes placed in inappropriate places. And in this case, it is plain that the NKJV translators corrected an inappropriate chapter division.

For it is plain that the actual account of future events begins in verse 2, with the words, **"And now I will tell you the truth: Behold, three more kings will arise in Persia, and the fourth shall be far richer than *them* all; by his strength, through his riches, he shall stir up all against the realm of Greece."** (Daniel 11:2)

We need to take particular notice of the first clause here, **"And now I will tell you the truth."** we need to compare this with the opening of chapter 10, which, as we noticed, is really only the introduction to this chapter. There we were told, **"the message was true, but the appointed time was long."** (Daniel 10:1) and again, in the last verse of that chapter, the messenger said, **"I will tell you what is noted in the Scripture of Truth."** (Daniel 10:21) Why did God so stress that this account was true? Because this prophecy (Daniel 11:2-12:13) is one of the most misrepresented and maligned of all the prophecies in the Bible. And the Holy Spirit wanted to stress that **"these are the true sayings of God,"** as we read in Revelation 19:9.

But then, as the actual account of coming events begins, we read, **"Behold, three more kings will arise in Persia, and the fourth shall be far richer than *them* all; by his strength, through his riches, he shall stir up all against the realm of Greece."**

We remember that this message was given **"in the third year of Cyrus king of Persia."** (Daniel 10:1) so **"three more kings"** were to **"arise"** after Cyrus. All three of these kings are explicitly mentioned in scripture. We remember that Cyrus was the king that originally gave the order to rebuild the Lord's temple in Jerusalem. (Ezra 1:1-4)

But then, as the book of Ezra unfolds, we find each of these **"three more kings"** mentioned by name, being **"Ahasuerus,"** (Ezra 4:6) **"Artaxerxes,"** (Ezra 4:7) and **"Darius."** (Ezra 4:24) These names are different from those given by the Greek historians, but our interest is in the names used by God.

But then the messenger said, **"and the fourth shall be far richer than *them* all; by his strength, through his riches, he shall stir up all against the realm of Greece."** This fourth king was Xerexes the Great, who assembled a huge army to conquer Greece, but his huge army was not enough to overcome the stubborn resistance of the Greeks.

But the messenger continued, **"Then a mighty king shall arise, who shall rule with great dominion, and do according to his will. And when he has arisen, his kingdom shall be broken up and divided toward the four winds of heaven, but not among his posterity nor according to his dominion with which he ruled; for his kingdom shall be uprooted, even for others besides these."** (Daniel 11:3-4)

This **"mighty king"** was Alexander the Great, who, in just a few short years, conquered all of the world known to the ancient middle eastern peoples. But while he was still young, he died, reportedly due to drunken accident, and his four generals divided his kingdom four ways.

But the purpose of God's prophecies is not to satisfy man's curiosity, nor to just prove that He can foretell the future, but to reveal His plans for His people. So in what follows, God only deals with two of the kingdoms that resulted from this breakup. These two kingdoms were those of Ptolemy whom God called **"the king of the south,"** and Selucius, whom God called **"the king of the north."**

As a result of the breakup of Alexander's kingdom, Ptolemy ended up with the southern portion, Egypt, and Selucius the eastern portion. But soon after, Selucius added the northern portion to his kingdom, thus becoming **"the king of the north."** And, as we just noted, the account given here does not even mention the other kingdoms. This is because what happened to those other kingdoms had no bearing on what God was revealing in this prophecy.

For we need to remember that the *purpose* of this entire prophecy was **"to make you understand what will happen to your people in the latter days."** (Daniel 10:14) The *purpose* of this account is not to reveal details along the way, but to reveal **"what will happen to"** Daniel's people (the Jews) **"in the latter days."** So all the information about what happened in ancient times had only an auxiliary purpose. And what was that auxiliary purpose? It was to reveal the meanings of the terms **"the king of the north"** and **"the king of the south"** in the portion of the account that deals with **"the latter days."** This is the portion that begins in verse 36. And until we understand this, we cannot even begin to understand what this prophecy is about.

So we need to examine the details that identify these two evil end time individuals, **"the king of the south"** and **"the king of the north."** But before we begin this analysis, we need to remember that when we consider the fact that the various accounts of current events are often radically different, depending on who is reporting them, it should come as no surprise to hear that the various accounts of almost every event of history almost never agree, And the historical accounts of this period are no exception. So the following analysis of the very long south-north war is drawn from those accounts that, in my personal opinion, seem to be those most likely to be correct.

So we first read in our NKJV, **"Also the king of the South shall become strong, as well as *one* of his princes; and he shall gain power over him and have dominion. His dominion *shall be* a great dominion."** (Daniel 11:5)

This seems to be saying that one of Alexander's princes would rebel against him. But no other scripture, even hints at this idea, and secular history reports no such rebellion. We notice that this wording is different from our familiar KJV, but even there, its meaning is not very clear, saying, "And the king of the south shall be strong, and one of his princes; and he shall be strong above him, and have dominion; his dominion *shall* be a great dominion." (Daniel 11:5, KJV)

The Hebrew text of this verse is difficult to understand, and various translators have rendered it various ways. After reviewing the comments by various translators., I have come to the conclusion that the best rendition of this verse is the one given in the JND translation, because it is a possible rendition of the Hebrew text, is clear, and is in agreement with both the rest of scripture and also with secular history. This translation reads:

"And the king of the south, who is one of his princes, shall be strong; but [another] shall be stronger than he, and have dominion: his dominion shall be a great dominion." (Daniel 11:5, JND)

Viewed thus, this is seen as an introductory comment on the two generals of Alexander the Great, Ptolemy. the first **"king of the south,"** and Selucius, the first **"king of the north."** But it also applies generally to the two dynasties they founded, clear down to the part of the account that applies to the end times, from verse 36 to the end of the chapter. For indeed, although both of them, and both of the dynasties they founded, were very great, both the original kingdom of Selucius and the Selucid dynasty, were greater than the original kingdom of Ptolemy and the Ptolemaic dynasty. And even in the part of this prophecy that deals with the end times, **"the king of the north"** is said to prevail over **"the king of the south."** We see this in verse 41, where, in describing the campaigns of **"the king of the north,"** it says, **"and the land of Egypt shall not escape."**

But then we read: **"And at the end of *some* years they shall join forces, for the daughter of the king of the South shall go to the king of the North to make an agreement; but she shall not retain the power of her authority, and neither he nor his authority shall stand; but she shall be given up, with those who brought her, and with him who begot her, and with him who strengthened her in *those* times."** (Daniel 11:6)

Throughout history, one of the common tools for making peace has been a marriage alliance. When successful, this has been a very effective method of making peace. But when it fails, it can fail miserably. And in this case, its failure led to a war that this prophecy describes through a span of six generations, and even then, it was not over.

We first need to notice the words **"And at the end of *some* years they shall join forces."** This, as the prophecy clearly states, did not take place right away. In fact it happened two generations later. For **"the daughter of the king of the South,"** who was named Berenice, was the daughter of the son of the original Ptolemy, so history calls that **"king of the south"** Ptolemy II, to distinguish him from the original Ptolemy, Ptolemy Soter, whom they call Ptolemy I.

Berenice married Antiochus Theos, that is, "Antiochus *the* god," whom historians also call Antiocus II, to distinguish him from his father, Antiochus Soter, whom they also call Antiochus I, who was the son of the original Seleucus, Seleucus Nicator, whom historians also call Seleucus I. So this marriage alliance was between the granddaughter of the original **"king of the south"** and the grandson of the original **"king of the north."**

But then we read, **"but she shall not retain the power of her authority, and neither he nor his authority shall stand; but she shall be given up, with those who brought her, and with him who begot her, and with him who strengthened her in *those* times."**

Antiochus II had been married to a woman named Laodice, whom historians call Laodice I to distinguish her from later queens of the same name. Berenice had persuaded him to disinherit the son of Laodice, so her own children could have the throne. But the marriage failed. For, about five years before his death, Antiochus II took Laodice back. And upon his death, Laodice seized the throne for her son Seleucus Callinicus, whom historians also call Seleucus II. And when he ascended the throne, he killed both Berenice and her son, who was the **"he"** whose **"authority"** would not stand.

But not only were both **"she"** and **"the power of her authority"** rejected, but also **"him who begot her,"** that is, Ptolemy II, was given up. That is, the alliance attempted through this marriage completely failed. And **"him who strengthened her in *those* times"** was Ptolemy Euergetes, the brother of Berniece, whom historians also call Ptolemy III. He came rushing to her aid when he heard that Laodice had seized the throne for her son Seleucus Callinicus. But he was too late, finding she was already dead when he arrived.

But next, Daniel was told, **"But from a branch of her roots** *one* **shall arise in his place, who shall come with an army, enter the fortress of the king of the North, and deal with them and prevail. And he shall also carry their gods captive to Egypt, with their princes** *and* **their precious articles of silver and gold; and he shall continue** *more* **years than the king of the North."** (Daniel 11:7-8)

This **"branch of her roots"** was again the same Ptolemy Euergetes, whom historians also call Ptolemy III. Being the brother of Berenice, he was enraged at her murder, and to avenge it, he launched a successful war against Seleucus II, doing everything this part of the prophecy said he would do. He is reported to have outlived Seleucus II by about four years.

Next, we read in he NKJV, "**Also** *the king of the North* **shall come to the kingdom of the king of the South, but shall return to his own land."** (Daniel 11:9) But the first thing we need to notice about this rendering is that the words *"the king of the north"* are in italics, clearly indicating that they are not present in the Hebrew text. Actually, an exact, word-for-word translation of the Hebrew words as they stand in the text is "shall come" "to the kingdom" "king" "of the south" "shall return" "to" "his own land." This more closely matches the KJV, "So the king of the south shall come into *his* kingdom, and shall return into his own land." (Daniel 11:9 KJV)

This KJV reading makes verse 9 a summary of the action of verses 7 and 8, rather than an account of another invasion. And this reading matches the historical records, while the NKJV reading seems to introduce an additional invasion that is not found in the historical records. So I am forced to conclude that again, as in the previous case we compared, The KJV reading of Daniel 11:9 is superior to the NKJV reading.

But the next verse most certainly prophesies a new action, at another time. **"However his sons shall stir up strife, and assemble a multitude of great forces; and** *one* **shall certainly come and overwhelm and pass through; then he shall return to his fortress and stir up strife."** (Daniel 11:10)

The **"his"** in this verse is a reference to **"the king of the north,"** who was the one whose kingdom had been invaded in verses 8-10. For Antiochus the Great, or Antiochus III, who was the third Selucid ruler after Seleucus II, set about to restore the territories lost under the attack of verses 8-10.

The statement that **"one shall certainly come and overwhelm and pass through"** is a reference to Daniel's land, not to the kingdom of **"the king of the south."** For in retaking lost territories, he retook the territory of the land of Judea. But instead of pressing his victories down into Egypt, he returned **"to his fortress"** in Phoenicia. And as a part of his strategies, he stirred up strife in various other places.

The prophecy continues, **"And the king of the South shall be moved with rage, and go out and fight with him, with the king of the North, who shall muster a great multitude; but the multitude shall be given into the hand of his *enemy*. When he has taken away the multitude, his heart will be lifted up; and he will cast down tens of thousands, but he will not prevail."** (Daniel 11:11-12)

The precise accuracy of these statements is startling. For Ptolemy Philopator, whom historians also call Ptolemy IV, who was the son of Ptolemy III, came out with a huge army in response to the belligerence of Antiochus III, handing him a decisive defeat on the southern border of Israel. But even as Antiochus III had failed to invade Egypt, Ptolemy III also failed to press his victory, returning instead to his homeland. So, even though he had **"cast down tens of thousands,"** he did not **"prevail."**

But then the prophecy says, **"For the king of the North will return and muster a multitude greater than the former, and shall certainly come at the end of some years with a great army and much equipment."** (Daniel 11:13) The first thing we notice about this is the words **"after some years."** For, about twenty years after his defeat, turmoil in Egypt after the death of Ptolemy IV and the succession of a very young Ptolemy Epiphanes, whom historians also call Ptolemy V allowed Antiochus III to resume his campaigns.

"Now in those times many shall rise up against the king of the South." (Daniel 11:14a) It was not only Antiochus III that rose up against this young Ptolemy, but also several other rulers, including Philip V of Macedonia and various other forces, even within Egypt itself.

But now we come to an amazing prophecy. **"Also, violent men of your people shall exalt themselves in fulfillment of the vision,**

but they shall fall." (Daniel 11:14) Again, I have to prefer the KJV rendition of the phrase **"in fulfillment of the vision,"** which is "to establish the vision." [34]

The audacity of mere mortals to exalt themselves to make God's word come to pass is amazing. If God clearly said that such-and-such will come to pass, it will come to pass, exactly as He said, regardless of what any man does or does not do.

We notice that the prophecy does not simply say, concerning these arrogant Jews, that "they shall fail," as if it would just happen. Instead of that, it says **"but they shall fall."** God is never pleased with arrogance, and in this case, He explicitly declared, ahead of time, that these men, who would presume **"to establish the vision,"** **"shall fall."** That is, they would be punished for their arrogance. The histories record that some of the Jews openly sided with the attacking Antiochus III. This prophecy plainly says this was **"to establish the vision."** But, although the campaign of Antiochus III was just as successful as God said it would be, after he had defeated **"the king of the south,"** he dealt brutally with these Jews, even as the prophecy about him clearly stated.

> "So the king of the North shall come and build a siege mound, and take a fortified city; and the forces of the South shall not withstand *him*. Even his choice troops *shall have no strength to resist*. But he who comes against him shall do according to his own will, and no one shall stand against him. He shall stand in the Glorious Land with destruction in his power." (Daniel 11:15-16)

This describes the final wresting of **"the Glorious Land"** from the control of the Ptolemies, completed when the forces of Antiochus III decisively defeated the forces of Ptolemy V at the battle of Panium, near what is now called the Golan heights.

---

34 The Hebrew word used here is עמד, *amad* in our alphabet. (word number 5975 in Strong's Hebrew Dictionary) This word translates literally as *"to stand."* So it seems to me that *"to establish"* more closely fits this sense than *"in fulfillment of."*

But the prophecy goes on, saying, **"He shall also set his face to enter with the strength of his whole kingdom, and upright ones with him; thus shall he do. And he shall give him the daughter of women to destroy it; but she shall not stand *with him*, or be for him."** (Daniel 11:17) The first sentence of this verse simply describes the end of this evil ruler's destructive campaign. But the second sentence needs particular notice.

"And he shall give him the daughter of women to destroy it; but she shall not stand *with him*, or be for him." (Daniel 11:17) [35] This describes a second attempt at a marriage alliance. And the two possible translations of this sentence discussed in the footnote only effect what sin would be in the heart of Antiochus III in this arrangement. If the correct reading is **"to destroy it,"** as the NKJV renders it, the meaning was that he would do this with an intent that his daughter should betray her husband. But if the correct reading is "corrupting her," as the KJV renders it, the meaning was that he would basically offer his daughter as a prostitute.

Either way, the end result would be the same. **"She shall not stand *with him*, or be for him."** The daughter so offered here was named Cleopatra. The Egyptians called her Cleopatra Syria because of her origin. And historians call her Cleopatra I to distinguish her from later Egyptian queens by the same name. And after her powerful father, Antiochus III, died, her husband, Ptolemy V, planned to attack her brother, Seleucus Philopator, whom historians also call Selucius IV. But before he could accomplish this, he died, and Cleopatra I seized the throne and canceled the planned attack, defeating her husband's plans.

But in this explanation, I have skipped ahead in the account. For the prophecy gave further details about the career of Antiochus III. **"After this he shall turn his face to the coastlands, and shall take many. But a ruler shall bring the reproach against them to an end;**

---

35   The Hebrew word here translated **"destroy"** is a form of שחת, *shahat* in our alphabet. (word number 7843 in Strong's Hebrew Dictionary) This word can alternately be translated *destroy* or *corrupt*. If the meaning intended by the Holy Spirit was *destroy*, then the NKJV rendering, **"destroy it"** is correct. But if the Holy Spirit meant *corrupt*, then the KJV rendering of **"corrupting her"** is correct. In this case, I see no reason to prefer either reading above the other.

and with the reproach removed, he shall turn back on him. Then he shall turn his face toward the fortress of his own land; but he shall stumble and fall, and not be found." (Daniel 11:18-19)

Rome had begun to exert its rising influence over the middle east. The main reason Antiochus III had so treacherously made his false peace with Ptolemy V, was because envoys from Rome, which was receiving its wheat from Egypt, had asked him to refrain from attacking it. So instead, he turned his attention to the Greek islands and coasts. But this time, the Romans made no request. Instead, they ordered him to withdraw. Afraid to face their wrath, he headed home. From that point, the historical accounts become contradictory. The one that seems most likely to be correct says that after having been humiliated in the west, he set off on an campaign toward the east. But on the way, he stumbled and fell from a path leading through a high mountain pass, and his body was never found.

Then the prophecy said, **"There shall arise in his place one who imposes taxes *on* the glorious kingdom; but within a few days he shall be destroyed,**(Daniel 11:20) The Romans had not only demanded that Antiochus III withdraw from Greece. They had also imposed a very high tribute on him for having made the invasion. As he was now dead, the responsibility to pay it fell upon his son, who, as we have noted, was called Selucius IV.

To raise this tribute, he imposed heavy **"taxes *on* the glorious kingdom,"** that is, upon Daniel's homeland, Judea. He sent a minister named Heliodorus to seize the treasures from the temple in Jerusalem, who, upon his return from Jerusalem, assassinated Selucius IV, who was thus **"destroyed" "within a few days," "but not in anger or in battle."**

Heliodorus tried to make himself king, but his plan failed, and the kingdom was seized by the worst of all the rulers of that dynasty, Antiochus Epiphanes, whom historians also call Antiochus IV.

One of the remarkable characteristics of scripture is that sometimes long periods of time are treated in just a few verses, and then much is said about a single individual. In this case, the first twenty verses of Daniel 11 had covered ten generations. But now the Holy Spirit devotes more than twelve verses to this one individual that would come. The reason for this was not only that he would be remarkably wicked, but the fact that his wickedness would be directed particularly against the Lord's own people.

The prophecy about this evil ruler begins with the words, **"And in his place shall arise a vile person, to whom they will not give the honor of royalty; but he shall come in peaceably, and seize the kingdom by intrigue. With the force of a flood they shall be swept away from before him and be broken, and also the prince of the covenant. And after the league *is made* with him he shall act deceitfully, for he shall come up and become strong with a small *number of* people."** (Daniel 11:21-23)

History says that, upon the murder of Selucius IV by Heliodorus, the rightful heir to the throne was his son Demetrius Soter. But, as Rome was still holding him hostage to ensure payment of the still incomplete tribute, Antiochus Epiphanes, who was the brother of Antiochus III, claimed a co-regency with the true heir's infant brother Antiochus. But then, about five years later, he had the child murdered, leaving himself the ruler. So he indeed came **"in peaceably,"** and seized **"the kingdom by intrigue."** But, like a **"flood,"** he **"swept away from before him"** all opposition, including **"the prince of the covenant."** That is, the child he murdered. And having acted **"deceitfully,"** he became **strong with a small *number of* people."**

But then the prophecy begins to describe his deceitful actions. **"He shall enter peaceably, even into the richest places of the province; and he shall do *what* his fathers have not done, nor his forefathers: he shall disperse among them the plunder, spoil, and riches; and he shall devise his plans against the strongholds, but *only* for a time."** (Daniel 11:24)

The words **"the providence"** here appear, from the historical records, to refer to Egypt. For the records show that he entered Egypt deceptively, coming as a friend, rather than a conqueror. But this artifice allowed him to **"do *what* his fathers have not done, nor his forefathers,"** in that he basically seized control of all of Egypt except the city of Alexandria. The **"them"** in the words **"he shall disperse among them the plunder, spoil, and riches,"** refers to his soldiers. For the historical records indicate that he gave them an entire year's wage at one time. And he devised **"his plans against the strongholds."** That is, even as he was feigning friendship, he was planning conquest. But he was only able to do this **"for a time."**

For next Daniel was told, **"He shall stir up his power and his courage against the king of the South with a great army. And the king of the South shall be stirred up to battle with a very great and mighty army; but he shall not stand, for they shall devise plans against him. Yes, those who eat of the portion of his delicacies shall destroy him; his army shall be swept away, and many shall fall down slain."** (Daniel 11:25-26)

Dropping his pretended peace, Antiochus Epiphanes finally attacked **"the king of the south,"** who, at this time, was Ptolemy Philometor, whom historians also call Ptolemy VI. The army of this Ptolemy VI should have been victorious, as it was much larger that of Antiochus Epiphanes. But he was betrayed by **"those who eat of the portion of his delicacies,"** that is, by some who ate at his table. And he was defeated.

But then the prophecy said, **"Both these kings' hearts *shall be* bent on evil, and they shall speak lies at the same table; but it shall not prosper, for the end *will* still *be* at the appointed time."** (Daniel 11:27) Afraid of the now ever threatening Roman forces, Antiochus Epiphanes resumed his pretense of peacefulness, and agreed to allow Ptolemy VI to continue to rule all of Egypt that he had subdued. That is, all except Alexandria, which by previous agreement with Ptolemy VI, continued to be ruled by this Ptolemy's brother. And it did not end well (for Antiochus Epiphanes.) but not immediately.

For the prophecy next said, **"While returning to his land with great riches, his heart shall be *moved* against the holy covenant; so he shall do *damage* and return to his own land."** (Daniel 11:28)

The earlier Selucid rulers had only been interested in physical rule over Judea, basically to obtain tribute monies. But this new king, Antiochus Epiphanes, had grander intentions. His goal was to enforce Hellenistic (Greek) culture upon all his realms, including Judea. This included the practice of total nudity (of both sexes) in the Greek games, which, of course, the Jews found totally unacceptable, and, worse yet, he tried to impose the worship of the Greek gods, even in the temple. This led to a revolt, led by a priest names Jason, which began while Antiochus Epiphanes was in Egypt for the first time. So he dealt with this revolt as he was returning from Egypt.

But then we read, **"At the appointed time he shall return and go toward the south; but it shall not be like the former or the latter. For ships from Cyprus shall come against him."** (Daniel 11:29-30a)

The historical records indeed indicate that, after returning to his home, Antiochus Epiphanes launched a second attack upon Egypt. But this time it was different. His path was blocked by a fleet from Rome. And the leader of that fleet demanded that he withdraw. Seeking time, He answered that he would consult with his council. But the Roman leader, whose name was Gaius Popillius Laenas, drew a circle around him in the sand, and demanded an answer before he stepped out of the circle. Fearing the power of Rome, as had his predecessor Antiochus III, he agreed to withdraw.

To understand the connection between these historical records and the text of this verse of the prophecy, we need to understand a Hebrew word that is not often discussed. That is the word here translated **"Cyprus,"** but in the KJV is translated **"Chittim."** [36] As this word is used in scripture, it indicates, not only the specific Island of Cyprus, the largest of the Islands in the Mediterranean Sea, but the islands of the sea generally, and the coast lands beyond them. And as Rome was located in the coast lands beyond the islands of the sea, in Hebrew terms, Rome was one of the *kittyyim*. And thus, the ships from Rome were indeed, **"ships from Cyprus."**

The results of this for Judea were indeed terrible. For next we are told, **"therefore he shall be grieved, and return in rage against the holy covenant, and do *damage*. So he shall return and show regard for those who forsake the holy covenant."** (Daniel 11:30b)

History tells us that he returned to Judea in a terrible rage, taking horrible vengeance against those Jews that remained faithful to their God, favoring only those Jews that had accepted his Hellenizing efforts. History says that "there were destroyed within the space of three whole

---

36 This Hebrew word is a form of מיתתכ, *kittyyim* in our alphabet. (word number 3794 in Strong's Hebrew Dictionary) This word does not translate literally as "Cyprus," for it ends with the Hebrew letter ם, that is, *m*, indicating that it is plural, so its actual meaning is *"the Cypruses."*

days fourscore thousand, whereof forty thousand were slain in the conflict; and no fewer sold than slain." (2 Maccabees 5:14 KJV)

But the prophecy continued, **"And forces shall be mustered by him, and they shall defile the sanctuary fortress; then they shall take away the daily** *sacrifices***, and place** *there* **the abomination of desolation."** [37] (Daniel 11:31)

And indeed, history records that, having wrought such extreme damage, this evil king defiled the temple, dedicating it instead to the Greek God Jupiter. It is widely reported that he even sacrificed a pig on the altar. But the historical records only say he erected an idol of Jupiter in the temple. Either one would fully match the words that **"they shall take away the daily** *sacrifices***, and place** *there* **the abomination of desolation."**

But then the prophecy says that **"Those who do wickedly against the covenant he shall corrupt with flattery; but the people who know their God shall be strong, and carry out** *great exploits***."** (Daniel 11:32) So this evil king gave great honors to those that accepted his Hellenizing attempts. But the people that remained faithful joined together, and led by Judas Maccabeus, they launched a rebellion, in fulfillment of the prophecy that **"the people who know their God shall be strong, and carry out** *great exploits***."**

But then the prophecy describes a long period of time with the words, **"And those of the people who understand shall instruct many; yet** *for many* **days they shall fall by sword and flame, by captivity and plundering. Now when they fall, they shall be aided with a little help; but many shall join with them by intrigue."** (Daniel 11:33-34)

---

37 We note in passing that the term **"the abomination of desolation,"** as found here, is an unfortunate error in translation. For the Hebrew word translated *desolation* in this verse is משומם, *meshomem* in our alphabet. This word form literally means *desolator*, not *desolation*. So this passage should read "the abomination of the desolator." The form of this word which means *desolation* is שמם, *shomem* in our alphabet. This form was used in both Daniel 8:13 and Daniel 12:11. As these are both forms of the Hebrew word שמם, *shamem* in our alphabet, Strong's Hebrew Dictionary lists them both under the same index number (8074). But such slight variations are significant in Bible prophecy. This passage refers to the actions of Antiochus Epiphanes But Daniel 8:13 and 12:11 refer to an event which was still future when our Lord spoke of it, when He called it **"the** *'abomination of desolation,'* **spoken of by Daniel the prophet."** (Matthew 24:15)

The faithful among the Jews instructed many. But still *"for many* **days"** they fell **"by sword and flame, by captivity and plundering."** Yet, as they fell, they were **"aided with a little help."** But many joined **"with them by intrigue."** This is a general description of the times of the Maccabees, during which there was much suffering, and in which they found many of those supposed friends to be false. You can read this sad account in the later chapters of 2 Maccabees.

But then we read, **"And *some* of those of understanding shall fall, to refine them, purify *them*, and make *them* white, *until* the time of the end; because *it is* still for the appointed time."** (Daniel 11:35) This general description of the long term persecution of the Jews clearly tells us how long this condition would last. **"*until* the time of the end; because *it is* still for the appointed time."**

Here we find, clearly stated in scripture, a long break in the account. The persecution so described would last **"*Until* the time of the end."** But after this break, in contrast to the highly detailed fulfillment of everything up to this point, nothing in the rest of this vision has ever taken place at all. Some Preterists claim that the rest of this has also been fulfilled, but, instead of the highly detailed fulfillment we found up to this point, their claims involve only historical events which only resemble the prophesied events in a very general way, with almost none of the details of the prophecies matching the details of the historical records alleged as their fulfillments.

And again, we need to note that it is wholly unreasonable to claim, as many do, that at this point in the prophecy **"the king of the north"** changes. This would mean that verses 5-32 of this very long prophecy were only to satisfy men's curiosity about the future, and not to show, as is clearly stated as the purpose of the vision, **"what will happen to your people in the latter days."** For the scriptural terms **"the latter days"** and **"the time of the end,"** speak of a short period of time just before the Lord returns. The point of these thirty verses was to identify **"the king of the north"** and **"the king of the south"** in the part of the prophecy that remains to be fulfilled in **"the time of the end."** In verses 36-45, as in the section we have just discussed, **"The king of the south"** is the end time ruler of Egypt. And **"the king of the north"** is the end time ruler of the area ruled by the ancient Selucid dynasty. Please carefully examine the map on the next page.

JAMES C. MORRIS

A Map of the Scene of Daniel's Vision

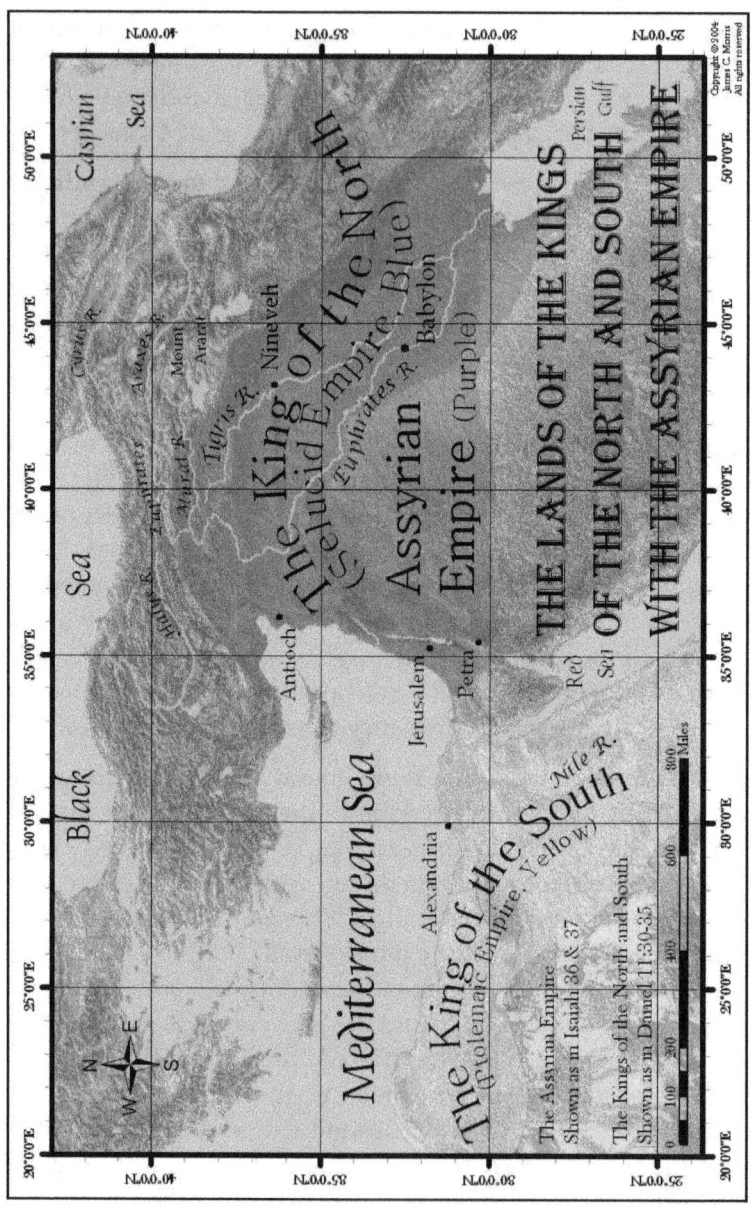

In this map, which is from page 230 of the author's book, "Keys to Bible Prophecy," the area ruled by the Selucid Dynasty, **"the king of the north,"** is shown in translucent blue. And the area ruled by the earlier Assyrian Empire, the kingdom of **"the Assyrian"** of Isaiah 7, 10, 14, 30, and 31, of Micah 5, and of Nahum, is shown in translucent purple. And thus we see that **"the king of the north"** and **"the Assyrian"** are two different representations of the same end time individual. For aside from a few sparsely settled areas around the edges, these two empires covered the same area at different times in history. And also in this map, the area ruled by the Ptolemaic dynasty, **"the king of the south"** is shown in translucent yellow, clearly showing that this is the land of Egypt.

Turning now to the part of this prophecy that remains to be fulfilled in the future, after the long break stated in verse 35, Daniel's informer continued, saying, **"Then the king shall do according to his own will: he shall exalt and magnify himself above every god, shall speak blasphemies against the God of gods."** (Daniel 11:36a)

Here, a new individual is suddenly introduced. The prophecy had already mentioned **"three more kings,"** and **"the fourth"** in verse 2, and then **"a mighty king"** in verse 3, and then **"the king of the south"** and **"the king of the north"** in verses 5-32. But now, it simply introduces this new individual as **"the king."** But it does not directly state where he rules.

Many think this blasphemous **"king"** is the Roman **"prince"** of Daniel 9:26. But the language of Bible prophecy is very precise. Every detail has meaning. This **"king"** is not the same person as **"the prince"** of Daniel 9:26.[38]

But if we are not told where he rules, how can we know? Here, we need to fall back on a standard rule of language, one that

---

38 The Hebrew word translated **"prince"** in Daniel 9:26 is נגיד, *nagiyd* in our alphabet. (word number 5057 in Strong's Hebrew Dictionary) This word means *leader* or *commander*. But the Hebrew word translated **"king"** in this passage is a form of מלך, *melek* in our alphabet. (word number 4428 in Strong's Hebrew Dictionary) This word literally means a *king*. In Bible prophecy, even such an apparently small difference as whether someone is called a *melek* or a *nagiyd* is important.

exists in all languages. When a leader is mentioned by his title, (King, President, etc.) without any introduction, the leader so mentioned is the leader of whatever group is under discussion. Thus, if we say "the President," if we are speaking of a corporation, we mean the President of that corporation. But if we are speaking of a nation, we mean the President of that nation.

So what nation is being spoken of here? We remember that Daniel was told that the subject of ths prophecy is **"what will happen to your people in the latter days"** (Daniel 10:14) And the prophecy has now progressed down to **"the time of the end."** so the subject is Daniel's people in **"the time of the end."** Thus we see that **"the king"** introduced here is the end time king of Daniel's people, Judah, the nation now called Israel.

So here we read of a **"king"** of Judah, who **"shall do according to his own will."** That is, he shall care nothing for the law of God, nor even for the laws of man. Instead, he shall do "whatever he jolly well pleases." And in his willfulness, **"he shall exalt and magnify himself above every god."** and, not content with that impiety, he **"shall speak blasphemies against the God of gods."**

We will temporarily skip over the rest of verse 36, to see that this impious **"king"** is indeed the end time **"king"** of Judah. For Daniel was next told of an evil king of Judah:

"He shall regard neither the God of his fathers nor the desire of women, nor regard any god; for he shall exalt himself above *them* all. But in their place he shall honor a god of fortresses; and a god which his fathers did not know he shall honor with gold and silver, with precious stones and pleasant things." (Daniel 11:37-38)

It is critical to notice that **"the king"** shall not regard **"the God of his fathers,"** (Daniel 11:37) but shall instead honor **"a god which his fathers did not know."** (verse 38) The term, **"the God of his fathers,"** is not just a generic reference to a god worshiped in past generations. Some form of this term is used of the God of Israel fifty-eight times in the Old Testament. When the Lord sent Moses to the children of Israel He told him **"Thus you shall say to the children of Israel: 'The LORD God of your fathers, the God of Abraham, the God of Isaac, and the God of Jacob·, has sent me to you. This *is* My name

forever, and this *is* My memorial to all generations." (Exodus 3:15) Thus we see that the God this king shall ignore is none other than the God of Israel; and that in calling Himself **"the God of his fathers,"** the Lord was identifying this **"king"** as an Israelite.

Most modern translations render this clause *"the gods of his fathers."* This is a possible translation because the Hebrew word for *God* [39] is plural. But the Hebrew scriptures use this word, *'elohiym*, for the one true *God* of Israel about two thousand four hundred times. (Including Deuteronomy 6:4, **"Hear, O Israel: The LORD our God, the LORD *is* one!"** While it was used of the *gods* of the heathen only about two hundred times. Whether *'elohiym* should be translated *God* or *gods* can only be determined from the context. Nothing in Daniel 11:37 implies a plural sense for this word. And if it were correct to translate this phrase, *"the gods of his fathers,"* this would be the only place the Holy Spirit ever used this phrase when speaking of false gods. Translators did not begin to use the plural word *gods* in this verse until the notion that **"the king"** is **"the prince"** became popular. So we realize this idea is the basis of the plural translation. Thus we understand that this plural translation does not prove this notion.

'Elohiym has a singular form. [40] But the fact that this singular form is not used never justifies translating *'elohiym* as *gods*. *'Elowahh* is used only sixteen times outside of the book of Job. [41] But it is used in every reference to false gods in the passage we are considering (the word rendered **"any god"** in verse 37 and the **"god"** worshiped by **"the king,"** mentioned twice in verse 38 and once in verse 39). This adds strength to the conclusion that the term **"the God of his fathers"** in this passage refers to the one true God of Israel, for a different word is used of all gods that are unquestionably false.

---

39 This Hebrew word is אלחים, *'elohiym* in our alphabet. (word number 430 in Strong's Hebrew Dictionary) As we end a word with the letter "s" to make it plural, the Hebrews made a word plural by ending it with the letter ם, or mem, their equivalent of our letter *"m."*

40 This is the Hebrew word אלוה, *'elowahh* in our alphabet. (word number 433 in Strong's Hebrew Dictionary)

41 Although unusual in the rest of scripture, *'elowahh* is used more than forty times in the book of Job.

The prophecy about the impiety of this **"king"** goes on, saying, **"Thus he shall act against the strongest fortresses with a foreign god, which he shall acknowledge,** *and* **advance** *its* **glory; and he shall cause them to rule over many, and divide the land for gain."** (Daniel 11:39) The fact that **"he shall acknowledge"** **"a foreign god,"** speaks again of the fact that he shall be a **"king"** of Daniel's people, Judah.

But this **"king"** will not only be evil, he will also be a coward. For in verse 41 **"the king of the North"** **"shall also enter the glorious land,"** which obviously means Judea. But, though his land is overrun, **"the king"** prospers **"till the wrath has been accomplished."** (verse 36) How does he escape? In Zechariah 11:17 **"the worthless shepherd"** **"leaves the flock!"** [42] The cowardice of this end time **"king"** of Judah is seen in several other scriptures, as the missing shepherd of Zechariah 10:2, the missing king of Micah 4:9, and the fainthearted king of Jeremiah 4:9.

We now need to go back and notice the rest of verse 36, which we previously skipped over. He **"shall prosper till the wrath has been accomplished; for what has been determined shall be done."** (Daniel 11:36b) Here we see two things specifically stated, One of them is that these things will not "just happen." God is here telling us that He is not simply speaking from His foreknowledge. Instead, He is telling us that He has planned these things. That they will happen because He will make them happen. But the other is the timing of this event. In the previous verse He had said this would be in **"the time of the end."** And why? **"because** *it is* **still for the appointed time."** But now He added that this evil **"king"** **"shall prosper till the wrath has been accomplished."**

We remember that in Daniel 9:24, the prophet had been told,

> "Seventy weeks are determined
> For your people and for your holy city."

And we remember that we saw that there was a break after the sixty-ninth week, leaving the seventieth week unfulfilled, even to this

---

42 We recognize this shepherd as a king of Judah because he will be raised up **"in the land."** (Zechariah 11:16)

day. So there remains an **"appointed time"** for Daniel's people (the Jews) and for Daniel's holy city (Jerusalem,) as Daniel was told in the introduction to this very long vision, **"Now I have come to make you understand what will happen to your people in the latter days, for the vision *refers* to *many* days yet *to come.*"** (Daniel 10:14)

And now we need to return to the description of this evil end time king of Judah. Daniel was told, **"He shall regard neither the God of his fathers nor the desire of women, nor regard any god; for he shall exalt himself above *them* all. But in their place he shall honor a god of fortresses; and a god which his fathers did not know he shall honor with gold and silver, with precious stones and pleasant things. Thus he shall act against the strongest fortresses with a foreign god, which he shall acknowledge, *and* advance *its* glory; and he shall cause them to rule over many, and divide the land for gain."** (Daniel 11:37-39)

We have already noticed the significance of the words that he shall not **"regard"** **"the God of his fathers,"** and that he shall honor **"a god which his fathers did not know,"** who is **"a foreign god."** but now we need to notice that he also shall not regard **"the desire of women."**

In the context of modern society, I can appreciate the opinion held by many that this means he will be a homosexual. But that conclusion neglects the context of this statement. In its context, we read, **"He shall regard neither the God of his fathers nor the desire of women, nor regard any god; for he shall exalt himself above *them* all."** We notice that the clause **"nor the desire of women,"** is in the middle of a list of the gods he will not regard. So I must take my stand with the commentators of the nineteenth century, who saw **"the desire of women"** as being the great **"Messiah,"** the long promised **"son of David."** Instead, **"he shall exalt himself above *them* all,** including the great **"Messiah," "the desire of women."**

But then this passage ends with the words, **"he shall cause them to rule over many, and divide the land for gain."** So this evil ruler will cause his own agents to rule over the many, which obviously refers to the people of Judah, and he will divide the land in a way that brings profit to himself.

This brings to mind another scripture which says **"For indeed I will raise up a shepherd in the land who will not care for those who are cut off, nor seek the young, nor heal those that are broken, nor feed those that still stand. But he will eat the flesh of the fat and tear their hooves in pieces."** (Zechariah 11:16) So this evil ruler will rule in a way that only benefits himself, rather than in a way that benefits the people.

And now, after this dismal description of this evil end time king of Judah, the prophecy takes up an end time attack on this evil king. **"At the time of the end the king of the South shall attack him; and the king of the North shall come against him like a whirlwind, with chariots, horsemen, and with many ships; and he shall enter the countries, overwhelm** *them,* **and pass through. He shall also enter the Glorious Land, and many** *countries* **shall be overthrown; but these shall escape from his hand: Edom, Moab, and the prominent people of Ammon."** (Daniel 11:40-41)

Most students of prophecy realize that the word **"him"** in the first part of verse 40 refers to **"the king."** But those who think **"the king"** is the Roman **"prince"** fail to see the change of actors in this verse. They think the repeated use of the word **"he"** in the last part of verse 40 and in the following verses also refer to **"the king."** Some defend this idea by saying it all turns on how we interpret this passage. But that is a serious error.

We are not free to interpret Scripture as we please. An interpretation of any part of the Bible is not correct if it disagrees with any other part of the Bible. If Daniel 11:40-41 were taken by itself, this interpretation would indeed be possible. But it completely fails to take into account the many scriptures about **"the Assyrian"** and **"the king."**

In the context of interpreting Daniel 11:40-41, one of the most important prophecies is Isaiah 7:17-20.

> "'The LORD will bring the king of Assyria upon you and your people and your father's house—days that have not come since the day that Ephraim departed from Judah.'
> "And it shall come to pass in that day
> *That* the LORD will whistle for the fly

> That *is* in the farthest part of the rivers of Egypt,
> And for the bee that *is* in the land of Assyria.
> They will come, and all of them will rest
> In the desolate valleys and in the clefts of the rocks,
> And on all thorns and in all pastures.
> In the same day the Lord will shave with a hired razor,
> With those from beyond the River, with the king of Assyria,
> The head and the hair of the legs,
> And will also remove the beard."

Here we see that the Lord will bring Assyria and Egypt upon the people of Ahaz (see verse 10) that is, upon Judah. From the way it is stated, the meaning is plainly that they will come at the same time. This cannot refer to Sennacherib's invasion of Judea, because at that time the king of Egypt was allied to Hezekiah. (see 2 Kings 18:21 and Isaiah 36:6) The Bible doesn't say much about this Egyptian king. But according to history he came to take part in the war, but was defeated by Sennacherib in the land of the Philistines before he reached Judea.

History also says the same thing had happened when the Assyrian king Sargon had attacked approximately 20 years earlier. Sargon also defeated the Egyptian army before it reached Judea. There has never been a time when Assyrian and Egyptian armies invaded Judea at the same time, so this prophecy remains to be fulfilled in the future.

When we realize the true identity of **"the king,"** as we have seen, and remember both **"the Assyrian,"** and the fact that Assyria and Egypt will invade Judea at the same time, we see that the only reasonable interpretation of Daniel 11:40 is that:

"The king of the South" (the king of Egypt) **"shall attack him,"** that is, **"the king"** (of Judah) and **"the king of the North"** (the Assyrian) **"shall come against him** [43] **like a whirlwind."** The actor has

---

43 I have interpreted this second **"him"** as a reference to **"the king."** If this interpretation is correct, the meaning is that **"the king of the South"** and **"the king of the North"** both attack **"the king."** But if this second **"him"** refers to **"the king of the South,"** the meaning is that when **"the king of the South"** attacks **"the king,"** **"the king of the North"** will in turn attack **"the king of the South."** To me, this interpretation seems less likely, but it is possible. But this is not a very important point, for in either case **"the king of**

changed from **"the king of the South"** to **"the king of the North,"** who, coming **"like a whirlwind, with chariots, horsemen, and with many ships... shall enter the countries, overwhelm** *them,* **and pass through."** But **"the king"** (of Judah) remains the object of the action, for it says **"He shall also enter the Glorious Land,"** which is plainly Daniel's land Judea. (verse 41) This interpretation agrees with all the prophecies about **"the Assyrian"** and **"the king."**

But the passage ends with the words, **"and many** *countries* **shall be overthrown; but these shall escape from his hand: Edom, Moab, and the prominent people of Ammon."**

It is critical to understand why **"Edom, Moab, and the prominent people of Ammon"** will be spared at this time. And that reason is not mercy. For other scriptures describe the judgments of these nations in great detail. [44] So why are they spared at this time?

We find the answer in our Lord's words, **" 'Therefore when you see the** *"abomination of desolation,"* **spoken of by Daniel the prophet, standing in the holy place'** (whoever reads, let him understand), **then let those who are in Judea flee to the mountains."** (Matthew 24:15-16) From, Jerusalem, the mountains were across the Jordan river to the lands of **"Edom, Moab, and... Ammon."**

Again, we read, **"Take counsel, execute judgment; Make your shadow like the night in the middle of the day; Hide the outcasts, Do not betray him who escapes. Let My outcasts dwell with you, O Moab; Be a shelter to them from the face of the spoiler. For the extortioner is at an end, Devastation ceases, The oppressors are consumed out of the land."** (Isaiah 16:3-4)

This time of exile is part of the Lord's design for His people, for He says, **"Therefore, behold, I will allure her, Will bring her into the**

---

the North" will "enter the glorious land." So the only question is why he will do it.

44 The judgment of all three is stated in Isaiah 11:14, and Jeremiah 9:25-26 and 25:15 with 21, The judgment of Edom is detailed in Isaiah 11:13-14 and 34:5-10, Jeremiah 49:20-22, Ezekiel 25:12-14, Amos 1:11, and Obadiah 7:8-16. The judgment of Moab is detailed in Isaiah 11:13-14, 15:1-16:12 and 25:10-12, Jeremiah 48:1-46 and 49:1-5, Ezekiel 25:8-11, Amos 2:1-3, and Zephaniah 2:8-11. And the judgment of Ammon is detailed in Jeremiah 49:1-5, Ezekiel 25:1-7, Amos 1:13-15, and Zephaniah 2:8-11.

wilderness, And speak comfort to her." (Hosea 2:14) He further says that **"The people who survived the sword Found grace in the wilderness; Israel, when I went to give him rest."** (Jeremiah 31:2) Again, in Isaiah 26:20 the Lord figuratively says, **"Come, my people, enter your chambers, And shut your doors behind you; Hide yourself, as it were, for a little moment, Until the indignation is past."**

So the reason that **"Edom, Moab, and the prominent people of Ammon"** will be spared at this time, is because this is where the righteous will have fled when they saw **"the *abomination of desolation,* spoken of by Daniel the prophet, standing in the holy place."** If **"the king of the north,"** who is also **"the Assyrian,"** were allowed by God to enter these lands, he would kill these refugees. But, as they will be under His special protection, this evil invader will not be allowed to enter these lands. But how he will be prevented from entering them is not revealed.

But Daniel's informer continued to describe the acts of this evil invader, saying, **"He shall stretch out his hand against the countries, and the land of Egypt shall not escape. He shall have power over the treasures of gold and silver, and over all the precious things of Egypt; also the Libyans and Ethiopians *shall follow* at his heels."** (Daniel 11:42-43)

We should here note that, in recent decades, there has been amassed a huge treasure **"of gold and silver"** in Saudi Arabia and in Kuwait. And of course, the treasures of Egypt, recovered from the pyramids, are well known.

This part of the account ends with these words: **"also the Libyans and Ethiopians *shall follow* at his heels."** In the original Hebrew, this is a difficult sentence and there is little agreement between the various translations. While several other translations use the same words as the New King James, which we are using, nearly as many **read "shall be at his steps"** or **"are at his steps."** Others give **"will surrender to him," "will submit to him," "will be his servants," "will obey him."** or **"in submission."** However this difficult sentence is translated, the thought expressed in the last clause **"*shall follow* at his heels"** is definitely not willing allegiance. Instead, it implies submitting through fear.

But the prophecy about the actions of this evil invader goes on to say, **"But news from the east and the north shall trouble him; therefore he shall go out with great fury to destroy and annihilate many."** (Daniel 11:44)

We remember that he will at this time be in Africa, having conquered Egypt, Libya, and Ethiopia. **"But news from the east and the north shall trouble him."** We are not told the nature of this news, but as it comes **"from the east and from the north"** it would appear that it involves preparations for, or threats of, attacks from these areas. We read of an attack from the east in Revelation 16:12, and of an attack from **"the far north"** in Ezekiel 38 and 39. But we are not told that either of these attacks will occur at this time.

The reason he returns is not the point of this prophecy, but rather the fact that he will do so, and that he will do it **"with great fury,"** and **"to destroy and annihilate many."**

The Hebrew word here translated **"many"** is the same word used in Daniel 9:27, where **"the prince that shall come," "shall confirm a covenant with many for one week."** [45] This word literally means *"many."* But in each case, the sense seems to be *"the many,"* that is, the bulk of the nation of Judah. For we remember that in Hebrew, as in Greek, the definite article is often not explicitly stated, even when that is the intended sense.

We remember that we are told concerning this time:

> " 'And it shall come to pass in all the land,'
> Says the LORD,
> *'That* two-thirds in it shall be cut off *and* die,
> But *one*-third shall be left in it:' "
> (Zechariah 13:8)

---

45 In each case, it is a form of the Hebrew word רב, *rab* in our alphabet. (word number 7227 in Strong's Hebrew Dictionary) Although it can be translated in various other ways, this word most often rendered as *many*.

And again:

> "O God, the nations have come into Your inheritance;
> Your holy temple they have defiled;
> They have laid Jerusalem in heaps.
> The dead bodies of Your servants
> They have given *as* food for the birds of the heavens,
> The flesh of Your saints to the beasts of the earth.
> Their blood they have shed like water
> all around Jerusalem,
> And *there was* no one to bury *them*."
> (Psalm 79:1-3)

And yet again:

> For behold, Your enemies make a tumult;
> And those who hate You have lifted up their head.
> They have taken crafty counsel against Your people,
> And consulted together against Your sheltered ones.
> They have said, "Come, and let us cut them off
> **from *being* a nation,**
> **That the name of Israel may be remembered no more."**
> **For they have consulted together with one consent**
> **They form a confederacy against You:**
> (Psalm 83:3-5)

So this campaign of attempted annihilation is a major subject of end time prophecy. But this is not God's vengeance against guilty Judah. Instead, it is His loving discipline, aimed at their restoration.

For we also read concerning this same time, that:

> " 'I will bring the *one*-third through the fire,
> Will refine them as silver is refined,
> And test them as gold is tested.
> They will call on My name,
> And I will answer them. I will say,

"This *is* My people;"
And each one will say, "The LORD *is* my God." ' " (Zechariah 13:9)

And:

"Therefore, behold, I will allure her,
Will bring her into the wilderness,
And speak comfort to her.
I will give her vineyards from there,
And the Valley of Achor as a door of hope;
She shall sing there,
As in the days of her youth,
As in the day when she came up from the land of Egypt."
(Hosea 2:14-15)

And yet again:

"Come, my people, enter your chambers,
And shut your doors behind you;
Hide yourself, as it were, for a little moment,
Until the indignation is past." (Isaiah 26:20)

So in this case, as He did at Calvary, the Lord will use the wickedness of Satan and mankind to accomplish the purpose He designed from ages past.

But Daniel's informer continued, saying, **"And he shall plant the tents of his palace between the seas and the glorious holy mountain; yet he shall come to his end, and no one will help him."** (Daniel 11:45) **"The glorious holy mountain"** is, of course, Mount Zion, the mountain of Jerusalem. And **"the seas"** refer to **"the eastern sea,"** the Dead Sea, and **"the western sea,"** Mediterranean Sea, as we find them mentioned in Joel 2:20 and Zechariah 14:8. So this scripture clearly states that **"the king of the north"** shall return from Egypt to the land of Judah.

Here ends the chapter, but not the prophecy revealed by Daniel's angelic messenger.

Daniel 12

This chapter is a continuation of the prophecy that began in chapter 11, with chapter 10 being the introduction to this long message delivered to Daniel by the angelic messenger.

The continuous nature of the narrative is revealed by the first words of this chapter, **"At that time."** So we read:

> "At that time Michael shall stand up,
> The great prince who stands watch over
> the sons of your people;
> And there shall be a time of trouble,
> Such as never was since there was a nation,
> *Even* to that time.
> And at that time your people shall be delivered,
> Every one who is found written in the book."
> (Daniel 12:1)

Matthew 24:21 says of this time, **"For then there will be great tribulation, such as has not been since the beginning of the world until this time, no, nor ever shall be."** And Revelation 7:14 calls this time **"the great tribulation."** But Jeremiah 30:7 says of this time:

> "Alas! For that day *is* great,
> So that none *is* like it;
> And it is the time of Jacob's trouble,
> But he shall be saved out of it."

The last line of Jeremiah 30:7 refers to the last two lines of Daniel 12:1:

> "And at that time your people shall be delivered,
> Every one who is found written in the book."

This last line is particularly important. The part of Daniel's people that would be delivered is **"Every one who is found written in the book.** This is the context of the passage in Romans 9:6b-8, which says, "For they *are* not all Israel who *are* of Israel, nor *are they* all children because they are the seed of Abraham; but, '*In Isaac your seed shall be called.*' That is, those who *are* the children of the flesh, these *are* not the children of God; but the children of the promise are counted as the seed."** And as God further said, "What shall we say then? *Is there* unrighteousness with God? Certainly not! For He says to Moses, '*I will have mercy on whomever I will have mercy, and I will have compassion on whomever I will have compassion.*' So then *it is* not of him who wills, nor of him who runs, but of God who shows mercy." (Romans 9:14-16) Some mere mortals dare to claim this is unfair. But God's answer to them is **"But indeed, O man, who are you to reply against God? Will the thing formed say to him who formed *it*, 'Why have you made me like this?' Does not the potter have power over the clay, from the same lump to make one vessel for honor and another for dishonor?** *What* if God, wanting to show *His* wrath and to make His power known, endured with much longsuffering the vessels of wrath prepared for destruction, and that He might make known the riches of His glory on the vessels of mercy, which He had prepared beforehand for glory, even us whom He called, not of the Jews only, but also of the Gentiles? As He says also in Hosea:

> '*I will call them My people, who were not My people,*
> *And her beloved, who was not beloved.*'
> '*And it shall come to pass in the place where*
> *it was said to them,*
> "*You are not My people,*"
> *There they shall be called sons of the living God.*' "
> (Romans 9:20-26)

So God's answer to this complaint is basically, "How do you *dare* to question *my* decree?" and it is important to realize that God said this in *direct* regard to his *authority* to make the choices revealed in the statement that the specific individuals that **"shall be delivered,"** would be **"Every one who is found written in the book."**

And then this very long message concluded with a description of the resurrection:

> **"And many of those who sleep in the dust of the earth shall awake,**
> **Some to everlasting life,**
> **Some to shame *and* everlasting contempt.**
> **Those who are wise shall shine**
> **Like the brightness of the firmament,**
> **And those who turn many to righteousness**
> **Like the stars forever and ever."** (Daniel 12:2-3)

Some have very deceptively pretended that this scripture proves that there will only be one resurrection. But what the Bible *does not* say is fully as important as what it *does* say. One of the most common errors in scriptural interpretation is drawing a person's own conclusion as to what a given scripture *means*, and then claiming that this is what it *says*.

We particularly need to notice the word **"many"** here it *does not* say, "all who sleep in the dust of the earth shall awake" at this time. (For the word **"And"** at the beginning of this statement ties this back to the words **"at that time"** in the previous verse.) Instead, it only says that **"many"** of these **"shall awake."** And the Hebrew word here translated **"many"** is again that same Hebrew word *"rab"* used in Daniel 9:27 and in Daniel 11:39 and 44. So this, again, seems to speak of the **"many"** righteous individuals among Daniel's people, Judah, or the Jews.

Here ends the prophetic portion of the message. But this is followed by an important instruction, unlike anything any other prophet of God was ever told to do.

"But you, Daniel, shut up the words, and seal the book until the time of the end." (Daniel 12:4a) This is stressed five verses later by telling him **"Go *your way,* Daniel, for the words *are* closed up and sealed till the time of the end."** (Daniel 12:9) We remember that in a previous day, God had said, **"And the dream was repeated to Pharaoh twice because the thing *is* established by God, and God will shortly bring it to pass."** (Genesis 41:32) So when God repeats himself in this way, He is stressing that this sealing was at His own direct command. That is, that God had chosen to give the prophecy at this time. But He had also chosen to not reveal its meaning at this time.

And this is the basis of the arrangement of this commentary, "Revelation and Daniel, Considered Together." For at the time the Revelation was given, the **"little book"** of Daniel was the only book in the entire Bible that had been so sealed. And although it is only interpretation, and is thus subject to error, I am firmly convinced that what God was saying in Revelation 10:9, when He told John to **"Take" "the little book" "and eat it,"** was that at that point in studying the book of Revelation, that is, after the seven seals on the **"scroll written inside and on the back,"** (Revelation 5:1) had been opened, we should go back and **"eat,"** that is, study and digest **"the little book"** (of Daniel,) until it simply becomes a part of ourselves, before trying to study the rest of the book of Revelation.

And, as was observed previously, The prophecies in Daniel concern end time actions of nations that have disappeared long ago, making their fulfillment seem to be impossible.

But the massive destruction and upheaval revealed in the opening of the seven seals, shows that the modern nations will be destroyed, making room for the old (natural) nations to rise up again. So the opening of the seals in the book of Revelation shows how the book of Daniel can indeed be fulfilled, even though the nations named there disappeared a very long time ago. But the symbols in the rest of the book of Revelation are based on the symbols in the book of Daniel. So what God was revealing in this, is that the book of Daniel cannot be understood without the part of the book of Revelation up to the point where John was told to **"Take" "the little book" "and eat it,"** and that the rest of the book of Revelation cannot be understood without the book of Daniel.

But this very important book of the Bible is not quite finished.

> "Then I, Daniel, looked; and there stood two others, one on this riverbank and the other on that riverbank. And *one* said to the man clothed in linen, who *was* above the waters of the river, 'How long shall the fulfillment of these wonders *be*?' Then I heard the man clothed in linen, who *was* above the waters of the river, when he held up his right hand and his left hand to heaven, and swore by Him who lives forever, that *it shall be* for a time, times, and half *a time*; and when the power of the holy people has been completely shattered, all these *things* shall be finished." (Daniel 12:5-7)

This new part of the vision adds two more messengers, one of which asks a question, **"How long shall the fulfillment of these wonders *be*?"** And the other answers in the strongest possible language. **"he held up his right hand and his left hand to heaven, and swore by Him who lives forever."** We remember that we read in Hebrews 6:13, **"For when God made a promise to Abraham, because He could swear by no one greater, He swore by Himself,"** adding, a few verses later, **"For men indeed swear by the greater, and an oath for confirmation *is* for them an end of all dispute. Thus God, determining to show more abundantly to the heirs of promise the immutability of His counsel, confirmed *it* by an oath, that by two immutable things, in which it *is* impossible for God to lie, we might have strong consolation, who have fled for refuge to lay hold of the hope set before *us*."** (Hebrews 6:16-18)

So this swearing **"by Him who lives forever"** is done to make the message *absolutely* sure and certain. This is not something that *might* happen, but something that will *most definitely* happen. **"It shall be for a time, times, and half *a time*."** We notice that this is half of the seventieth week of Daniel 9:27, where we noticed that the **"one who makes desolate"** shall come **"in the middle of the week."**

But then, still under his oath, he continued, **"and when the power of the holy people has been completely shattered, all these *things* shall be finished." "The holy people"** can mean nothing other than Daniel's people, the Jews. But we see that the end of **"all these things"** will be when their **"power"** **"has been completely shattered."**

Again we remember that the point of all this was **"to make you** [that is, Daniel] **understand what will happen to your people** [that is, the Jews] **in the latter days."** (Daniel 10:14) So, according to this prophecy, all of this was working up to a final point. And that final point would be **"when the power of the holy people has been completely shattered."**

Daniel could not comprehend such a prophecy. He doubtless knew about the many prophesies of Isaiah, depicting such a rosy end as:

> **"For the LORD will comfort Zion,**
> **He will comfort all her waste places;**
> **He will make her wilderness like Eden,**
> **And her desert like the garden of the LORD;**
> **Joy and gladness will be found in it,**
> **Thanksgiving and the voice of melody"**. (Isaiah 51:3)

And:

> **"For Zion's sake I will not hold My peace,**
> **And for Jerusalem's sake I will not rest,**
> **Until her righteousness goes forth as brightness,**
> **And her salvation as a lamp** *that* **burns."** (Isaiah 62:1)

So how, then could **"all these *things*... be finished"** **"when the power of the holy people has been completely shattered."** It did not even make sense. So Daniel said, **"Although I heard, I did not understand."** (Daniel 12:8a)

This is one of the places in the Bible where we see the error of the false principle that, in order to understand a scripture, we must seek the intent of the human author in writing the text. Here we see that the human author did not even understand the message he was transmitting. The Holy Spirit pointed this out in 1 Peter 1:10-11, saying, **"Of this salvation the prophets have inquired and searched** carefully, who prophesied of the grace that *would come* to you, searching what, or what manner of time, the Spirit of Christ who was in them was indicating when He testified beforehand the sufferings of Christ and the glories that would follow."

And in the following verse the Holy Spirit further explained, **"To them it was revealed that, not to themselves, but to us they were ministering the things which now have been reported to you."** (1 Peter 1:12) So we are explicitly told, not only that the prophets themselves did not understand what they were being commanded to say, but that they were also told that the messages they were delivering were not even intended for the original hearers. This disproves a second false principle of scriptural interpretation that is often taught, the notion that we should always interpret a text of scripture in the light of how it would have been interpreted by the original hearers of the words.

But, not understanding, Daniel inquired as to its meaning. And instead of being given an answer, he was told, as 1 Peter 1:12 says, **"Go *your way*, Daniel, for the words *are* closed up and sealed till the time of the end."** (Daniel 12:9) So, as we noted earlier, this is the only book of the Bible that had ever been so sealed before the Revelation was given.

But then Daniel's informer continued, saying, **"Many shall be purified, made white, and refined, but the wicked shall do wickedly; and none of the wicked shall understand, but the wise shall understand."** (Daniel 12:10) Here we see the principle applied in Matthew 13:10-12, when the disciples asked Jesus, **"Why do You speak to them in parables?"** And **"He answered and said to them, 'Because it has been given to you to know the mysteries of the kingdom of heaven, but to them it has not been given. For whoever has, to him more will be given, and he will have abundance; but whoever does not have, even what he has will be taken away from him.'"** So we are explicitly told that some of God's message is intentionally given in a way that would hide its meaning from unbelievers. But we are also told that **"the wise shall understand."**

But this is not all that is contained in this short statement, for he also said, **"Many shall be purified, made white, and refined."** So this is the purpose, the reason, why **"the power of the holy people"** shall be **"completely shattered."** it is so that they might **"be purified, made white, and refined."**

Many imagine that ths is accomplished through the suffering involved. But that is not the case. This always was, and always will be, accomplished only through the sacrifice made by our Lord at Calvary. Instead, this suffering is what God uses to bring His own to repentance, so He can then righteously bless them.

But then some numerical details were added.

> "And from the time *that* the daily *sacrifice* is taken away, and the abomination of desolation is set up, *there shall be* one thousand two hundred and ninety days. Blessed *is* he who waits, and comes to the one thousand three hundred and thirty-five days." (Daniel 12:11-12)

The first of these periods is just one month more than the **"time, times, and half *a time*"** of Daniel 12:7, which is half of the **"week"** of Daniel 9:27, which we are told would be divided by a signal event in its **"middle."** Since half a week is 1260 days, the time of trouble will end one Hebrew month (30 days) after the end of the seventieth week, and the time of blessing will begin one and a half Hebrew months (45 days) later. For more information on the time periods of Bible prophecy, see the comments on Revelation 11:2-3.

And then Daniel was given a personal message. **"But you, go your way till the end; for you shall rest, and will arise to your inheritance at the end of the days."** (Daniel 12:13)

The wording **"arise to your inheritance,"** as given in the NKJV, is a possible rendition of the Hebrew text. [46] But it is worded **"stand in thy lot"** in the King James Version, the American Standard Version, the Douay-Rheims Version, and the literal translations by Darby and Young. The English Standard Version renders this **"stand**

---

46   The Hebrew word rendered "arise" in the NKJV and some other translations, is עָמַד, *amad* in our alphabet, word number 5975 in Strong's Hebrew Dictionary. In the KJV, this word is rendered "stand" or "stood" 308 times, and "raise" or "stand up" only 42 times.

in your alloted place." And the Bible in Basic English renders it "be in your place."

But the words "at the end of the days" are a literal rendition of the Hebrew text. For the Hebrew word here translated "the days" is יוֹם, *yom* in our alphabet, word number 3117 in Strong's Hebrew Dictionary. This word is in the plural, and has a definite article prefix. So this promise was not just for "the end of" *days*, as if it meant *time*, but "the days." That is, the promise applies to the end of a specific period of days. And here, the specific period of days has to be "the one thousand three hundred and thirty-five days" mentioned in the previous verse. If this interpretation is correct, and I believe it is, then Daniel 12:13 indicates that the Old Testament saints will be included in "the first fesurrecton," which will be before the millennium, as we read in Revelation 20:4b-5, "And they lived and reigned with Christ for a thousand years. But the rest of the dead did not live again until the thousand years were finished. This is the first resurrection."

REVELATION 11

Having now "eaten" **"the little book"** of Revelation 10:8-10, the book of Daniel, whose seals of Daniel 12:4 and 9 were opened in Revelation 6-8, we are now ready to consider the rest of this unusually important book of Revelation. I say unusually important because the Revelation is the only book in the entire Bible which contains a specific blessing upon **"he who reads and those who hear"** [heed] its words **"and keep those things which are written in it."** (Revelation 1:3)

Revelation 11 opens with the words: **"Then I was given a reed like a measuring rod. And the angel stood, saying, 'Rise and measure the temple of God, the altar, and those who worship there. But leave out the court which is outside the temple, and do not measure it, for it has been given to the Gentiles. And they will tread the holy city underfoot *for* forty-two months. And I will give *power* to my two witnesses, and they will prophesy one thousand two hundred and sixty days, clothed in sackcloth.' "** (Revelation 11:1-3)

The prophet's attention is here re-directed from heaven to earth. He had been beholding heavenly scenes. But now he is told to **"Rise and measure the temple of God, the altar, and those who worship there."** For, as the prophet is now instructed to pay careful attention to, (**"measure,"**) **"the temple of God, the altar, and those who worship there,"** God is now pointing out things on the earth, rather than in heaven.

Some have erroneously argued that the fact that the temple is here mentioned as physically existing proves that this had to have been written before the temple was destroyed, which took place in approximately 70 A. D. But that neglects the fact that the temple is seen as existing, and worship in that temple is seen as taking place, in numerous other end time prophecies.

An end time existence of the temple is found in the words, **"Let no one deceive you by any means; for that Day *will not come* unless the falling away comes first, and the man of sin is revealed, the son of perdition, who opposes and exalts himself above all that is called God or that is worshiped, so that he sits as God in the temple of God, showing himself that he is God."** (2 Thessalonians 2:3-4)

And end time worship in that temple is found in the words, **"He even exalted *himself* as high as the Prince of the host; and by him the daily *sacrifices* were taken away, and the place of His sanctuary was cast down. Because of transgression, an army was given over *to the horn* to oppose the daily *sacrifices*; and he cast truth down to the ground. He did *all this* and prospered."** (Daniel 8:11-12) And **"Then he shall confirm a covenant with many for one week; But in the middle of the week He shall bring an end to sacrifice and offering. And on the wing of abominations shall be one who makes desolate, Even until the consummation, which is determined, Is poured out on the desolate."** (Daniel 9:27)

So it is clear that here will indeed be a temple in the end times. And the fact that God will recognize those that will be worshiping in that temple is shown by the fact that the prophet was instructed to **"measure the temple of God, the altar, and those who worship there."**

This recognition of the worshipers is highlighted by the words, **"But leave out the court which is outside the temple, and do not measure it, for it has been given to the Gentiles."** That is, measure my people, but *only* measure the ones that are mine. But that is not all these words reveal. For in scripture, the word **"gentiles"** is used in contrast to the word **"Jews."** So, although it does not distinctly state it, this sentence shows that the ones **"who worship"** in **"the temple of God,"** whom the prophet is instructed to **"measure,"** are **"Jews."** That is, that this passage shows that God himself will recognize this end time worship of **"Jews"** in the **"temple of God."**

But that is not all this shows. We had seen in chapter 7 that the opening of the seventh seal had been delayed until **"the servants of our God"** had been sealed. But when these **"servants of our God"** were sealed, they were **"twelve thousand"** from each of the twelve tribes of Israel. (There were others as well, but that is not the point at the moment.) And now, the worshipers in **"the temple of God"** are measured, specifically omitting **"the gentiles."** These two passages together show, and clearly show, that at this time God will resume direct dealings with the nation of Israel, as such. This enrages those that deny the testimony of Bible prophecy. But God's word prevails over all the opinions of mere mortals.

But then we come to some important time periods. Speaking of **"the gentiles,"** John was told that **"they will tread the holy city underfoot for forty-two months."** And then it says, **"And I will give power to my two witnesses, and they will prophesy one thousand two hundred and sixty days, clothed in sackcloth."** These are two statements of the same period of time, the first half of the seventieth week of the prophecy of the **"seventy weeks."** We remember who these **"seventy weeks"** were **"determined upon."**

They were not **"determined upon"** **"the church,"** but upon Daniel's **"people"** [the Jews] and upon Daniel's **"holy city"** [Jerusalem.] So this is yet another indication that God is here dealing specifically, not with **"the church,"** but with **"Israel."**

We remember wording of the prophecy about the last of the **"seventy weeks:"**

> "Then he shall confirm a covenant with many for one week;
> But in the middle of the week
> He shall bring an end to sacrifice and offering.
> And on the wing of abominations shall be
> one who makes desolate,
> Even until the consummation, which is determined,
> Is poured out on the desolate." (Daniel 9:27)

So we are explicitly told that there would be a major event **"in the middle of the week."** This event divides the **"week"** into two half weeks, which are alternately designated as **"a time, times, and half a time," "forty-two months,"** and **"one thousand, two hundred and sixty days."** When we realize that the Hebrew year consisted of twelve months of thirty days each, we realize that each of these three time periods is *precisely* and *exactly* half of a Hebrew **"week."**

God, in the precision of his statements, knowing that an actual year was different from a Hebrew year, never used the word "year," but instead words that would be understood to mean that, but actually referred to the Hebrew method of measuring time, saying **"time"** rather than "year" and **"week,"** rather than "seven years." These details show the awesome precision of God's statements. For Bible prophecy, instead of only being general and indistinct, as many imagine it to be, is highly detailed and precisely accurate, with every word, and indeed, even the very spelling of each word, being both highly significant and precisely accurate. As it is sometimes stated, "God means what He says, and says what He means." and others correctly add, "and He does not mean anything He does not say."

But, after telling how long His **"two witnesses"** will prophesy, God says, **"These are the two olive trees and the two lampstands standing before the God of the earth."** (Revelation 11:4)

This is an unmistakable reference to Zechariah 4:2-3; **"And he said to me, 'What do you see?' So I said, 'I am looking, and there *is* a lampstand of solid gold with a bowl on top of it, and on the *stand* seven lamps with seven pipes to the seven lamps. Two olive trees *are* by it, one at the right of the bowl and the other at its left.'"** This is explained a few verses later: **"Then I answered and said to him, 'What *are* these two olive trees; at the right of the lampstand and at its left?' And I further answered and said to him, 'What *are these* two olive branches that *drip* into the receptacles of the two gold pipes from which the golden *oil* drains?' Then he answered me and said, 'Do you not know what these *are?*' And I said, 'No, my lord.' So he said, 'These *are* the two anointed ones, who stand beside the Lord of the whole earth.'"** (Zechariah 4:11-14)

The context and grammar of the Hebrew text used here indicates that these two were already standing **"beside the Lord of the whole earth"** in Zechariah's day. They can be neither angels nor resurrected men, for they will be killed. And Luke 20:26 shows us that neither angels nor resurrected men can die. It is interesting to note that Scripture tells us of two men who were in heaven at that time, but have not died and are therefore not resurrected. Enoch and Elijah were taken to heaven without passing through death. (Genesis 5:24, 2 Kings 2:11)

From all this we understand that these **"two witnesses"** were long ago anointed by God for this particular mission, and have been held in reserve for thousands of years, even though the time for their mission has still not arrived.

But next their mission is described. **"And if anyone wants to harm them, fire proceeds from their mouth and devours their enemies. And if anyone wants to harm them, he must be killed in this manner. These have power to shut heaven, so that no rain falls in the days of their prophecy; and they have power over waters to turn them to blood, and to strike the earth with all plagues, as often as they desire."** (Revelation 11:5-6)

Because the miracles done by these **"two witnesses"** resembles the miracles done by Elijah and Moses, many have assumed that these two witnesses will be Moses and Elijah. But we have already noticed that the only two men that we re in heaven in the time of Zechariah, and can still die, are Enoch and Elijah.

For next we are told, **"When they finish their testimony, the beast that ascends out of the bottomless pit will make war against them, overcome them, and kill them. And their dead bodies *will lie* in the street of the great city which spiritually is called Sodom and Egypt, where also our Lord was crucified. Then *those* from the peoples, tribes, tongues, and nations will see their dead bodies three- and-a-half days, and not allow their dead bodies to be put into graves. And those who dwell on the earth will rejoice over them, make merry, and send gifts to one another, because these two prophets tormented those who dwell on the earth."** (Revelation 11:7-10)

We need to notice that everything from the end of verse 2 through verse 10 is an explicit statement of future events. That is, these **"two witnesses"** are not merely symbolic representations of things that will happen. They are two literal individuals that will appear in the end times and testify for God for a literal period of **"a thousand two hundred and sixty days,"** after which they will be killed.

But where will they be killed? **"their dead bodies *will lie* in the street of the great city which spiritually is called Sodom and Egypt, where also our Lord was crucified."**

Many want to pretend that the name Babylon represents Jerusalem. But here we are explicitly told that **"the great city" "where also our Lord was crucified"** (which is unquestionably Jerusalem) is **"spiritually" "called Sodom and Egypt,"** not Babylon.

Having rejected their testimony, **"those who dwell on the earth"** will celebrate their deaths, and disrespect their dead bodies by denying them a decent burial. **"Those who dwell on the earth,"** as we noted earlier, are a moral class, those whose entire occupation is with the things of the earth, rather than with heavenly things.

But, although hated and despised by **those who dwell on the earth,"** these men are loved and publicly honored by God. And here God, as He so often does, uses the very wickedness of the enemy to defeat him. For, since their bodies had been left lying in the street, everyone saw it when:

"Now after the three-and-a-half days the breath of life from God entered them, and they stood on their feet, and great fear fell on those who saw them. And they heard a loud voice from heaven saying to them, 'Come up here.' And they ascended to heaven in a cloud, and their enemies saw them." (Revelation 11:11-12)

So the whole world will, even while they are celebrating their death, actually see them arise and then ascend into heaven. And the obvious result will be that **"great fear fell upon them."** and that fear will be well justified, for, **"In the same hour there was a great earthquake, and a tenth of the city fell. In the earthquake seven thousand people were killed, and the rest were afraid and gave glory to the God of heaven."** (Revelation 11:13) Of course, **"the city"** here is Jerusalem, for that is where their dead bodies had lain.

But then we read, **"The second woe is past. Behold, the third woe is coming quickly."** (Revelation 11:14)

It has been so long since we discussed the three woes and the first woe, that we need to go back and review.

In Revelation 8, when the seventh seal was opened, seven angels were given seven trumpets, and as the first four angels sounded their trumpets, severe disasters followed.

But then, in verse 13, we read, **"And I looked, and I heard an angel flying through the midst of heaven, saying with a loud voice, 'Woe, woe, woe to the inhabitants of the earth, because of the remaining blasts of the trumpet of the three angels who are about to sound!'"** (Revelation 8:13) Then in chapter 9, the fifth angel sounded his trumpet, and after the description of the disasters that fell at that time, we read, **"One woe is past. Behold, still two more woes are coming after these things."** (Revelation 9:12)

Then the sixth angel sounded in chapter 9, and everything from there to our present verse followed, up to these words, **"The second woe is past. Behold, the third woe is coming quickly."** (Revelation 11:14) So the second woe consists of all the disasters depicted between Revelation 8:13 and Revelation 11:14. But one more woe, the third woe, **"is coming quickly."**

> "Then the seventh angel sounded: And there were loud voices in heaven, saying, 'The kingdoms of this world have become *the kingdoms* of our Lord and of His Christ, and He shall reign forever and ever!'" (Revelation 11:15)

It is truly amazing that, in the face of this clearly stated prophecy, so many still claim that it is false to teach that there will be a physical kingdom in this earth. They argue that our Lord is reigning now, and thus, that any teaching of a future kingdom is necessarily false. But in so doing, they are ignoring many scriptures like this one, and more particularly, the scripture that Quotes Psalm 8:6 saying, ***"You have put all things in subjection under his feet."*** and then explicitly says, **"For in that He put all in subjection under him, He left nothing *that is* not put under him. But now we do not yet see all things put under him."** (Hebrews 2:8)

So the scriptures very explicitly say that the time for all things to be put under His feet has not yet come, and this verse clearly depicts it as coming at a time that is still future.

But we need to notice that, rather than being announced as a blessing, this is announced as the final of the three woes. Many scriptures speak of the blessedness of this coming kingdom. So how could its coming be a **"woe"**?

To understand this, we need to go back and see upon whom these three woes were pronounced. It said, **"Woe, woe, woe to the inhabitants of the earth, because of the remaining blasts of the trumpet of the three angels who are about to sound!"** (Revelation 8:13) So the woes are pronounced upon **"the inhabitants of the earth."** And we remember that we have already seen that this is not simply a generic term for "all mankind," but speaks of a moral class, those whose entire thoughts and hearts are occupied with th things of this earth, as opposed to the things of the Spirit of God. For such, this blessed coming is not a joy, but a disaster. As Amos 5:18-20 says:

> "Woe to you who desire the day of the Lord!
> For what good is the day of the Lord to you?
> It *will* be darkness, and not light.
> It *will* be as though a man fled from a lion,
> And a bear met him!
> Or *as though* he went into the house,
> Leaned his hand on the wall,
> And a serpent bit him!
> *Is* not the day of the Lord darkness, and not light?
> *Is it not* very dark, with no brightness in it?"

So, to **"the inhabitants of the earth,"** that is, to those whose entire being is wrapped up in the things of this world, this event is indeed **"very dark, with no brightness in it."**

But what is it to the saints of God? **"And the twenty-four elders who sat before God on their thrones fell on their faces and worshiped God, saying:**

> 'We give You thanks, O Lord God Almighty,
> The One who is and who was and who is to come,
> Because You have taken Your great power and reigned.
> The nations were angry, and Your wrath has come,
> And the time of the dead, that they should be judged,
> And that You should reward Your servants
> the prophets and the saints,
> And those who fear Your name, small and great,
> And should destroy those who destroy the earth.' "
> (Revelation 11:16-18)

So this great event, which, to **"the inhabitants of the earth"** is **"very dark, with no brightness in it,"** is, for the inhabitants of heaven, a cause for great celebration.

And **"Then the temple of God was opened in heaven, and the ark of His covenant was seen in His temple. And there were lightnings, noises, thunderings, an earthquake, and great hail."** (Revelation 11:19)

In Hebrews 9:24 we are told that **"the holy places made with hands...** *are* **copies of the true."** The ark in the Holy place **"made with hands"** was repeatedly called **"the ark of the covenant."** and the one in the true temple is called the same.

And when we remember God's ancient covenant with His people, we see the typical symbols of judgment, **"lightnings, noises, thunderings, an earthquake, and great hail."**

Here ends chapter eleven, But there is far more to be revealed.

REVELATION 12

In this chapter a new subject begins with the words, **"Now a great sign appeared in heaven: a woman clothed with the sun, with the moon under her feet, and on her head a garland of twelve stars. Then being with child, she cried out in labor and in pain to give birth."** (Revelation 12:1-2)

This is immediately followed by the words, **"And another sign appeared in heaven: behold, a great, fiery red dragon having seven heads and ten horns, and seven diadems on his heads. His tail drew a third of the stars of heaven and threw them to the earth. And the dragon stood before the woman who was ready to give birth, to devour her Child as soon as it was born."** (Revelation 12:3-4)

The fact that these are called "signs" clearly shows they are symbols. This is not about a woman and a dragon. It is about things represented by a woman and a dragon. To understand these symbols we first need to notice that the woman **"bore a male Child who was to rule all nations with a rod of iron. And her Child was caught up to God and His throne."** (Revelation 12:5) This **"male Child"** is plainly our Lord Jesus, who will **"rule all nations with a rod of iron."** (See Psalm 2:7-9) We are expressly told that the dragon is **"that serpent of old, called the Devil and Satan."** (Revelation 12:9) But why is he seen with seven heads and ten horns?

We see such a beast again in Revelation 17, where we are told that **"The seven heads are seven mountains on which the woman sits."** (verse 9) But the woman there is not the same woman as the one we are considering here.

In chapter 17 the prophet was told that **"the woman whom you saw is that great city which reigns over the kings of the earth."** (verse 18) Rome was unquestionably the city that was reigning **"over the kings of the earth"** at the time that was written. And since ancient times, Rome has always been widely called "the city of seven hills."

So the seven heads clearly represent Rome. But what of the ten horns? In Daniel 7, Daniel saw **"four great beasts"** come up. (verse 3) And the fourth one **"had ten horns"** (verse 7) He was then told that **"Those great beasts, which are four, *are* four kings *which* arise out of the earth."** (verse17) And both that **"The fourth beast shall be A fourth kingdom on earth,"** (verse 23) and **"The ten horns *are* ten kings *Who* shall arise from this kingdom."** (verse24)

So the beast that had the ten horns was unquestionably **"a fourth kingdom on earth."** But the fourth of what four kingdoms? We had previously seen these four kingdoms as men saw them in Daniel 2, where they were magnificent, and verse 38 says that the first kingdom was that of Nebuchadnezzar. And in Daniel 8:20-21 the next two kingdoms are identified as the kingdoms of Medo-Persia and of Greece. The fourth kingdom was not named, but was described, first, in Daniel 2:40 **"as strong as iron, inasmuch as iron breaks in pieces and shatters everything; and like iron that crushes, *that kingdom* will break in pieces and crush all the others."**

And then we read in Daniel 7:23:

> **"The fourth beast shall be**
> **A fourth kingdom on earth,**
> **Which shall be different from all *other* kingdoms,**
> **And shall devour the whole earth,**
> **Trample it and break it in pieces."**

These two descriptions both perfectly fit the fourth ancient world kingdom, which is well known to history as the Roman Empire.

So there can be no doubt that the ten horns, like the seven heads, speak of Rome. This means there can be little doubt that the **"dragon having seven heads and ten horns"** speaks of Satan acting through the power of Rome. This becomes even more clear when we notice that **"the dragon stood before the woman who was ready to give birth, to devour her Child as soon as it was born."** We remember that when our Lord was born, the Roman governor tried to kill him. (Matthew 2:12-16)

But who is the woman? If she represented Mary, the mother of Jesus, she would not be **"a great sign."** This would simply be an account of the birth of Jesus. Besides, **"the woman was given two wings of a great eagle, that she might fly into the wilderness to her place, where she is nourished for a time and times and half a time, from the presence of the serpent."** (Revelation 12:14) Scripture contains no account of such a flight of Mary into the wilderness. Her flight (with Joseph) was into Egypt, not into the wilderness, and it lasted until Herod died (Matthew 2:19), not for three and a half years. Again, we read that **"her child was caught up to God and His throne. Then the woman fled into the wilderness."** (Revelation 12:5-6) Mary's flight into Egypt was long before Jesus ascended into heaven. But this woman fled into the wilderness after **"her Child was caught up to God and to His throne."**

Alternately, if the woman spoke of mankind as having given birth to Jesus, she would represent the entire human race. If that were the case, who would she be fleeing from, and who would be left to persecute her as we read in Revelation 12:13. Further, no other scripture speaks of such a flight of all mankind.

If the woman represents neither Mary nor mankind, she must represent Israel, the nation that bore our Lord. Many scriptures speak of such a flight of the righteous remnant of Israel. This is further suggested by the **"garland of twelve stars"** that was on her head. Taken by itself, this might speak either of the twelve tribes of Israel or of the twelve apostles. But if it represented the twelve apostles, the woman would be the church. This would not fit the rest of the sign, for the church did not give birth to Jesus. Thus we see it is unreasonable to think the woman represents anything but Israel. And this again shows that at the time spoken of here, God will again be dealing directly with he nation of Israel, as such.

But in this respect it is important to understand that in God's sight **"they *are* not all Israel, who *are* of Israel, nor *are they* all children because they are the seed of Abraham; but *'In Isaac your*** *seed shall be called.'* That is, those who are the children of the flesh, these *are* not the children of God; but the children of the promise are counted as the seed." (Romans 9:6-8) Thus, in the vision of the woman, as in many other scriptures, the righteous remnant of Israel is looked upon as the entire nation. That is, the wicked among them are not recognized as true Israelites. The Lord says of these, that **"I will purge the rebels from among you, and those who transgress against Me; I will bring them out of the country where they dwell, but they shall not enter the land of Israel."** (Ezekiel 20:38)

The period during which the woman was fed in the wilderness, which is specified in verse 6 as **"one thousand two hundred and sixty days,"** is also called **"a time and times and half a time"** in verse 14. This speaks of the half week of trouble for Daniel's people, the time Jesus spoke of when He said, **"Therefore when you see the *'abomination of desolation,'* spoken of by Daniel the prophet, standing in the holy place (whoever reads, let him understand), then let those who are in Judea flee to the mountains. Let him who is on the housetop not go down to take anything out of his house. And let him who is in the field not go back to get his clothes. But woe to those who are pregnant and to those who are nursing babies in those days! And pray that your flight may not be in winter or on the Sabbath. For then there will be great tribulation, such as has not been since the beginning of the world until this time, no, nor ever shall be."** (Matthew 24:15-21) Jeremiah 30:7 calls this period **"the time of Jacob's trouble."**

But we were told that the dragon's **"tail drew a third of the stars of heaven and threw them to the earth."** many think this means that Satan drew away a third of the angels in heaven, to join his rebellion against God. This conclusion would seem to be reinforced by the next part of the vision. **"And war broke out in heaven: Michael and his angels fought with the dragon; and the dragon and his angels fought, but they did not prevail, nor was a place found for them in heaven any longer. So the great dragon was cast out, that serpent of old, called the Devil and Satan, who deceives the whole world; he was cast to the earth, and his angels were cast out with him."** (Revelation 12:7-9) So there can be no doubt that some of the angels of heaven are sided with the Devil in this war.

But this part of the vision, like the flight of the woman, rather than referring to the past, refers to the future. We know this from the declaration that accompanied it.

> "Then I heard a loud voice saying in heaven, 'Now salvation, and strength, and the kingdom of our God, and the power of His Christ have come, for the accuser of our brethren, who accused them before our God day and night, has been cast down. And they overcame him by the blood of the Lamb and by the word of their testimony, and they did not love their lives to the death. Therefore rejoice, O heavens, and you who dwell in them! Woe to the inhabitants of the earth and the sea! For the devil has come down to you, having great wrath, because he knows that he has a short time.' " (Revelation 12:10-12)

In this declaration, we first see, as we saw in the end of the last chapter, **"Now salvation, and strength, and the kingdom of our God, and the power of His Christ have come."** Then, at its end, we also see that **"the devil"** will have **"great wrath, because he knows that he has a short time."** So it is clear that this is a prophecy of the end times.

And what does this show? That in the end times, **"the devil,"** along with **"his angels,"** will be expelled from heaven, where he currently accuses **"our brethren"** **"before our God day and night."** And, being cast down, he will have **"great wrath,"** which he will pour on **"the inhabitants of the earth and the sea."** It has been pointed out that in the context of this comparison, **"the earth"** speaks of that portion of the world which is under stable government, while **"the sea"** speaks of that portion of the world which is in a state of unrest, as we read, **"the wicked *are* like the troubled sea, When it cannot rest."** (Isaiah 57:20)

The woman flees: **"Now when the dragon saw that he had been cast to the earth, he persecuted the woman who gave birth to the male *Child*. But the woman was given two wings of a great eagle, that she might fly into the wilderness to her place, where she is nourished for a time and times and half a time, from the presence of the serpent. So the serpent spewed water out of his mouth** like a flood after the woman, that he might cause her to be carried away by the flood. But the earth helped the woman, and the earth opened its mouth and swallowed up the flood which the dragon had spewed out of his mouth." (Revelation 12:13-16)

The time when **"the dragon"** (Satan) persecutes **"the woman,"** (the faithful remnant of Israel) is the same length as the time mentioned in Daniel 7:25, where **"the saints shall be given into his hand For a time and times and half a time." "But the woman was given two wings of a great eagle, that she might fly into the wilderness to her place, where she is nourished for a time and times and half a time, from the presence of the serpent."** Here we notice two different periods of time, although they are both the same length. In the first period, **"*the saints* are given into his hand,"** and in the second period, **"the woman"** whom, as we have seen, represents the same group as **"the saints," "is nourished" "from the presence of the serpent."** We thus understand that these two periods are the two halves of the seventieth week. For we remember that a great disturbance will take place **"in the middle of the week."** (Daniel 9:27)

A flight of the righteous remnant of Israel is mentioned in numerous scriptures. Jesus spoke of it, saying, **"When you see the 'abomination of desolation,' spoken of by Daniel the prophet, standing in the holy place"** (whoever reads, let him understand), **then let those who are in Judea flee to the mountains. Let him who is on the housetop not go down to take anything out of his house. And let him who is in the field not go back to get his clothes."** (Matthew 24:15-18)

This exile is part of God's plan for His people, for He said:

> "The people who survived the sword
> Found grace in the wilderness;
> Israel, when I went to give him rest." (Jeremiah 31:2)

And:

> "Therefore, behold, I will allure her,
> Will bring her into the wilderness,

And speak comfort to her." (Hosea 2:14)

Again, in Isaiah 26:20 the Lord figuratively said,

> "Come, my people, enter your chambers,
> And shut your doors behind you;
> Hide yourself, as it were, for a little moment,
> Until the indignation is past."

The emotions of those who fled at this time are described in passages such as:

> "As the deer pants for the water brooks,
> So pants my soul for You, O God.
> My soul thirsts for God, for the living God.
> When shall I come and appear before God?
> My tears have been my food day and night,
> While they continually say to me,
> 'Where is your God?'
> When I remember these *things*,
> I pour out my soul within me.
> For I used to go with the multitude;
> I went with them to the house of God,
> With the voice of joy and praise,
> With a multitude that kept a pilgrim feast.
> Why are you cast down, O my soul?
> And *why* are you disquieted within me?
> Hope in God, for I shall yet praise Him
> For the help of His countenance.
> O my God, my soul is cast down within me;
> Therefore I will remember You fro
> the land of the Jordan,
> And from the heights of Hermon,
> From the Hill Mizar." (Psalm 42:1-6)

And:

> "O God, You *are* my God;
> Early will I seek You;
> My soul thirsts for You;
> My flesh longs for You
> In a dry and thirsty land
> Where there is no water." (Psalm 63:1)

In these Psalms we notice that they long to **"come and appear before God,"** but they cannot. They **"used to go with the multitude… to the house of God,"** but this is no longer possible. Instead, they can only remember their God **"from the land of the Jordan,"** **"from the heights of Hermon,"** and **"From the hill Mizar."** They are **"In a dry and thirsty land Where there is no water."** That is where they have fled.

And the Lord instructed Moab, which is one of the nations into which they will flee, saying:

> "Take counsel, execute judgment;
> Make your shadow like the night in the middle of the day;
> Hide the outcasts,
> Do not betray him who escapes.
> Let My outcasts dwell with you, O Moab;
> Be a shelter to them from the face of the spoiler.
> For the extortioner is at an end,
> Devastation ceases,
> The oppressors are consumed out of the land."
> (Isaiah 16:3-4)

But, returning now to Revelation 12, what did **"the serpent"** do when **"the woman"** fled? He **"spewed water out of his mouth like a flood after the woman, that he might cause her to be carried away by the flood."** In the Bible, invading armies are often compared to a flood. So **"the serpent,"** who is acting through Roman power, sends an army to overwhelm the fleeing saints, who are depicted as **"the woman."**

But something stops this army. For **"the earth helped the woman, and the earth opened its mouth and swallowed up the flood which the dragon had spewed out of his mouth."** Suddenly, a new player enters the stage. This new player is not named here in the Revelation but he is seen in numerous Old Testament prophecies.

We read of thu=is new player in Isaiah 10:28-32, which calls him **"the king of Assyria,"** (verse 12) and says,

> "He has come to Aiath,
> He has passed Migron;
> At Michmash he has attended to his equipment.
> They have gone along the ridge,
> They have taken up lodging at Geba.
> Ramah is afraid, Gibeah of Saul has fled.
> Lift up your voice,
> O daughter of Gallim!
> Cause it to be heard as far as Laish--
> O poor Anathoth!
> Madmenah has fled,
> The inhabitants of Gebim seek refuge.
> As yet he will remain at Nob that day;
> He will shake his fist at the mount of the daughter of Zion,
> The hill of Jerusalem."

It is critical to understand that no ancient attacker has ever invaded Judea by approaching along the path described here. And we have already noticed the very strong evidence that this **"king of Assyria,"** or **"the Assyrian,"** as he is also called in verse 24 and five other places in the Bible (Isaiah 14:25, 30:31, and 31:8, and in Micah 5:5 and 6) is another designation for **"the king of the north"** that is the subject of Daniel 11:40-41, where we read of an impious king of Judah, and then it says, **"At the time of the end the king of the South shall attack him; and the king of the North shall come against him like a whirlwind, with chariots, horsemen, and with many ships; and he shall enter the countries, overwhelm them, and pass through. He shall also enter the Glorious Land, and many** *countries* **shall be overthrown; but these shall escape from his hand: Edom, Moab, and the prominent people of Ammon."** (Daniel 11:40-41)

We notice that this attacker will overthrow many countries, **"but these shall escape from his hand: Edom, Moab, and the prominent people of Ammon."** These three ancient nations make up the modern nation of Jordan which is just over the Jordan river from Judea, which is now called Israel. This is the place where our Lord warned those who would be heeding His words to flee **"when you see the *"abomination of desolation'* spoken of by Daniel the prophet."**

And how did **"the dragon"** react to this frustration of his plans? He **"was enraged with the woman, and he went to make war with the rest of her offspring, who keep the commandments of God and have the testimony of Jesus Christ."** (Revelation 12:17)

REVELATION 13

In Revelation 13 we see two beasts rise up. The first one rises in verse 1, and the second one in verse 11. And the Holy Spirit stresses that these two beasts are not the same by repeating three times over that the second one is a different beast. Verse 11 calls him **"another beast,"** and after he rises up, verse 12 twice refers to the other one as **"the first beast."** So this second beast is not simply a different representation of the same end time person, but a different person. And until we realize this, we cannot even begin to understand this chapter.

So, looking first at the first beast, we read, **"Then I stood on the sand of the sea. And I saw a beast rising up out of the sea, having seven heads and ten horns, and on his horns ten crowns, and on his heads a blasphemous name. Now the beast which I saw was like a leopard, his feet were like the feet of a bear, and his mouth like the mouth of a lion. The dragon gave him his power, his throne, and great authority."** (Revelation 13:1-2)

The seven heads and ten horns clearly identify this beast as yet another representation of Rome. But now we need to notice something we skipped over in the last chapter. In verse 2 of chapter 12, the beast had **"seven diadems on his heads."** But here, he has **"ten crowns" "on his horns."** Why is this beast seen first with **"seven diadems,"** and then with **"ten crowns"**? The difference in wording is an artifice of the translation. [47] We also notice that the **"seven diadems"** are on his **"seven heads,"** while the **"ten crowns"** are on his **"ten horns."**

---

47 This is because the Greek word used is the same in both places. It is διάδημα, or *diadema* in our alphabet. (word number 1238 in Strong's Greek Dictionary)

We see the reason for this when we examine other prophecies about this beast. For while, as we have seen, his seven heads refer to the seven hills of Rome, they also represent seven successive kings, that is, governments, of Rome. We will examine this in more detail when we get to chapter 17. For this is revealed in Revelation 17:10. But the ten horns represent ten kings that will voluntarily unite to revive the Roman empire, as we are explicitly told in Revelation 17:12-13.

Further, **"the beast which I saw was like a leopard, his feet were like the feet of a bear, and his mouth like the mouth of a lion."** **"A leopard"** was the third beast of Daniel 7. (verse 6) **"A bear"** was the second beast of that chapter, (verse 5) while **"a lion"** was the first beast. So this beast is a combination of all the previous kingdoms, and the reversal of the order in which they are mentioned reflects looking backward to them here, while Daniel 7 was looking forward to these same beasts.

But beyond his appearance, the character of this beast is revealed, not only in the fact that he is seen as a beast, but also in the two details of this description. He had **"on his heads a blasphemous name."** And, **"The dragon gave him his power, his throne, and great authority."**

When **"the devil"** came to tempt Jesus, he **"showed Him all the kingdoms of the world in a moment of time."** and told our Lord that, if He would worship himself, he would give Him **"All this authority,"** saying, **"for this has been delivered to me, and I give it to whomever I wish."** (Luke 4:5-7) So here, in Revelation 13:2. We see that it was **"the devil"** that gave this beast **"his power, his throne, and great authority."**

But next we read, **"And *I saw* one of his heads as if it had been mortally wounded, and his deadly wound was healed."** (Revelation 13:3a) Many have interpreted this to mean that the final ruler of the Roman Empire will be killed and then resurrected. And others have more rationally interpreted it to only mean that he will appear to have been killed. In defense of this idea, many quote Zachariah 11:17:

> "Woe to the worthless shepherd,
> Who leaves the flock!
> A sword *shall be* against his arm
> And against his right eye;
> His arm shall completely wither,
> And his right eye shall be totally blinded."

But in sayting this, they fail to notice that an injury to the arm or to the eye, though indeed serious, is not life threatening. A wound in the arm or in the eye would not kill a person. And the heads do not represent individual kings. Those are represented by horns. The heads represent the successive governments of Rome. And one of these governments fell, apparently killed. But, instead of dying, Rome lives on, and the healing of the deadly wound speaks of the Roman Empire being revived.

But then it says, **"And all the world marveled and followed the beast."** (Revelation 13:3b) in addition to this statement, verse 8 says that **"All who dwell on the earth will worship him."** And verse 7 it says **"authority was given him over every tribe, tongue, and nation."** [48] [49]

---

[48] The Greek word translated **"all"** in verses 3,8 and 16, and **"every"** in verse 7, is πας, *pas* in our alphabet. (word number 3956 in Strong's Greek Dictionary) This Greek word literally means *all*. But like our English word *all*, it does not necessarily mean *absolutely* all. *Pas* is the Greek word used in Matthew 27:1, where we read that **"all the chief priests and elders of the people plotted against Jesus to put Him to death."** But Luke 23:50-51 says that Joseph of Arimathea was a member of the council and **"had not consented to their decision and deed."** Also, Nicodemus opposed the council in John 7:50-51 and came with Joseph to bury Jesus in John 19:39. In English, we add the word *absolutely* to the word *all* to make it absolute. In Greek, this was done by adding a syllable to *pas*, making it *hapas*. (word number 537 in Strong's Greek Dictionary) This is the word used in Luke 17:27, where we read that **"Noah entered the ark, and the flood came and destroyed them all."** If the Holy Spirit had meant that **"the beast"** would be given authority over *absolutely* all tribes, tongues, and nations, it would seem that He would have used the word *hapas*. But He said *pas*, not *hapas*.

[49] The Greek word translated *authority* here (and in verses 2, 4, 5, and 12) is ἐξουσία, *exousia* in our alphabet. (word number 1849 in Strong's Greek Dictionary) This word is often used of *official authority*, but that is not its only meaning. It also

These two footnotes show that the actual Greek words used in the original text of this chapter do not *necessarily* mean the Beast's power will be either universal or official. And in recent years, we have seen that it is indeed possible, through use of the world's computer systems, to gain *nearly* total control over *basically* **"every tribe, tongue, and nation"** without any need for that power to be *official*.

So, while the Greek words used in this chapter *seem* to *imply* that **"the beast"** will become the ruler of the entire world. That is not what they *actually* say. And other scriptures show that this is not what will happen. In this regard the first thing we need to notice is that in *every* other scripture where this power is mentioned, it is described only as a revival of the ancient Roman empire.

The next thing we need to notice is that other kings will continue to exist throughout the time of this evil ruler's reign. We see this in Revelation 16. While **"the beast"** is gathering his last great army, we read of **"the kings of the East"** in verse 12 and **"the kings of the earth and of the whole world."** in verse 14. These references are only general, but scripture specifically speaks of two great powers that will continue to exist during that time.

The first of these is **"the Assyrian."** Isaiah 10:12 says that this evil invader will be punished **"when the Lord has performed all His work on mount Zion and on Jerusalem."** Verse 20 of the same chapter says **"And it shall come to pass in that day *That* the remnant of Israel, And such as have escaped of the house of Jacob, Will never again depend on him who defeated them, But will depend on the Lord, the Holy One of Israel, in truth."**

It should be clear to even the most casual student of prophecy that the Lord's **"work on mount Zion and on Jerusalem"** will not be completed until He returns in power and glory, nor will Israel learn to **"depend on the Lord, the Holy One of Israel, in truth"** until that time.

And the second of these powers is Gog. Ezekiel 39:7 says that after Gog is destroyed the Lord **"will not *let them* profane"** His holy name **"anymore."** Again, Ezekiel 39:22 says that **"the house of Israel shall know that I *am* the LORD their God from that day forward"**

---

means *power*, as in the ability to control. For this use of *exousia* see Romans 9:21 and 1 Corinthians 7:37.

Neither of these could possibly apply until after the time when they allow **"the man of sin"** to sit **"as God in the temple of God, showing himself that he is God."** (2 Thessalonians 2:3-4)

So we see that it is an error to assume that **"the beast"** will become the official ruler of the entire world.

But returning to where we left off in Revelation 13, we read: **"So they worshiped the dragon who gave authority to the beast; and they worshiped the beast, saying, 'Who is like the beast? Who is able to make war with him?' And he was given a mouth speaking great things and blasphemies, and he was given authority to continue for forty-two months."** (Revelation 13:4-5) So the devil manages to get basically the entire world to worship, not only **"the beast,"** but himself. And **"the beast"** will be allowed to speak **"great things and blasphemies."** For the mouth to do this **"was given to him."** And he also **"was given"** great power. But only for a time, for **"he was given authority to continue for forty-two months."** This is the same half week we keep seeing again and again in various prophecies. But then we are told:

> "Then he opened his mouth in blasphemy against God, to blaspheme His name, His tabernacle, and those who dwell in heaven. It was granted to him to make war with the saints and to overcome them. And authority was given him over every tribe, tongue, and nation. All who dwell on the earth will worship him, whose names have not been written in the Book of Life of the Lamb slain from the foundation of the world." (Revelation 13:6-8)

So, using the mouth he had been given, he blasphemes **"God," "His name, His tabernacle, and those who dwell in heaven."** That is, everything sacred. But there is more. He is not only **"given"** the power to blaspheme, and **"authority"** **"over every tribe, tongue, and nation."** Also **"It was granted to him to make war with the saints and to overcome them."**

We need to understand that God is specifically and explicitly *allowing* all this, including this beast's abuse of **"the saints."** He is not only allowed **"to make war with"** them, but **"to overcome"** them. Why would a loving God allow this? We find an answer in Daniel 11:35. **"And *some* of those of understanding shall fall, to refine them, purify *them*, and make *them* white."** And again, in the context of the word, **"You have not yet resisted to bloodshed, striving against sin,"** (Hebrews 12:4) we read, **"If you endure chastening, God deals with you as with sons; for what son is there whom a father does not chasten? But if you are without chastening, of which all have become partakers, then you are illegitimate and not sons. Furthermore, we have had human fathers who corrected *us*, and we paid *them* respect. Shall we not much more readily be in subjection to the Father of spirits and live? For they indeed for a few days chastened *us* as seemed *best* to them, but He for *our* profit, that *we* may be partakers of His holiness. Now no chastening seems to be joyful for the present, but painful; nevertheless, afterward it yields the peaceable fruit of righteousness to those who have been trained by it."** (Hebrews 12:7-11)

So, even though the minds of the men who will do all this will be nothing but pure evil, God will use them to accomplish His own purpose, even as He did at Calvary.

But then, after revealing all this about **"the beast,"** He adds a word for His own. **"If anyone has an ear, let him hear. He who leads into captivity shall go into captivity; he who kills with the sword must be killed with the sword. Here is the patience and the faith of the saints."** (Revelation 13:9-10) So He tells His own to endure patiently, and wait for Him to act, when the proper time comes.

We now come to the second beast. The first one had risen up **"out of the sea,"** but this one comes up **"out of the earth."** When **"the sea"** and **"the earth"** are contrasted in this way, **"the sea"** seems to represent nations in a state of confusion, while **"the earth"** represents them in a stable condition. We remember that the seal and trumpet visions had depicted a general collapse of government, resulting in a state of anarchy. And that a revival of the Roman Empire will rise out of this state of anarchy. Now, this vision represents a new power rising up out of the newly established condition of stability.

"Then I saw another beast coming up out of the earth, and he had two horns like a lamb and spake like a dragon." (Revelation 13:11) This beast looked like a lamb; (**"the Lamb of God,"** John 1:29, 36) but he could be recognized when he spoke, for he **"spake like a dragon."** ("the great dragon... that serpent of old, called the Devil and Satan," Revelation 12:9) So here, we see a beast who looks like the Lord, but can be recognized when he speaks, for he speaks like Satan.

Since ancient times, men have consistently called the first **"beast"** in this chapter, the one that represents the head of the revived Roman Empire, "the Antichrist." But here we see a different ruler, stressed by repeating three times over, that it is a different **"beast,"** presented as looking like the Lord Jesus but speaking like Satan.

We are told of this second beast, **"And he exercises all the authority of the first beast in his presence, and causes the earth and those who dwell in it to worship the first beast, whose deadly wound was healed. He performs great signs, so that he even makes fire come down from heaven on the earth in the sight of men. And he deceives those who dwell on the earth by those signs which he was granted to do in the sight of the beast, telling those who dwell on the earth to make an image to the beast who was wounded by the sword and lived. ⁵⁰ He was granted** *power* **to give breath to the image of the beast, that the image of the beast should both speak and cause as many as would not worship the image of the beast to be killed."** (Revelation 13:12-15)

Many think that, because the second **"beast"** **"causes the earth and those who dwell in it to worship the first beast,"** then **"the first beast"** must be "the Antichrist." But they forget that Jesus taught men to worship the Father. (see John 4:21-24) The Antichrist will imitate the true Christ. Even as the true Christ taught us to worship the Father, the Antichrist will teach men to worship **"the first beast."** Likewise, even as the true Christ **"always"** did **"those things**

---

50   This does not refer to the worthless shepherd's sword wound of Zechariah 11:17, but to the beast's deadly wound of Revelation 13:3. Although a sword is mentioned in Zechariah 11:17 but not Revelation 13:3, the worthless shepherd's wounds will not be healed. We are specifically told that **"His arm shall completely wither, And his right eye shall be totally blinded."** (Zechariah 11:17) Further, the worthless shepherd's wounds, though serious, will not be life threatening. There would be nothing remarkable about such wounds being healed. But the beast's wound in Revelation 13:3 was mortal. It will seem unreasonable that the beast could have survived. The world will therefore marvel that the beast's **"deadly wound was healed."** (Revelation 13:3)

that please" "the Father," (John 8:29) the Antichrist will exercise "**all the authority of the first beast in his presence.**" And even as the true Christ did signs and wonders to make men believe, (see John 4:48) the Antichrist will perform "**great signs, so that he even makes fire come down from heaven on the earth in the sight of men.**"

But then it says, "**He causes all, both small and great, rich and poor, free and slave, to receive a mark on their right hand or on their foreheads, and that no one may buy or sell except one who has the mark or the name of the beast, or the number of his name.**" (Revelation 13:16-17)

When I was young, I thought this meant that he would make a law prohibiting anyone from buying or selling without the mark. But now that the use of computers has become so all-prevalent, and particularly the scanners now used in stores everywhere, it has become obvious that this will not just be a law. It now seems obvious that it will be made impossible to buy or to sell anything without the mark.

A system known as "the cashless society" has been in the planning process for some years now. In this system, all money will be reduced from a physical symbol of value to simply credits in banks.

This is advocated as a way to make it impossible to steal money, because there simply will not be any money to steal. But then, the advocates of this system point out that it would still be possible to steal the credit cards currently used to access this system, which is already partly in place. So they have proposed replacing the credit cards with a tattoo made with ink invisible to the human eye, but visible to scanners. And they have specifically recommended the location of this tattoo - in the right hand, or, if that has been maimed, in the forehead! The scanners that are already being used in essentially all stores can read such tattoos, so the cost of instituting such a system would be minimal.

But the advocates of this system keep quiet about its dark side, for whoever controls the computer system that keeps track of all the transactions, would have complete control over everyone, and everything. For without access to the system, it would be literally impossible to buy or to sell anything.

It is a serious error to interpret Bible prophecy on the basis of current events. But this is not interpretation. The system being currently advocated by the banking community and by many governments is, *literally* and *exactly*, the system described in Revelation 13:16-17!

Finally, it says **"Here is wisdom. Let him who has understanding calculate the number of the beast, for it is the number of a man: His number *is* 666."** (Revelation 13:18) This is commonly interpreted to mean that the numerical values of the letters in the name of **"the beast"** will add up to 666. Various schemes of applying values to the letters of the alphabet have been used to find this sum in current names ranging all the way from a title claimed by the Pope to the names of many different past or current political leaders. All this is error. The time covered in Bible prophecy has not yet begun. The beast is not yet revealed. But when he comes, **"him who has understanding"** will recognize him from the many descriptions in Scripture. The correct way to calculate his number will then be apparent, and will confirm his identity.

REVELATION 14

A Lamb stands on mount Zion with 144,000

"Then I looked, and behold, a Lamb standing on Mount Zion, and with Him one hundred *and* forty-four thousand, having His Father's name written on their foreheads. And I heard a voice from heaven, like the voice of many waters, and like the voice of loud thunder. And I heard the sound of harpists playing their harps. They sang as it were a new song before the throne, before the four living creatures, and the elders; and no one could learn that song except the hundred *and* forty-four thousand who were redeemed from the earth. These are the ones who were not defiled with women, for they are virgins. These are the ones who follow the Lamb wherever He goes. These were redeemed from *among* men, *being* firstfruits to God and to the Lamb. And in their mouth was found no deceit, for they are without fault before the throne of God." (Revelation 14:1-5)

We should note here that, although when He comes, He will come as a mighty conqueror, to His own people, He is **"a lamb."** For it is only in that character that we have any claim upon Him. For we must always remember that we **"were not redeemed with corruptible things,** *like* **silver or gold, from your** aimless conduct *received* by tradition from your fathers, but with the precious blood of Christ, as of a lamb without blemish and without spot."** (1 Peter 1:18-19) So it is only in His character as **"a Lamb as though it had been slain"** (Revelation 5:6) that we have any caim upon Him. So he is here seen among His own **"one hundred *and* forty-four thousand"** as **"a lamb."**

The number, **"one hundred *and* forty-four thousand"** seems to be symbolic. In scripture, twelve seems to represent a complete witness. There were twelve sons of Jacob, whose families were the twelve tribes of Israel. There were twelve Apostles. There were twelve wells of water from which God provided for His people in the wilderness. (Exodus 15:27) Here, we see twelve times twelve, and that a thousand times over. That is, a complete witness multiplied completely, and that, a thousand times over. In other words, far, far, more than a complete witness to a wicked world. These are gathered with the **"Lamb,"** that is, with Jesus, **"on Mont Zion."** The number here is the same as in Revelation 7, indicating that this is that same group, now gathered for their reward. We are told nothing of what they do at this time, other than that they sing. But we are told at length of their righteousness.

We need to no notice that, although they are here seen standing with the **"Lamb,"** it is not **"a Lamb as though it had been slain."** And it is not His name that is written on their foreheads. Instead, they have **"His Father's name written on their foreheads."** We remember that in Revelation 3:12 any overcomer from **"the church in Philadelphia"** had been promised that **"I will write on him the name of My God and the name of the city of My God, the New Jerusalem, which comes down out of heaven from My God. And *I will write on him* My new name."** These do not have all this, but only **"His Father's name written on their foreheads."**

I stress this because we are explicitly told that when He comes, **"*one* shall say unto him, What *are* these wounds in thine hands? Then he shall answer, *Those* with which I was wounded *in* the house of my friends."** (Zechariah 13:6 KJV) Here the KJV reading appears to capture the sense far better than the NKJV. But we notice that, in both translations, the word **"*one*"** is in italics. That is, it is not in the Hebrew text. It is not just **"*one*"** (an individual) that shall ask this question, but "they" shall ask it.

So the inhabitants of the land will not come to faith in Jesus until after He comes. And, although the people in this vision **"were redeemed from the earth,"** and **"were redeemed from *among* men, *being* firstfruits to God and to the Lamb,"** the ones mentioned here are not here commended for their faith, but only for their righteous deeds, saying, **"These are the ones who were not defiled with women, for they are virgins. These are the ones who follow the Lamb wherever He goes."** And **"in their mouth was found no deceit, for they are without fault before the throne of God."** This reinforces the idea that these are righteous members of the tribe of Judah, that is, Jews, whose hearts have long been right toward God, but will not realize until He appears, that the great Messiah for whom they had been longing, is that same Jesus whose name they had despised from their youths. So to them, He will not yet be, at this time, **"a Lamb as though it had been slain."**

And this is why they **"shall say unto him, What *are* these wounds in thine hands?"** And when He answers them, their reaction will be like those of Jacob's brothers, when he revealed himself to them, saying, **" 'I *am* Joseph; does my father still live?' But his brothers could not answer him, for they were dismayed in his presence."** (Genesis 45:3)

We see their reaction to this answer in Zechariah 12 10-14: **"They will look on Me whom they pierced. Yes, they will mourn for Him as one mourns for *his* only *son*, and grieve for Him as one grieves for a firstborn. In that day there shall be a great mourning in Jerusalem, like the mourning at Hadad Rimmon in the plain of Megiddo. And the land shall mourn, every family by itself: the family of the house of David by itself, and their wives by themselves; the family of the house of Nathan by itself, and their wives by themselves; the family of the house of Levi by itself, and their wives by themselves; the family of Shimei by itself, and their wives by themselves; all the families that remain, every family by itself, and their wives by themselves."**

So the faithfulness of these men whose hearts had been right toward God, but whose faith had been lacking will eventually be rewarded with a true faith. Our Lord commented on this when He said to Thomas, **"because you have seen Me, you have believed. Blessed** *are* those who have not seen and *yet* have believed." (John 20:29) Even so these, who will believe when they see Him, will indeed be blessed, but not nearly so blessed as those who had believed in Him before the rapture.

And in this regard we need to notice where this **"one hundred and forty-four thousand"** are seen, **"standing," "with"** the **"Lamb."** It is **"on Mount Zion."** We realize that the **"Lamb"** will not be **"standing on Mount Zion."** until after He comes in power and glory to judge the world and to deliver Israel. So these are the redeemed Jews who have believed in Jesus after He has returned, the ones we have been discussing.

And the fact that they will not come to a true faith in Christ until afer He appears is also the explanation for a scriptural statement that has been the occasion of much bad doctrine. This statement, which is found in Matthew 10:22 and 24:13 and again in Mark 13:13, is **"But he who endures to the end shall be saved."** All three of these passages are speaking of the time after the rapture and before the Lord returns to deliver Israel. The faithful in that day, although their hearts will be right toward God, will not have actually trusted in that name of which **"there is no other name under heaven given among men by which we must be saved."** (Acts 4:12) And, as it is **"not by works of righteousness which we have done, but according to His mercy He saved us,"** (Titus 3:5) those that do not endure **"to the end"** will not be **"saved."** For **"the end"** is when Messiah returns and they will finally come to a true and living faith in that only name that can save them.

But next we read, **"Then I saw another angel** [51] **flying in the midst of heaven, having the everlasting gospel to preach to those**

---

51   The Greek word here translated **"another"** is ειδον, *eidon* in our alphabet. This is a first person form of the Greek word ειδω, *eido* in our alphabet, word number 1492 in Strong's Greek Dictionary, which translates literally as **"another."**. But as the last time any angel of God had been mentioned was six chapters back in Revelation 8:13, and as *eido* can also be translated as "an," It seems to me that here, this Greek word should be translated as "an," making the passage read, "I saw an angel flying in the midst of heaven, having the everlasting gospel." For, although, this was indeed **"another angel,"** in the sense that he was different from any angel that had previously been mentioned, he is unquestionably the first in a group of three angels. For immediately after this passage, we come to a statement in which the Greek word used should unquestionably be translated as **"another"** (angel) for this one is the second angel in the series, and the next

who dwell on the earth--to every nation, tribe, tongue, and people--saying with a loud voice, 'Fear God and give glory to Him, for the hour of His judgment has come; and worship Him who made heaven and earth, the sea and springs of water.' "** (Revelation 14:6-7)

The Bible speaks of various gospels. **"The gospel of the kingdom of God"** is **"The time is fulfilled, and the kingdom of God is at hand. Repent, and believe in the gospel."** (Mark 1:14-15) And Paul was sent to preach **"the gospel of the grace of God."** (Acts 20:24) Which seems to be the same as **"the gospel of Christ"** and **"the gospel of God"** we read about in numerous passages. But **"the everlasting gospel"** is neither **"the gospel of the grace of God"** nor **"The gospel of the kingdom of God."** Instead, **"the everlasting gospel"** is **"Fear God and give glory to Him."** This is called **"the everlasting gospel"** because it has always applied, and always will apply.

"The gospel of the kingdom of God" could only be preached when **"the time"** was **"fulfilled,"** and **"the kingdom of God"** was **"at hand."** And **"the gospel of the grace of God"** could not be preached before Calvary, and will no longer apply when the current "day of grace" is over. But **"the everlasting gospel"** can be preached at any time, in any place, under any condition. For it is **"fear God and give glory to Him... and worship Him who made heaven and earth, the sea and springs of water."** And the reason this will be preached at that time will be because **"the hour of His judgment has come."**

"And another angel followed, saying, 'Babylon is fallen, is fallen, that great city, because she has made all nations drink of the wine of the wrath of her fornication.' " (Revelation 14:8) We will leave a discussion of the meaning of the typical name **"Babylon"** until we get to chapter 17, where its meaning is explicitly stated.

Finally, the united voices of the three angels in this chapter have closely related messages. First, is the everlasting gospel, which is

---

angel mentioned is called **"a third angel."**

My suggestion of this change in the translation of verse 6, but not of verse 8, is based entirely on the construction of the overall passage, not because the Greek word used the second time is different, For the second time the Greek word was αλλος, *allos* in our alphabet, word number 243 in Strong's Greek Dictionary. And this Greek word also translates literally as **"another,"**

"Fear God and give glory to Him." This is followed by the announcement that **"Babylon is fallen,"** and then a clear warning of the wrath of God against **"anyone"** who **"worships the beast."**

> "Then a third angel followed them, saying with a loud voice, 'If anyone worships the beast and his image, and receives *his* mark on his forehead or on his hand, he himself shall also drink of the wine of the wrath of God, which is poured out full strength into the cup of His indignation. He shall be tormented with fire and brimstone in the presence of the holy angels and in the presence of the Lamb. And the smoke of their torment ascends forever and ever; and they have no rest day or night, who worship the beast and his image, and whoever receives the mark of his name.' " (Revelation 14:9-11)

Many seem to think that simply taking the tattoo necessary to use this proposed new monetary system will automatically condemn a person to hell. But that is not what this says. The God who shed His own blood to save us, would not automatically condemn a person to hell for merely accepting a credit card. And this warning was not simply about receiving the mark. What it says is, **"If anyone worships the beast and his image, and receives *his* mark on his forehead or on his hand."** So we see that receiving the mark will involve some kind of a blasphemous recognition of the beast's claim to be God. And without such blasphemy, the mark will be unavailable.

But then there is a parenthetical note. **"Here is the patience of the saints; here *are* those who keep the commandments of God and the faith of Jesus. Then I heard a voice from heaven saying to me, "Write: 'Blessed *are* the dead who die in the Lord from now on.' 'Yes,' says the Spirit, 'that they may rest from their labors, and their works follow them.' "** (Revelation 14:12-13) So, while the Spirit of God warns of the dreadful punishment of **"anyone"** who **"worships the beast,"** He also promises a great reward to all who remain faithful, and refuse to take part in this blasphemy, even at the cost of their lives. This promise was not even given to the **"one hundred and forty-four thousand"** on **"Mount Zion."**

And then we find one final symbolic vision in this chapter. "Then I looked, and behold, a white cloud, and on the cloud sat *One* like the Son of Man, having on His head a golden crown, and in His hand a sharp sickle. And another angel came out of the temple, crying with a loud voice to Him who sat on the cloud, 'Thrust in Your sickle and reap, for the time has come for You to reap, for the harvest of the earth is ripe.' So He who sat on the cloud thrust in His sickle on the earth, and the earth was reaped.

"Then another angel came out of the temple which is in heaven, he also having a sharp sickle. And another angel came out from the altar, who had power over fire, and he cried with a loud cry to him who had the sharp sickle, saying, 'Thrust in your sharp sickle and gather the clusters of the vine of the earth, for her grapes are fully ripe.' So the angel thrust his sickle into the earth and gathered the vine of the earth, and threw *it* into the great winepress of the wrath of God. And the winepress was trampled outside the city, and blood came out of the winepress, up to the horses' bridles, for one thousand six hundred furlongs." (Revelation 14:14-20)

As the result of trampling the winepress is that **"blood came out of the winepress,"** the meaning of this symbol is obvious. And this is made even more obvious by the extreme nature of the bloodshed. For the **"blood came out" "up to the horses' bridles, for one thousand six hundred furlongs."** [52] This symbol apparently represents the great battle of Armageddon.

This same symbolism had been used in a previous prophecy:

> **For there I will sit to judge all the surrounding nations.**
> **Put in the sickle, for the harvest is ripe.**
> **Come, go down;**
> **For the winepress is full,**
> **The vats overflow--**

---

52 The Greek word here translated **"furlongs"** was σταδιων, *stadion* in our alphabet. (word number 4712 in Strong's Greek Dictionary) This was 600 Greek feet, which are thought to equal 607 of our feet. So 1600 *stadion* would be (607 x 1600 = 971,200 feet) / 5280 ft/mile = 184 miles. So this passage describes a stream of blood about four feet deep, flowing out of the winepress for a distance of 184 miles.

> For their wickedness *is* great.'
> Multitudes, multitudes in the valley of decision!
> For the day of the LORD *is* near
> in the valley of decision." (Joel 3:11-14)

Joel 2:20 informs us that this will be God's punishment on **"the northern army,"** and in Joel 3:17 the result will be that:

> "Then Jerusalem shall be holy,
> And no aliens shall ever pass through her again."

This has to speak of a time that is still in the future, for aliens have continued to pass through Jerusalem throughout the thousands of years since this was written. But the battle represented in Revelation 14:17-20 appears to be even bigger than the battle in Joel 3:11-14, which is why I conclude it represents Armageddon

# Revelation 15

This chapter is an introduction to the following ones.

> "Then I saw another sign in heaven, great and marvelous: seven angels having the seven last plagues, for in them the wrath of God is complete." (Revelation 15:1)

But before these **"seven last plagues"** are introduced, there is another parenthesis:

> "And I saw *something* like a sea of glass mingled with fire, and those who have the victory over the beast, over his image and over his mark *and* over the number of his name, standing on the sea of glass, having harps of God. They sing the song of Moses, the servant of God, and the song of the Lamb, saying:
> 'Great and marvelous *are* Your works,
> Lord God Almighty!
> Just and true *are* Your ways,
> O King of the saints!
> Who shall not fear You, O Lord, and glorify Your name?
> For *You* alone *are* holy.
> For all nations shall come and worship before You,
> For Your judgments have been manifested.'"
> (Revelation 15:2-4)

The fact that these have died is shown by the fact that they are in heaven. But who are they? **"Those who have the victory over the beast, over his image and over his mark *and* over the number of his name."** These, having **"the victory over the beast,"** have been killed, as we saw in chapter 12, **"they did not love their lives to the death."** (Revelation 12:11)

So this vision reveals the persecution of these that have resisted **"the mark of he beast."** But that is not all it reveals. They sing that **"Your judgments have been manifested."** The fact that they have been killed, and are now in heaven, manifests the righteousness of the judgments that are about to fall. As we read in 2 Thessalonians 1:4-6, where, in speaking of **"all your persecutions and tribulations that you endure,"** the Holy Spirit said,**"*which is* manifest evidence of the righteous judgment of God, that you may be counted worthy of the kingdom of God, for which you also suffer; since *it is* a righteous thing with God to repay with tribulation those who trouble you."**

And after this parenthesis, whose purpose is to demonstrate the righteousness of the judgments which are coming, it says:

"After these things I looked, and behold, the temple of the tabernacle of the testimony in heaven was opened. And out of the temple came the seven angels having the seven plagues, clothed in pure bright linen, and having their chests girded with golden bands. Then one of the four living creatures gave to the seven angels seven golden bowls full of the wrath of God who lives forever and ever. The temple was filled with smoke from the glory of God and from His power, and no one was able to enter the temple till the seven plagues of the seven angels were completed." (Revelation 15:5-8)

Here we see the temple being called by a different name, **"the temple of the tabernacle of the testimony in heaven."** Earlier, in chapter 11, we read about **"the temple of God,"** which was **"in heaven,"** and in chapter 14 of **"the temple which is in heaven."** But here it is called **"the temple of the tabernacle of the testimony in heaven."**

And **"Seven angels"** come out of the temple. These **"seven angels"** have **"the seven last plagues."** We need to notice the details given about these angels. First, they are **"clothed in pure bright linen."** We are explicitly told that **"fine linen"** **"is,"** that is, represents,

"the righteous acts of the saints." (Revelation 19:8) But they also have **"their chests girded with golden bands."** Throughout scripture, gold seems to speak of the righteousness of God. Their chests, that is, their hearts, are restrained by the righteousness of God.

We are repeatedly told of the love of God, and many imagine that a loving God would never punish harshly. But our God is not only a loving God, but also a righteous one. And here, righteousness required His love to be restrained.

But **"Then one of the four living creatures gave to the seven angels seven golden bowls full of the wrath of God who lives forever and ever."** **"The four living creatures"** is a reference back to chapter 4, where these **"four living creatures"** were seen, not only **"around the throne,"** but **"in the midst of the throne."** That is, it was God himself who gave the **"golden bowls"** to the angels.

But what was in the **"golden bowls?"** They were **"full of the wrath of God who lives forever and ever."** the time has come for the wrath of God to be poured out on the earth.

And **"The temple was filled with smoke from the glory of God and from His power."** We remember how, in a day long before, **"Mount Sinai *was* completely in smoke, because the LORD descended upon it in fire. Its smoke ascended like the smoke of a furnace."** (Exodus 19:18) In Exodus, the righteous Judge was about to give His law. And here, that same righteous judge is about to punish the wicked for their rebellion.

And the smoke was so intense that **"no one was able to enter the temple till the seven plagues of the seven angels were completed."** when God is sitting as judge, no one can stand before Him, for all are guilty. How wonderful that **"we have an Advocate with the Father, Jesus Christ the righteous."** (1 John 2:1) For without that all sufficient advocate, we could have no hope. **"For our God is a consuming fire."** (Hebrews 12:29)

Revelation 16

And now the dreadful command comes. **"Then I heard a loud voice from the temple saying to the seven angels, 'Go and pour out the bowls of the wrath of God on the earth.' "** (Revelation 16:1) And even as the **"seven bowls"** had been given to **"the seven angels"** by God himself, the **"loud voice"** comes **"from the temple."** That is, the command is given by God himself. And the judgment begins.

"So the first went and poured out his bowl upon the earth, and a foul and loathsome sore came upon the men who had the mark of the beast and those who worshiped his image." (Revelation 16:2)

Here we see a detail that reveals the meaning of several terms often used in Bible prophecy. The angels were told to **"pour out the bowls of the wrath of God on the earth."** And when **"the first went and poured out his bowl upon the earth," "a foul and loathsome sore came upon"** a particular group of men. It **"came upon the men who had the mark of the beast and those who worshiped his image."** So the prophetic term **"the earth"** is associated with the kingdom of **"the beast."** And we will see this distinguished from the term **"the sea"** when the next angel pours out his bowl.

But what of the **"foul and loathsome sore"**? We saw a similar judgment fall upon Egypt in Exodus 9:8-11, upon the Philistines in 1 Samuel 5:6-12. and upon Israel in Isaiah 1:6. So this **"foul and loathsome sore"** is the mark of God's wrath **"upon the men who had the mark of the beast and those who worshiped his image."** They took **"the mark of the beast"** and God marks them in judgement.

"**Then the second angel poured out his bowl on the sea, and it became blood as of a dead *man*; and every living creature in the sea died.**" (Revelation 16:3) It would seem obvious that there would be very little point in God killing all the fish in the sea. This is not about the death of sea creatures, but about the part of the world that is typified by the term **"the sea."** We saw in Revelation 7 that this prophetic term represents that portion of the world that is in a state of confusion, as opposed to the kingdom of the beast, which, being stable, is called **"the earth."** And it would seem that the death of **"every living creature"** in **"the sea"** would indicate that, throughout the area called **"the sea,"** all pretense of being Christians is given up. They no longer even profess to be Christians. They have died, as far as the faith is concerned.

This is quickly followed by the third terrible judgment. **"Then the third angel poured out his bowl on the rivers and springs of water, and they became blood."** (Revelation 16:4)

In the scriptures, water speaks of the word of God. As we read in Ephesians 5:26 of **"the washing of water by the word."** So the rivers and springs of water being turned to blood would represent the normal sources of the truth of God, that is, the pulpits of the so-called "churches," beginning to spew forth deadly lies, instead of the truth of God. But we need to notice that this is not presented as something that will just happen, but rather, that it will be a punishment from God.

We remember that **"because they did not receive the love of the truth, that they might be saved... God will send them strong delusion, that they should believe the lie, that they all may be condemned who did not believe the truth but had pleasure in unrighteousness."** (2 Thessalonians 2:9-12)

And again, **"Just as they have chosen their own ways, And their soul delights in their abominations, So will I choose their delusions, And bring their fears on them; Because, when I called, no one answered, When I spoke they did not hear; But they did evil before My eyes, And chose *that* in which I do not delight."** (Isaiah 66:3-4)

In the first of these two passages, **"God will send them strong delusion, that they should believe the lie."** We need to realize that the Greek text does not read "a lie," as we find it in the KJV, but **"the lie."** [53] We need to remember that, as the definite article is optional in the Greek language, its normal use is for stress. This is not just some general kind of a lie, but a particular lie. And that is why, in the second passage quoted above He said, **"So will I choose their delusions."** So we see that, as a punishment for their willful choice to reject His truth, God will turn them over to be deceived by this delusion.

And this is unquestionably a punishment for having willfully turned away from His truth, for in Isaiah, the stated reason for this action was **"Because, when I called, no one answered, When I spoke they did not hear; But they did evil before My eyes, And chose *that* in which I do not delight."** And in 2 Thessalonians, it was **"because they did not receive the love of the truth, that they might be saved."**

It does not say that what they had refused was simply **"the truth,"** but **"the love of the truth."** That is, because they had rejected any desire for the truth. So, as a punishment for *that* decision, He will turn them over to **"believe the lie."** He will **"choose their delusions."** And why? **"that they all may be condemned who did not believe the truth but had pleasure in unrighteousness."**

As this *seems* unfair to those who only know the ways of God in a superficial way, the righteousness of this punishment is very strongly declared:

"And I heard the angel of the waters saying:
'You are righteous, O Lord,
The One who is and who was and who is to be,
Because You have judged these things.
For they have shed the blood of saints and prophets,
And You have given them blood to drink.
For it is their just due.'

---

53   The Greek words here are τω φευδει, *te pseudei* in our alphabet, The Greek word "te" is a form of their word "ho," which means **"the."** And the word "pseudei" is a form of their word *pseudos*, word number 5579 in Strong's Greek Dictionary, which is the source of our English prefix "pseudo," which means "false." So the correct translation of these two Greek words is unquestionably **"the lie."**

> And I heard another from the altar saying, 'Even so, Lord God Almighty, true and righteous *are* Your judgments.' "(Revelation 16:5-7)

But the sore judgments are not over yet.

> "Then the fourth angel poured out his bowl on the sun, and power was given to him to scorch men with fire. And men were scorched with great heat, and they blasphemed the name of God who has power over these plagues; and they did not repent and give Him glory." (Revelation 16:8-9)

And **"Then the fifth angel poured out his bowl on the throne of the beast, and his kingdom became full of darkness; and they gnawed their tongues because of the pain. They blasphemed the God of heaven because of their pains and their sores, and they blasphemed the name of God who has power over these plagues; and they did not repent and give Him glory."** (Revelation 16:10-11)

As these judgments are similar, we will discuss them together. We first need to realize that these prophecies, being symbolic, do not speak of the physical sun first becoming very hot and then going out. In Bible prophecy, the sun speaks of the ultimate earthly power. So the heat of the sun scorching them **"with fire"** speaks of the ultimate earthly power, that is, the authority of **"the beast,"** becoming oppressive.

In our own recent history, we have repeatedly observed this happening. In nation after nation, a new ruler has come in, and the people have welcomed him as a deliverer. Yet before long, they have realized that their imagined deliverer was far more oppressive than the previous one. But by the time they have realized that, it has been too late to do anything about it. In similar fashion, the rule of **"the beast"** will become oppressive. But by the time that happens he will already be in full control, and by the time the people realize that, it will be too late to resist. So instead, they will blaspheme God for allowing it to happen.

Likewise, the **"kingdom"** of **"the beast"** being filled with **"darkness"** does not mean that the physical sun will go out, but rather, that there will be a total lack of understanding. The scriptures say **"whatever makes manifest is light,"** (Ephesians 5:13) so they have no comprehension of the cause of their pain. But **"they blasphemed the God of heaven because of their pains and their sores."**

But then we are given one more detail which is worded exactly the same in each case, and is why we are treating these two judgments as one. Speaking of **"God"** in both cases, it says, **"they did not repent and give Him glory."**

In Jeremiah 18:7-10, the Lord said, **"The instant I speak concerning a nation and concerning a kingdom, to pluck up, to pull down, and to destroy it, if that nation against whom I have spoken turns from its evil, I will relent of the disaster that I thought to bring upon it. And the instant I speak concerning a nation and concerning a kingdom, to build and to plant** *it***, if it does evil in My sight so that it does not obey My voice, then I will relent concerning the good with which I said I would benefit it."**

On the basis of this scripture, many have imagined that Bible prophecy is always conditional, that the prophesied judgments will only fall if people do not repent. And the prophesied blessings will only come if the people continue to serve God. But that is an error. For here we are specifically told that these people will not repent. So these judgments will definitely fall upon them. [54] For we remember that, in our previous comments on the third bowl judgment, (Revelation 16:4) we discussed the fact that, as a punishment for their previous rejection of His admonitions, God will take away their understanding, leaving them incapable of repenting. This *seems* unlike our God. But we need to remember that the time for God's judgment will have come.

> **"Then the sixth angel poured out his bowl on the great river Euphrates, and its water was dried up, so that the way of the kings from the east might be prepared. And I saw three un-**

---

[54] Likewise, in Zechariah 12:10-14 we are explicitly told that **"all the families that remain"** (in Jerusalem) will repent with bitter weeping. So they will definitely receive the promised blessings.

> clean spirits like frogs *coming* out of the mouth of the dragon, out of the mouth of the beast, and out of the mouth of the false prophet. For they are spirits of demons, performing signs, *which* go out to the kings of the earth and of the whole world, to gather them to the battle of that great day of God Almighty. 'Behold, I am coming as a thief. Blessed is he who watches, and keeps his garments, lest he walk naked and they see his shame.' And they gathered them together to the place called in Hebrew, Armageddon." (Revelation 16:12-16)

Here we see three distinct things happening. But they do not just happen. They happen under the direct control of God. The **"water"** of the **"Euphrates"** river **"was dried up."** And why? **"So that the way of the kings from the east might be prepared."** That is, God himself makes provision for a way to cross this mighty barrier. Then, **"demons"** **"go out to the kings of the earth and of the whole world."** And why this? **"To gather them to the battle of that great day of God Almighty."** And finally, **"They gathered them together to the place called in Hebrew, Armageddon."**

And then God makes a side comment. **"Behold, I am coming as a thief. Blessed is he who watches, and keeps his garments, lest he walk naked and they see his shame."** So, even though He causes this to happen, God still warns men to not take part in this fateful project. For those who do so will be destroyed.

> "Then the seventh angel poured out his bowl into the air, and a loud voice came out of the temple of heaven, from the throne, saying, 'It is done!' And there were noises and thunderings and lightnings; and there was a great earthquake, such a mighty and great earthquake as had not occurred since men were on the earth. Now the great city was divided into three parts, and the cities of the nations fell. And great Babylon was remembered before God, to give her the cup of the wine of the fierceness of His wrath. Then every island fled away, and the mountains were not found. And great hail from heaven fell upon men, *each hailstone* about the weight of a talent. Men blasphemed God because of the

plague of the hail, since that plague was exceedingly great." (Revelation 16:17-22)

We remember that in Ephesians 2:2, Satan is called **"the prince of the power of the air."** So this bowl is poured out on the kingdom of Satan. And what happens? **"A loud voice came out of the temple of heaven, from the throne, saying, 'It is done!' "** It is not only a voice, but a **"loud"** voice. And where does it come from? **"Out of the temple of heaven, from the throne."** That is, God himself *loudly* declares **"It is done!"** And this awesome declaration is accompanied by the usual symbols of judgment - **"noises and thunderings and lightnings."** But not only the usual symbols, but also **"there was a great earthquake."** And this was no ordinary earthquake. Instead, **"such a mighty and great earthquake as had not occurred since men were on the earth."** That is, this would be the most mighty earthquake that has ever taken place **"since men were on the earth."**

We notice that the earthquake causes things. **"The great city was divided into three parts,"** and **"the cities of the nations fell."** We remember that, in both Greek and Hebrew, the definite article, being optional, is normally used only for stress. So when it occurs, it specifically designates something as specific or particular. So this is a reference to a particular **"great city,"** which could only be Jerusalem. So, at the time of this **"earthquake,"** Jerusalem will be divided into three parts.

But also, **"the cities of the nations"** will **"fall."** This is a generic term, simply meaning the cities of the gentiles, cities which were not part of Israel. And this term being opposed to the term **"the great city"** makes it clear that **"the great city"** is Jerusalem. How many **"cities of the nations"** will fall is not stated, but the implication is that this will extend over a wide area. For further down it says, **"Then every island fled away, and the mountains were not found."**

But in between these **"great Babylon"** is specifically noticed. This is an obvious reference to the mystic Babylon of Revelation 17, where it is clearly identified by showing a woman in verse 5, labeled "MYSTERY BABYLON," followed by the statement in verse 18 that "**the woman whom you saw is that great city which reigns over the kings of the earth.**"

We need to notice that it does not say that **"great Babylon"** fell as part of the damage of the earthquake, but rather, that, at that time, **"great Babylon was remembered before God, to give her the cup of the wine of the fierceness of His wrath."** For this great and guilty city is singled out for particular punishment, separate and distinct from the general punishments of the rest of the world.

And finally, we see one final commonly used symbol of judgment. **"And great hail from heaven fell upon men, *each hailstone* about the weight of a talent."** The **"talent"** was a measure of weight which at different times and places was somewhat different. But it seems that the most common meaning of **"a talent"** in New Testament days was the weight of water held by a standard amphora, the two handled jar so commonly found in ancient ruins. This was around 70 pounds, with various modern estimates ranging from 66 to 75 pounds. So we see that the meaning is plainly a hailstone so heavy it would totally destroy whatever it hit.

So we see that the destruction symbolized in this vision, although general and widespread, is particularly directed towards two centers of false worship, Jerusalem and Rome. For, beyond any possibility of rational debate, Rome was **"that great city"** which was reigning **"over the kings of the earth"** at the time the Revelation was given. (Revelation 17:5,18)

But, as in two of the previous bowls, instead of repenting, **"men blasphemed God because of the plague of the hail, since that plague was exceedingly great."** For God will have hardened their hearts, so much so that they will be unable to repent, **"that they all may be condemned who did not believe the truth but had pleasure in unrighteousness."** (2 Thessalonians 2:12)

REVELATION 17

Now, in chapter 17, begins a vision of this judgment of Babylon.

> **"Then one of the seven angels who had the seven bowls came and talked with me, saying to me, 'Come, I will show you the judgment of the great harlot who sits on many waters, with whom the kings of the earth committed fornication, and the inhabitants of the earth were made drunk with the wine of her fornication.'"** (Revelation 17:1-2)

In considering this, we first need to think about what a harlot is. Of course, we know that the modern word for such a person is a prostitute. That is a woman who wickedly takes the place of a wife, and who does it for gain. In the Bible, the worship of false gods was often called harlotry. We see this in 2 Chronicles 21:11-13, Jeremiah 3:9, Jeremiah 13:27, Ezekiel 16:15-41, Ezekiel 23:5-44, Hosea 1:2, Hosea 4:12-15, Hosea 5:3, and Hosea 6:10. And in like manner, those who worshiped these false gods were called harlots. We see this in Exodus 34:15-16, Leviticus 17:17, Deuteronomy 31:16, 1 Chronicles 5:25, Psalm 106:39, Jeremiah 2:21, Jeremiah 3:1-8, Ezekiel 6:9, Hosea 9:1, Micah 1:7, and Nahum 3:4. So it is clear that this label **"harlot"** represents an idolatrous system of worship. But then we read:

> "So he carried me away in the Spirit into the wilderness. And I saw a woman sitting on a scarlet beast *which was* full of names of blasphemy, having seven heads and ten horns."
> (Revelation 17:3)

So John is shown a **"woman,"** who has already been identified as an **"harlot,"** sitting on a beast which has **"seven heads and ten horns."** And now, that we have eaten the **"little book,"** we go to Daniel to learn what this **"beast"** represents.

Daniel was told:

> "The fourth beast shall be
> A fourth kingdom on earth,
> Which shall be different from all *other* kingdoms,
> And shall devour the whole earth,
> Trample it and break it in pieces.
> The ten horns *are* ten kings
> *Who* shall arise from this kingdom." (Daniel 7:23-24)

It is a simple matter of history, that the fourth kingdom to rise in the ancient world after the time of Daniel was the Roman Empire. So we realize that the beast with the ten horns represents Roman power. But now it also has seven heads. In Daniel 7, the **"little horn"** speaks **"pompous words** in verses 8, 11, and 20. And in verse 25 these **"*pompous* words"** are directed **"against the Most High."** and now, this **"beast"** in Revelation 17 is **"full of names of blasphemy."**

So, although Revelation 17 contains additional symbols, it is clear that the Holy Spirit is identifying this **"beast"** as the Roman Empire. And the **"woman"** is seen **"sitting on"** this **"beast."** All doubt about this is eliminated in the last verse of the chapter, where John was explicitly told that **"the woman whom you saw is that great city which reigns over the kings of the earth."** (Revelation 17:18) For there can be zero doubt that, at the time the Revelation was given, Rome was reigning **"over the kings of the earth."**

And we all know well of the great religious system that is seated in Rome, which teaches men to worship "the Queen of heaven" more than the Lord himself, and teaches men to pray to "saints" instead of to God himself. This idolatrous worship truly qualifies that evil system to be called an **"harlot."**

And we need to notice that this **"harlot"** was one **"with whom the kings of the earth committed fornication, and the inhabitants of the earth were made drunk with the wine of her fornication."** And we remember that the great idolatrous system which is centered in Rome has been worshiped by many earthly kings. And not only by **"the kings of the earth,"** but also by **"the inhabitants of the earth."** We remember that we saw that this term **"the inhabitants of the earth,"** is a moral class. It is those whose whole thought and being is centered in the earth, rather than in heaven. And such would also seem to be implied in the term **"the kings of the earth."** That is, that those who commit **"fornication"** with this **"harlot"** are those whose entire minds and hearts are centered on this present earth, rather than on heavenly things.

But now we need to notice the woman herself:

> "And on her forehead a name *was* written:
> MYSTERY,
> BABYLON THE GREAT,
> THE MOTHER OF HARLOTS
> AND OF THE ABOMINATIONS
> OF THE EARTH."
> (Revelation 17:5)

The fact that this is not a representation of the literal city of **"BABYLON"** is clearly signified by the word **"MYSTERY."** For a **"MYSTERY"** is something that is hidden. So if this woman actually represented the city of **"BABYLON,"** she would not be a **"MYSTERY."** We have already noticed that the last verse of this chapter tells us what she represents, saying, **"the woman whom you saw is that great city which reigns over the kings of the earth."** (Revelation 17:18) So this woman clearly represents Rome.

Yet in spite of this very clear statement of scripture, there are many that try to pretend that this **"woman"** represents Jerusalem. These deceivers point out that the Greek word translated **"earth"** in Revelation 17:18, can also be translated "land," and pretend that Jerusalem was ruling over the kings of the land. But the hard truth is that, at the time the Revelation was given, Jerusalem was not ruling over anything. Instead, she was being ruled over by Rome. It is true that the Roman government had an administrative center in the city of Jerusalem. But that governmental center was not controlled by Jerusalem, but by Rome. And we have already seen that Revelation 11:8 tells us that **"the great city"** **"where also our Lord was crucified," "spiritually is called Sodom and Egypt."** So there is no excuse for even trying to pretend that this **"woman"** represents the city of Jerusalem.

Then we read, **"I saw the woman, drunk with the blood of the saints and with the blood of the martyrs of Jesus. And when I saw her, I marveled with great amazement."** (Revelation 17:6) These same deceivers correctly point out that Jerusalem martyred many of the saints of God. But the number of those so wickedly killed by Jerusalem is dwarfed by those killed by Rome. Even in ancient times, Rome killed far more of the saints than did Jerusalem. But her sins in that respect did not end in ancient times, but were vastly multiplied in the times of the reformation.

> **"But the angel said to me, 'Why did you marvel? I will tell you the mystery of the woman and of the beast that carries her, which has the seven heads and the ten horns. The beast that you saw was, and is not, and those who dwell on the earth will marvel, whose names are not written in the Book of Life from the foundation of the world, when they see the beast that was, and is not, and yet is.'"** (Revelation 17:7-8)

So now the angel begins to explain this marvelous vision, both **"of the woman and of the beast carries her."** And we notice that the fact that the beast has **"seven heads and ten horns"** is again mentioned. But he explains that **"The beast that you saw was, and is not, and will ascend out of the bottomless pit and go to perdition."** The first part of this prophecy appears to be projecting forward from the time it was given to a later day. For the Roman Empire indeed **"was, and is not."** But the prophecy goes on to explicitly tells us that it **"will**

ascend out of the bottomless pit and go to perdition." There are many that claim that no scripture tells us that the Roman Empire will be revived. But this scripture clearly says it.

We remember that in Daniel 2:34-35. The **"stone cut out without hands"** **"struck the image on its feet."** And the entire system of human government, consisting of four successive kingdoms, collapsed. And in Daniel 7:11, the fourth **"beast was slain"** **"because of the pompous words"** of the **"horn"** which was on the fourth beast. But when was it slain? When **"the Ancient of Days"** was seated, not as a savior, but as a judge. (Daniel 7:9-12) So we see that in both of these visions, the fourth kingdom, which was undoubtedly the Roman Empire, would continue all the way down to the end. How so, when it **"was, and is not"**? Because it **"will ascend out of the bottomless pit."** So we see that the scriptures do indeed teach us that the Roman Empire will be revived.

But it not only says that this **"beast,"** which **"was, and is not,"** **"will ascend out of the bottomless pit."** It also says that this beast **"was, and is not, and yet is."** And indeed, although the political power of Rome has been completely destroyed, it still exerts near total control over much of the world through the idolatrous system centered there.

And finally, we are told that **"those who dwell on the earth will marvel"** **"when they see the beast."** But then it defines the group it so labels. It is those **"whose names are not written in the Book of Life from the foundation of the world."** That is, this group is composed of unbelievers. The unbelievers **"will marvel"** **"when they see the beast."**

But then we are told, **"Here *is* the mind which has wisdom: The seven heads are seven mountains on which the woman sits."** (Revelation 17:9) Since ancient times, Rome has been called "the city of seven hills." This can be clearly seen in the photograph on the next page, which shows a coin minted within twenty years of the time the Revelation was given. On this coin, Rome is depicted as a woman (the goddess Roma) sitting on seven hills.

The Roma Sestertius of Vespasian

Retouched photo from "The Goddess Roma In the Art of the ·Roman Empire" by Cornelius C. Vermeule III, Cambridge (Massachusetts) and London, 1959, Plate III, figure 24. Used by permission of the Museum of Fine Arts, Boston.

Those who try to pretend that **"BABYLON THE GREAT"** represents Jerusalem pretend that Jerusalem was built on seven hills. But Josephus clearly said Jerusalem was built on two hills, not seven. [55]

So there can be no reasonable debate that Revelation 17 clearly presents **"BABYLON THE GREAT"** as a Roman power, and **"the beast that carries her, which has the seven heads and the ten horns"** as Rome itself.

But then it says, **"There are also seven kings. Five have fallen, one is, *and* the other has not yet come. And when he comes, he must continue a short time."** (Revelation 17:10) Rome was first ruled by kings, then by consuls; followed by decemvirs and then by consular tribunes. During these governments, the Roman Senate had occasionally appointed dictators in extreme emergencies. These had

---

[55] "The Jewish War", by Flavius Josephus, Book 5, chapter 4, sec. 1, from "The New Complete Works of Josephus," translated by William Whiston, revised by Paul L. Maier, Grand Rapids: Kregel, 1999, pg. 851.

always been given power for only six months or until the emergency was over. [56] But Rome's fifth form of government was different. One after another, military commanders began to violently seize dictatorial power by force of arms, as recorded by the ancient historian Appian in a book called "The Civil Wars." This continued for a period of about a hundred years, finally ending when the Senate granted absolute power to Augustus Caesar, thus establishing Rome's sixth government, the line of emperors called Caesars. This government was in power when the Revelation was given and lasted until the fall of the Roman empire. So the one which **"has not yet come"** has to be future.

So the seven heads speak, not only of the seven hills of Rome, but of its seven governments, (kings.) Five of these successive governments had already fallen at the time the Revelation was given, and the one currently in power, the Empire, was the sixth. This says that there would be one more government (king.) But when it arose, it would only **"continue for a short time."** What would happen?

"And the beast that was, and is not, is himself also the eighth, and is of the seven, and is going to perdition." (Revelation 17:11) So this tells us that a new government of Rome will arise, and only a **"short time"** later it will be replaced by **"the beast that was, and is not,"** which **"is of the seven,"** but is **"the eighth."**

In Daniel 7, as the prophet was considering the ten horns on the beast, he saw **"another horn, a little one, coming up among them, before whom three of the first horns were plucked out by the roots."** (verse 8) But after telling him the ten horns represented ten kings, Daniel's informer added that **"another shall rise after them; He shall be different from the first ones, And shall subdue three kings."** (verse 24)

Here we find three more details to help in the early identification of this king. First, we are specifically told that he will **"rise after"** the first ten kings. Second, when this king first appears, he will seem insignificant; for when this horn first appeared, it was **"a little one."** And third, **"He shall be different from the first ones."** [57] This word

---

56   "The History of Rome," by Livy, book 5, chapter 2. And "the Annals of Imperial Rome," by Tacitus, book 1, chapter 1.

57   The Chaldean word here translated *different* is שׁנה, "shena" in our alphabet. (word number 8133 in Strong's Hebrew and Chaldee Dictionary)

does not just mean that this king is not one of the first ten. It means that there is a basic difference between him and all of the rest.

But now, in Revelation 17, we are given details about how this will come to pass. **"The ten horns which you saw are ten kings who have received no kingdom as yet, but they receive authority for one hour as kings with the beast. These are of one mind, and they will give their power and authority to the beast."** (Revelation 17:12-13)

We need to realize that Daniel 7:24 very specifically says that

> "The ten horns *are* ten kings
> *Who* shall arise from this kingdom."

That prophecy did not speak of the rise of a world government. It spoke of a revival of the Roman Empire. And now this one adds the fact that these **"ten kings" "have received no kingdom as yet."** This rules out all interpretations that assume that these **"ten horns"** were some of the of the various ancient kingdoms. And then two more details about them are added. First, the **"ten kings"** represented by these **"ten horns"** will **"receive authority for one hour as kings with the beast."** And second, **"they will give their power and authority to the beast,"** because they **"are of one mind."** Since the day this was written, there has never been a time when ten kings have voluntarily united to give their power to a Roman ruler. Since this has not yet happened, we know it will happen in the future.

Since **"they will give their power and authority to the beast,"** many have imagined that this wicked ruler will come into power by peaceful means. But as Daniel was considering the horns he saw **"three of the first horns... plucked out by the roots" "before"** the **"little"** horn. (Daniel 7:8) Daniel was specifically told that the king represented by this horn **"shall subdue three kings."** (verse 24) And verse 20 says that the three **"fell"** before this one. So we see that, although the final union will indeed be voluntary, this evil ruler will most certainly not rise to power solely "by peaceful means."

But now we are told of the end of this evil union. **"These will make war with the Lamb, and the Lamb will overcome them, for**

He is Lord of lords and King of kings; and those *who are* with Him *are* called, chosen, and faithful." (Revelation 17:14) This also corresponds to what was revealed in the visions in Daniel.

In Daniel 2:34-35, **"a stone was cut out without hands, which struck the image on its feet of iron and clay, and broke them in pieces. Then the iron, the clay, the bronze, the silver, and the gold were crushed together, and became like chaff from the summer threshing floors; the wind carried them away so that no trace of them was found. And the stone that struck the image became a great mountain and filled the whole earth."**

And in Daniel 7:24-26, the king that **"shall arise after"** the **"ten kings," "Shall persecute the saints of the Most High, And shall intend to change times and law. Then *the saints* shall be given into his hand For a time and times and half a time. 'But the court shall be seated, And they shall take away his dominion, To consume and destroy *it* forever."**

But **"Then he said to me, "The waters which you saw, where the harlot sits, are peoples, multitudes, nations, and tongues. And the ten horns which you saw on the beast, these will hate the harlot, make her desolate and naked, eat her flesh and burn her with fire. For God has put it into their hearts to fulfill His purpose, to be of one mind, and to give their kingdom to the beast, until the words of God are fulfilled."** (Revelation 17:15-17)

The adherents of this wicked system have long argued that the long delay of God's judgment on her wickedness is proof that she is of God. For, they pretend, that, if she were not of God, He would have punished her long ago. But this flies in the face of numerous scriptures, such as **"Because the sentence against an evil work is not executed speedily, therefore the heart of the sons of men is fully set in them to do evil."** (Ecclesiastes 8:11) And **"But, beloved, do not forget this one thing, that with the Lord one day is as a thousand years, and a thousand years as one day. The Lord is not slack concerning *His* promise, as some count slackness, but is longsuffering toward us, not willing that any should perish but that all should come to repentance."** (2 Peter 3:8-9)

And we remember that, although it was spoken of a different prophecy, our God said, **"For the vision *is* yet for an appointed time; But at the end it will speak, and it will not lie. Though it tarries, wait for it; Because it will surely come, It will not tarry."** (Habakkuk 2:3) So the judgment on this wicked system will most certainly come.

But our God has not only told us *that* it will come, but *how* it will come. **"The ten horns,"** which we are explicitly told represent **"ten kings" "will hate the harlot, make her desolate and naked, eat her flesh and burn her with fire."** So, although she indeed, for a time, rides **"the beast,"** She will finally be destroyed by the very **"beast"** she so dominated. And why? Because these **"ten kings" "will hate the harlot."**

This hatred is already being manifested throughout the world, as the world wide hatred of this evil system becomes increasingly manifested in the daily news.

The harlot nature of this Roman system is not revealed in Daniel, but only when we come to the Revelation. We realize the reason for this when we remember that Ephesians 3:3-9 says the church was a **"mystery" "which in other ages was not made known to the sons of men."** For it seems obvious that it would have been inappropriate to reveal a false church before the true church had been revealed.

And, as we have already noticed, the last verse of this chapter explicitly identifies this idolatrous system by saying, **"And the woman whom you saw is that great city which reigns over the kings of the earth."** (Revelation 17:18) So it is unreasonable to even question the fact that the **"harlot"** of this chapter represents the idolatrous religious system centered in Rome.

REVELATION 18

After having revealed this harlot as a Roman power, the Holy Spirit now describes the wickedness of that foul system.

> "After these things I saw another angel coming down from heaven, having great authority, and the earth was illuminated with his glory. And he cried mightily with a loud voice, saying, 'Babylon the great is fallen, is fallen, and has become a dwelling place of demons, a prison for every foul spirit, and a cage for every unclean and hated bird! For all the nations have drunk of the wine of the wrath of her fornication, the kings of the earth have committed fornication with her, and the merchants of the earth have become rich through the abundance of her luxury.' " (Revelation 18:1-3)

First, we are told that **"Babylon the great"** **"is fallen."** This clearly indicates a loss of a former position. She fell from something, but what? Then we see that she **"has become a dwelling place of demons."** When we see this, we remember that, long before, God's people had been warned that **"the Spirit expressly says that in latter times some will depart from the faith, giving heed to deceiving spirits and doctrines of demons, speaking lies in hypocrisy, having their own conscience seared with a hot iron, forbidding to marry,** *and commanding* **to abstain from foods which God created to be received with thanksgiving by those who believe and know the truth."** (1 Timothy 4:1-3) So commanding to abstain from certain foods, and forbidding to marry, are explicitly identified as **"doctrines of demons."** and we know that the evil system centered in Rome forbids its leaders to marry and for a long time commanded all its adherents to abstain from certain foods at certain times.

The statement that she had become **"a dwelling place of demons"** was heightened by saying she had also become **"a prison for every foul spirit, and a cage for every unclean and hated bird."** Remember that in Ephesians 2:2, Satan is called **"the prince of the power of the air."** So **"unclean and hateful"** things that fly in the air would represent Satanic spirits, as does **"every foul spirit."** So what had once been a witness for Christ had become a foul cesspool of Satanic forces.

But then we read, **"For all the nations have drunk of the wine of the wrath of her fornication, the kings of the earth have committed fornication with her."** And indeed, there is essentially no nation which has not partaken of her idolatrous worship, and *many* **"kings of the earth"** have enthusiastically participated in her idolatry.

And finally, the Holy Spirit says, **"and the merchants of the earth have become rich through the abundance of her luxury."** And indeed the trade in "religious items" has become a very big business within that system, And the luxurious life enjoyed its leaders is well known.

But then we have what is both a command and a loving call.

"And I heard another voice from heaven saying, "Come out of her, my people, lest you share in her sins, and lest you receive of her plagues. For her sins have reached to heaven, and God has remembered her iniquities." (Revelation 18:4-5) Sadly, many people who have truly trusted in the Lord Jesus Christ as their Savior, and thus are truly His people, remain in that wicked system. Some do this from ignorance, and others from a misguided imagination that they will be able to reform it. But God did not tell them to reform it from within, but to **"come out of her."** And why did He say to **"come out of her"**? **"lest you share in her sins, and lest you receive of her plagues."**

He explained this warning, saying, **"For her sins have reached to heaven, and God has remembered her iniquities."** And then He said, **"Render to her just as she rendered to you, and repay her double according to her works; in the cup which she has mixed, mix** double for her. In the measure that she glorified herself and lived luxuriously, in the same measure give her torment and sorrow; for she says in her heart, 'I sit *as* queen, and am no widow, and will not see sorrow.' Therefore her plagues will come in one day--death and mourning and famine. And she will be utterly burned with fire, for strong is the Lord God who judges her."** (Revelation 18:6-8)

We need to notice that this evil system will be judged, not only for its open wickedness, but for the way **"she glorified herself and lived luxuriously."** It is well known how the main leaders of this evil system glorify themselves, and live lives of luxury, while their devotees grovel in poverty. And beyond that, God, who reveals **"the thoughts and intents of the heart,"** (Hebrews 4:12) says of this wicked system, that, **"she says in her heart, 'I sit *as* queen, and am no widow, and will not see sorrow.' "** But what is His answer? **"Therefore her plagues will come in one day--death and mourning and famine. And she will be utterly burned with fire."** And then He adds, **"for strong is the Lord God who judges her."** So the God of heaven reminds these mere mortals of His almighty power and irresistible might.

So the judgment against this evil system is sure and certain, even though it has been long delayed. For the Holy Spirit warned, **"be sure your sin will find you out."** (Numbers 32:23)

But here in this vision, the voice of God continued, saying, **"The kings of the earth who committed fornication and lived luxuriously with her will weep and lament for her, when they see the smoke of her burning, standing at a distance for fear of her torment, saying, 'Alas, alas, that great city Babylon, that mighty city! For in one hour your judgment has come.' "** (Revelation 18:9-10)

These evil rulers who had partaken in her idolatry and in the luxuries of her wickedness, will stand **"at a distance"** from her. And why? **"For fear of her torment."** How often it is that false friends desert people in their hour of need. So these evil rulers, who will have been delighted to partake of her luxuries, will desert her in her hour of distress. Instead, they **"will weep and lament for her, when they see the smoke of her burning."** And their cry will be, **"Alas, alas, that great city Babylon, that mighty city! For in one hour your judgment has come."**

"And the merchants of the earth will weep and mourn over her." (Revelation 18:12a) But we need to notice that they are not weeping and mourning out of love for this wicked system. Instead, the cause of their sorrow is strictly loss of income. For the cause of their mourning will be **"for no one buys their merchandise anymore:"** (Revelation 18:12b).

These wicked merchants will have become rich through trading in the luxuries of that evil system But now, that will be over. And what kind of merchandise will they have been trading? **"merchandise of gold and silver, precious stones and pearls, fine linen and purple, silk and scarlet, every kind of citron wood, every kind of object of ivory, every kind of object of most precious wood, bronze, iron, and marble; and cinnamon and incense, fragrant oil and frankincense, wine and oil, fine flour and wheat, cattle and sheep, horses and chariots, and bodies and souls of men."** (Revelation 18:12-13)

We need to notice here that this wicked system has long been known, not only for its trade in luxuries, but even for its support of slavery, to say nothing of its making merchandise of the souls of men.

Then God observes, **"The fruit that your soul longed for has gone from you, and all the things which are rich and splendid have gone from you, and you shall find them no more at all."** (Revelation 18:14) It will be all gone forever, and this will indeed be a cause for weeping and mourning.

But then God repeats, **"The merchants of these things, who became rich by her, will stand at a distance for fear of her torment, weeping and wailing, and saying, 'Alas, alas, that great city that was clothed in fine linen, purple, and scarlet, and adorned with gold and precious stones and pearls! For in one hour such great riches came to nothing.'"** (Revelation 18:15-17a) As before, caring nothing for her, but only for the loss of their incomes, they **"will stand at a distance for fear of her torment,"** and bemoan their own loss at her miserable end.

But in addition, **"Every shipmaster, all who travel by ship, sailors, and as many as trade on the sea, stood at a distance and cried out when they saw the smoke of her burning, saying, 'What *is* like this great city?' They threw dust on their heads and cried out, weeping and wailing, and saying, 'Alas, alas, that great city, in which all who had ships on the sea became rich by her wealth! For in one hour she is made desolate.' " (Revelation 18:17b-19) So the reaction of those that made profit by transporting all these luxuries, is the same as the merchants. They also **"stood at a distance,"** and mourned in similar fashion. But, like the merchants, they also stated the reason for their sorrow. And it was not love for the evil system, but rather, **"all who had ships on the sea became rich by her wealth!"**

But the reaction of heaven is completely different. For God calls them to **"Rejoice over her, O heaven, and *you* holy apostles and prophets, for God has avenged you on her!"** (Revelation 18:20) So what brings sorrow on earth brings joy in heaven.

And **"Then a mighty angel took up a stone like a great millstone and threw *it* into the sea, saying, 'Thus with violence the great city Babylon shall be thrown down, and shall not be found anymore.'** " (Revelation 18:21) So the fall of this evil system will not just happen, but it will come suddenly and with great violence, and as a direct judgment from God.

But the **"mighty angel"** continues, **"The sound of harpists, musicians, flutists, and trumpeters shall not be heard in you anymore. No craftsman of any craft shall be found in you anymore, and the sound of a millstone shall not be heard in you anymore. The light of a lamp shall not shine in you anymore, and the voice of bridegroom and bride shall not be heard in you anymore."** (Revelation 18:22-23a)

So all entertainment will cease, but not only entertainment, but crafts of every sort, and not only crafts, but even the ordinary business of life will come to an end. Even weddings will cease. Everything will stop.

And then the **"mighty angel"** recites the reasons for the severity of this awesome judgment.

> "For your merchants were the great men of the earth, for by your sorcery all the nations were deceived. And in her was found the blood of prophets and saints, and of all who were slain on the earth." (Revelation 18:23b-24)

Three reasons for the seveirety of this judgment are stated. First, **"For your merchants were the great men of the earth."** We remember that Abraham told the rich man, **"remember that in your lifetime you received your good things, and likewise Lazarus evil things; but now he is comforted and you are tormented."** (Luke 16:25) So being **"the great men of the earth"** is, itself, a reason to be punished, when it is not accompanied by righteousness.

But then, the second reason, is far greater, **"for by your sorcery all the nations were deceived."** Having deceived **"all the nations"** by **"sorcery"** was indeed a crime to be severely punished.

But then the third and greatest reason is stated. **"And in her was found the blood of prophets and saints, and of all who were slain on the earth."** We remember that long before, God had said, **"blood defiles the land, and no atonement can be made for the land, for the blood that is shed on it, except by the blood of him who shed it."** (Numbers 35:33) These were guilty of the blood **"of all who were slain on the earth."** But not only for the blood **"of all who were slain on the earth,"** but **"the blood of prophets and saints."** These had dared to touch those that had been particularly loved by the very king of the entire universe. And now, the time for vengeance had come, and He had finally poured out His wrath on that ancient and guilty system.

Revelation 19

From time to time, we see cases where we have to remember that the chapter and verse divisions we find in our Bibles are made by man, and thus are not inspired. And here we find a prime case of that. For the first five verses of Revelation 19 are heaven's response to the command in Revelation 18:20, **"Rejoice over her, O heaven, and *you* holy apostles and prophets, for God has avenged you on her!"**

Heaven's response is, **"After these things I heard a loud voice of a great multitude in heaven, saying, 'Alleluia! Salvation and glory and honor and power *belong* to the Lord our God! For true and righteous *are* His judgments, because He has judged the great harlot who corrupted the earth with her fornication; and He has avenged on her the blood of His servants *shed* by her.' Again they said, 'Alleluia! Her smoke rises up forever and ever!' And the twenty-four elders and the four living creatures fell down and worshiped God who sat on the throne, saying, 'Amen! Alleluia!' Then a voice came from the throne, saying, 'Praise our God, all you His servants and those who fear Him, both small and great!'"** (Revelation 19:1-5)

Here we notice, not only the general celebration, but the celebration of two particular things. The first was the judgment of her **"fornication."** We have already noticed that this speaks of idolatry. That is, that God has finally judged her systematic affront to His majesty by causing **"the earth"** to worship and serve **"the creature rather than the Creator."** (Romans 1:25)

And the second thing being celebrated is that **"He has avenged on her the blood of His servants *shed* by her."** This wicked system is guilty of the blood of untold thousands of the saints of God. And she will most certainly be held to account for it.

This chorus of praise ends with a passage that applies to both what had just happened and to what is about to happen. **"And I heard, as it were, the voice of a great multitude, as the sound of many waters and as the sound of mighty thunderings, saying, 'Alleluia! For the Lord God Omnipotent reigns!' "** (Revelation 19:6) This applies to both the last and the next events because when a man is preparing to get married, but someone other than His bride has been falsely claiming to be His wife, He must deal with her lies before He can proceed with his wedding. But now that God had dealt with the **"harlot,"** who was falsely claiming to be the bride of Christ, almost in the same breath with this final celebration, comes the great proclamation:

"Let us be glad and rejoice and give Him glory, for the marriage of the Lamb has come, and His wife has made herself ready." (Revelation 19:7)

The love our God has for us is so great it transcends the ability of a mere human to even comprehend it. So, in the scriptures, He compares it to each of our most loving relationships. He calls us His children, both by birth, (John 3:3,7, and 1 Peter 1:23) and by adoption. (Romans 8:15 and Ephesians 1:5) But the most loving relationship He expresses to us is when He calls us His bride. He does not just call us His wife, as here, but also His bride, in John 3:29, and in Revelation 21:9 and 17.

That is, He refers to this closest of human relationships, not only in the stability of its long term commitment, but also in the passion of its first beginnings. But in each of these comparisons, the stress is not in our delight in Him, but in His delight in us. We remember that, although it is indeed **"not by works of righteousness which we have done, but according to His mercy He saved us."** (Titus 3:5) Yet **"our great God and Savior Jesus Christ... gave Himself for us, that He might redeem us from every lawless deed and purify for Himself *His* own special people, zealous for good works."** (Titus 2:13-14) So the good works of the saints of God are His special delight, and these are what will adorn His bride at the time of her wedding. For **"And to her it was granted to be arrayed in fine linen, clean and bright, for the fine linen is the righteous acts of the saints.' "** (Revelation 19:7-8)

This is followed by a wonderful pronouncement, **"Then he said to me, 'Write: "Blessed *are* those who are called to the marriage supper of the Lamb!'"** (Revelation 19:9a)

But this brings up the question, who are **"those who are called to the marriage supper of the Lamb!"** This is obviously something different from being a part of the bride. For John the Baptist said, speaking under the leadership of the Holy Ghost, (for he was speaking as a prophet of God,) **"He who has the bride is the bridegroom; but the friend of the bridegroom, who stands and hears him, rejoices greatly because of the bridegroom's voice. Therefore this joy of mine is fulfilled."** (John 3:29) Here we notice that John was not part of the bride of Christ, but **"the friend of the bridegroom."** Yet our Lord himself said of this man, that, **"Assuredly, I say to you, among those born of women there has not risen one greater than John the Baptist; but he who is least in the kingdom of heaven is greater than he."** (Matthew 11:11)

Here, our Lord himself drew a clear distinction between those saints which had gone before and those that would come after. For He very clearly said that **"he who is least in the kingdom of heaven is greater than"** the one of whom He, in the same breath, said, **"among those born of women there has not risen one greater than John the Baptist."** This is a clear statement that **"he who is least in the kingdom of heaven."** is greater that *any* Old Testament saint. *You*, if you have truly trusted in Jesus, are greater than David, Moses, or even Abraham. For John the Baptist was at least as great as the greatest of these, but **he who is least in the kingdom of heaven is greater than he."**

This helps us to understand why John the Baptist was only **"the friend of the bridegroom,"** and not a part of **"the bride."** So he will be one of those **"blessed"** ones **"who are called to the marriage supper of the Lamb."** And this pronouncement reveals that, although there will indeed be those that enjoy a closer relationship with the Lord, every one of His saints will be exceedingly blessed in that wonderful day. For God told Abraham, who, being an Old Testament saint, is only a **"friend of tbe bridegroom,"** rather than part of **"the bride,"** yet, God told him, **"do not be afraid, Abram. I am your shield, your exceedingly great reward."** (Genesis 15:1)

And finally, the truth of all these pronouncements is stressed. **"And he said to me, "These are the true sayings of God."** (Revelation 19:9b)

There are many that wrest the numerous scriptures that teach that, in Christ, all are one, whether they be Jew or Gentile. They use this as an excuse to pretend that all the people of God, throughout all ages, are a single people. Thus, they try to blur the clear distinction between Israel and the church, which runs throughout scripture.

While many pretend it is not there, This distinction could not be more clear. The promises to Israel are all centered on eventual blessing in this earth, such as Ezekiel 36:1-10, where the **"mountains of Israel,"** along with **"the hills, the rivers, the valleys, the desolate wastes, and the cities that have been forsaken,"** (verse 4) are promised that **"I will multiply men upon you, all the house of Israel, all of it; and the cities shall be inhabited and the ruins rebuilt."** (verse 10) But the promises to the church are all centered in heaven, such as **"For we know that if our earthly house, *this* tent, is destroyed, we have a building from God, a house not made with hands, eternal in the heavens."** (2 Corinthians 5:1)

All these revelations were simply too much of an emotional strain on the prophet. So he responded inappropriately. For we read, **"And I fell at his feet to worship him. But he said to me, "See *that you do* not *do that!* I am your fellow servant, and of your brethren who have the testimony of Jesus. Worship God! For the testimony of Jesus is the spirit of prophecy'"** (Revelation 19:10) We see two things here. First, of course, that we should only worship God himself, and none other. But then we have these words that are critical to understanding the entire Bible. **"For the testimony of Jesus is the spirit of prophecy"** Some have observed that, if we do not see Jesus in a pssage of scripture, we have missed its entire spirit, regardless of how many details about it we may get right. And indeed, throughout the prophetic scriptures, we are not simply being informed about what is going to happen, but about what our Lord is going to do, either Himself directly, or by causing others to do Hs will.

"Now I saw heaven opened, and behold, a white horse. And He who sat on him *was* called Faithful and True, and in

righteousness He judges and makes war. His eyes *were* like a flame of fire, and on His head *were* many crowns. He had a name written that no one knew except Himself. He *was* clothed with a robe dipped in blood, and His name is called The Word of God." (Revelation 19:11-13)

We remember that John 1:1 says, **"The beginning was the Word, and the Word was with God, and the Word was God."** and then thirteen verses farther down it says, **"And the Word became flesh and dwelt among us, and we beheld His glory, the glory as of the only begotten of the Father, full of grace and truth."** (John 1:14) So the one whose **"name is called The Word of God"** is none other than the Lord Jesus himself.

Here, He is no longer the Savior, but the King. So He is seen riding on **"a white horse"** and crowned with **"many crowns."** But He is seen both as a Judge, with **"eyes" "like a flame of fire,"** and as a mighty Warier **"clothed with a robe dipped in blood."**

His coming as a warier is further stressed by saying, **"Now out of His mouth goes a sharp sword, that with it He should strike the nations. And He Himself will rule them with a rod of iron. He Himself treads the winepress of the fierceness and wrath of Almighty God."** (Revelation 19:15) This is the time spoken of in Psalm 45:5, where we read, **"Your arrows *are* sharp in the heart of the King's enemies."**

But not only is this Warrior Judge **"called Faithful and True,"** and **"called The Word of God."** He also now comes with another title:

"And He has on *His* robe and on His thigh a name written:
KING OF KINGS
AND LORD OF LORDS."
(Revelation 19:16)

This last label finally ends all possibility of doubt about the identity of this great Warrior Judge. He is none other than the great God of heaven, the creator of heaven and earth. The One we call **"the Lord."**

Preparations are now made for what is about to take place. **"Then I saw an angel standing in the sun; and he cried with a loud voice, saying to all the birds that fly in the midst of heaven, 'Come and gather together for the supper of the great God, that you may eat the flesh of kings, the flesh of captains, the flesh of mighty men, the flesh of horses and of those who sit on them, and the flesh of all** *people***, free and slave, both small and great.'"** (Revelation 19:17-18)

The birds having gathered, all is now ready. **"And I saw the beast, the kings of the earth, and their armies, gathered together to make war against Him who sat on the horse and against His army."** (Revelation 19:19) We saw, three chapters ago, that **"they gathered them together to the place called in Hebrew, Armageddon."** (Revelation 16:16)

There could only be one outcome to such an unequal battle. **"Then the beast was captured, and with him the false prophet who worked signs in his presence, by which he deceived those who received the mark of the beast and those who worshiped his image. These two were cast alive into the lake of fire burning with brimstone. And the rest were killed with the sword which proceeded from the mouth of Him who sat on the horse. And all the birds were filled with their flesh."** (Revelation 19:20-21)

Two men (Enoch, in Genesis 5:22-24, and Elijah, in 2 Kings 2:11-12) were so holy that they were taken to heaven without tasting death. **"The beast"** and **"the false prophet"** will be so evil that they will be **"cast alive into the lake of fire,"** only to be joined later by the devil himself. (Revelation 20:10) And their followers will be fed to the birds.

One of the least understood subjects in Bible prophecy is the various battles that will take place when the Lord comes. Most people simply assume that there will only be one great battle, and everything will be finished. But that is far from correct. The scriptures actually describe five different battles or campaigns that will be fought when He returns.

When the Lord first appears, Jerusalem will be under siege, surrounded by many nations, for we read in Zechariah 14:2, **"For I will gather all nations against Jerusalem to battle; and the city shall be taken, and the houses rifled, and the women ravished; and half** of the city shall go forth into captivity, and the residue of the people shall not be cut off from the city."

The Lord will deal with this in summary manner. **"Then the LORD will go forth And fight against those nations, As He fights in the day of battle. And in that day His feet will stand on the Mount of Olives, Which faces Jerusalem on the east. And the Mount of Olives shall be split in two, From east to west,** *Making* **a very large valley; Half of the mountain shall move toward the north And half of it toward the south."** (Zechariah 14:3-4) So the Lord's campaigns start at the Mount of Olives.

Joel 3:1-2 says these nations will not come against Jerusalem of their own accord. They will be brought there by the Lord. But this passage also tells us where He will force them as they flee.

> "For behold, in those days and at that time,
> When I bring back the captives of Judah and Jerusalem,
> I will also gather all nations,
> And bring them down to the Valley of Jehoshaphat;
> And I will enter into judgment with them there
> On account of My people, My heritage Israel,
> Whom they have scattered among the nations;
> They have also divided up My land."

He will **"enter into judgment with them"** in **"the Valley of Jehoshaphat."** We are not told the location of this valley. But In Joel 2:20 the Lord declared:

> "But I will remove far from you the northern *army*,
> And will drive him away into a barren and desolate land,
> With his face toward the eastern sea
> And his back toward the western sea;
> His stench will come up,
> And his foul odor will rise,
> Because he has done monstrous things."

This is the outcome of the first battle.

After this comes the Lord's campaign against Edom, Which is the southern part of modern Jordan and the northern part of modern Saudi Arabia. The Lord said:

> "**Therefore hear the counsel of the LORD**
> **that He has taken against Edom,**
> **And His purposes that He has proposed**
> **against the inhabitants of Teman:**
> **Surely the least of the flock shall draw them out;**
> **Surely He shall make their dwelling places**
> **desolate with them.**
> **The earth shakes at the noise of their fall;**
> **At the cry its noise is heard at the Red Sea.**
> **Behold, He shall come up and fly like the eagle,**
> **And spread His wings over Bozrah;**
> **The heart of the mighty men of Edom in that day shall be**
> **Like the heart of a woman in birth pangs."**
> (Jeremiah 49:20-22)

So this judgment begins at Bozrah, about thirty miles south of the Dead Sea. From there it goes some twenty five miles south to Teman, and from there to within hearing of the Red Sea. Habakkuk 3:3 mentions His coming from Mount Paran, which is approximately one hundred and sixty miles southeast of Teman, and is on the shore of the Red Sea. This entire area will receive the same judgment as Sodom and Gomorrah.

God returns to Jerusalem after destroying Edom. But when He returns, it is not yet in blessing. It is still in judgment, for we read in Habakkuk 3:3-6 that:

> "**God came from Teman,**
> **The Holy One from Mount Paran.**
> **Selah.**
> **His glory covered the heavens,**
> **And the earth was full of His praise.**
> *His* **brightness was like the light;**
> **He had rays** *flashing* **from His hand,**
> **And there His power** *was* **hidden.**

> Before Him went pestilence,
> And fever followed at His feet.
> He stood and measured the earth;
> He looked and startled the nations.
> And the everlasting mountains were scattered,
> The perpetual hills bowed.
> His ways *are* everlasting."

And in Malachi 3:1-3 we read,

> "'And the Lord, whom you seek,
> Will suddenly come to His temple,
> Even the Messenger of the covenant,
> In whom you delight.
> Behold, He is coming,'
> Says the LORD of hosts.
> 'But who can endure the day of His coming?
> And who can stand when He appears?
> For He *is* like a refiner's fire
> And like launderer's soap.
> He will sit as a refiner and a purifier of silver;
> He will purify the sons of Levi,
> And purge them as gold and silver,
> That they may offer to the LORD
> An offering in righteousness.'"

But we remember that the righteous had been cast out three and a half years earlier. All who are left are wicked. This coming is not deliverance, but a terror, as we read in Isaiah 66:6:

> "The sound of noise from the city!
> A voice from the temple!
> The voice of the LORD,
> Who fully repays His enemies!"

After the Lord returns to Jerusalem, the beast and the armies of the world come down to Armageddon. "**The kings of the earth and of the whole world**" assemble. This is the Lord's third battle, but their first one. Armageddon is on the edge of the plain of Megiddo, about 55 miles north of Jerusalem. Many call it the "valley of Armageddon," but it is not called that in scripture. There is a reference to the **"Valley of Megiddo"** in 2 Chronicles 35:22 and in some translations of Zechariah 12:11. But it is important to realize that the Hebrew word translated *valley* in these places is distinctly different from the Hebrew word used for the **"valley of Jehoshaphat."** [58] Thus we understand that the prophesied judgment in the **"valley of Jehoshaphat"** is not just another description of the battle of Armageddon.

Demons go out performing signs, to gather all the nations. (Revelation 16:13-14) The ten kings allied with the Beast are particularly noticed. **"The ten horns which you saw are ten kings who have received no kingdom as yet, but they receive authority for one hour as kings with the beast. These are of one mind, and they will give their power and authority to the beast. These will make war with the Lamb, and the Lamb will overcome them, for He is Lord of lords and King of kings; and those *who are* with Him *are* called, chosen, and faithful."** (Revelation 17:12-14)

> "And I saw the beast, the kings of the earth, and their armies, gathered together to make war against Him who sat on the horse and against His army. Then the beast was captured, and with him the false prophet who worked signs in his presence, by which he deceived those who received the mark of the beast and those who worshiped his image. These two were cast alive into the lake of fire burning with brimstone. And the rest were killed with the sword which proceeded from the mouth of Him who sat on the horse. And all the birds were filled with their flesh." (Revelation 19:19-21)

---

58 Megiddo is a בִּקְעָה, *biq'ah* in our alphabet. (word number 1237 in Strong's Hebrew Dictionary) This indicates a wide level valley between mountains, or a *plain*. This Hebrew word is also used for Megiddo in Zechariah 12:11, where our translation renders it as a **"plain,"** rather than a *valley*. We have already noticed that the **"valley of Jehoshaphat"** is an עֵמֶק, *'emeq* in our alphabet. (word number 6010 in Strong's Hebrew Dictionary) this means a *vale*. This plainly shows that these are different places.

The survivors from this battle will be sent to call all Israel home. "'I will gather all nations and tongues; and they shall come and see My glory. I will set a sign among them; and those among them who escape I will send to the nations: *to* Tarshish and Pul and Lud, who draw the bow, and Tubal and Javan, *to* the coastlands afar off who have not heard My fame nor seen My glory. And they shall declare My glory among the Gentiles. Then they shall bring all your brethren for an offering to the LORD out of all nations, on horses and in chariots and in litters, on mules and on camels, to My holy mountain Jerusalem,' says the LORD, 'as the children of Israel bring an offering in a clean vessel into the house of the LORD.'"** (Isaiah 66:18-20)

But the Lord has come to judge the nations, and His work is not yet finished. The nations that have hated Israel must now be punished. So, after He has gathered Israel back to their land, the Lord, in His justice, decrees that the punishment of these nations must be dispensed by the very ones they have so long tried to destroy. So He commands Israel to destroy them. The justice of this is pointed out in Habakkuk 2:8; **"Because you have plundered many nations, All the remnant of the people shall plunder you, Because of men's blood And the violence of the land *and* the city, And of all who dwell in it."** We see this again in Isaiah 49:26. **"I will feed those who oppress you with their own flesh, And they shall be drunk with their own blood as with sweet wine. All flesh shall know That I, the LORD, *am* your Savior, And your Redeemer, the Mighty One of Jacob."** Again, in Isaiah 51:22-23, the Lord says, **"See, I have taken out of your hand The cup of trembling, The dregs of the cup of My fury; You shall no longer drink it. But I will put it into the hand of those who afflict you, Who have said to you, 'Lie down, that we may walk over you.' And you have laid your body like the ground, And as the street, for those who walk over."**

In keeping with this decree, the Lord gives Israel a most awesome charge: **"Cursed *is* he who does the work of the LORD deceitfully, And cursed *is* he who keeps back his sword from blood."** (Jeremiah 48:10) This may seem unlike the gracious God we know, but we must remember that the present age of grace will be ended, and it will now be **"the Day of the LORD."** As we read in Psalm 110:6,

"The Lord *is* at Your right hand; He shall execute kings in the day of His wrath. He shall judge among the nations, He shall fill *the places* with dead bodies, He shall execute the heads of many countries."

This is the fourth battle or campaign of the Lord. But the nations will still not be completely subdued. One final battle must take place. Gog will come down after the Lord has brought Israel **"back from the sword,"** after they have been **"brought out of the nations."** (Ezekiel 38:8) Gog's thought will only be evil, but it will be the Lord Himself who brings him down. Why? **"So that the nations may know Me, when I am hallowed in you, O Gog, before their eyes."** (verse 16)

The millennium will be about to begin. It will be time to put an end to all thought of rebellion. To do this, the Lord will need one final display of His power. So He says **"Thus I will magnify Myself and sanctify Myself, and I will be known in the eyes of many nations. Then they shall know that I *am* the LORD."** (Ezekiel 38:23) Gog will provide the occasion, but **"all the nations shall see My judgment which I have executed, and My hand which I have laid on them."** (Ezekiel 39:21)

The Lord will strike down this rebellion in an awesome display of power. **"'Surely in that day there shall be a great earthquake in the land of Israel, so that the fish of the sea, the birds of the heavens, the beasts of the field, all creeping things that creep on the earth, and all men who *are* on the face of the earth shall shake at My presence. The mountains shall be thrown down, the steep places shall fall, and every wall shall fall to the ground. I will call for a sword against Gog throughout all My mountains,' says the Lord GOD. 'Every man's sword will be against his brother. And I will bring him to judgment with pestilence and bloodshed; I will rain down on him, on his troops, and on the many peoples who *are* with him, flooding rain, great hailstones, fire, and brimstone.'"** (Ezekiel 38:18-22)

Many Imagine that this battle will take place before the tribulation, but five different details of this prophecy clearly show that it will take place after the tribulation, and before the millennium. The most significant of these is Ezekiel 39:22, where the Lord says, that **"the house of Israel shall know that I *am* the LORD their God from that day forward"** This fixes the date as after the seven years of tribulation and before the millennium. That is because during the tribulation, Judah (which is all of **"the house of Israel"** that will be in the land at that time) will be worshiping the antichrist. But during the millennium, "**No more shall every man teach his neighbor, and every man his brother, saying, 'Know the Lord,' for they all shall know Me, from the least of them to the greatest of them.**" (Jeremiah 31:34) So Ezekiel 39:22 places the time of Gog's defeat at the time of this change.

Revelation 20

This chapter is the only place in the entire Bible where we are told that the future kingdom on this earth will last **"a thousand years."** But is the thousand year duration stated for this future kingdom intended to be taken literally? There are many that, failing to realize that how long this future earthly kingdom will last is only a detail, argue long and loud that scripture consistently uses the term **"a thousand years"** as a metaphor for "a very long time." And indeed, this is unquestionably correct. For, outside of Revelation 20, every place where the Bible uses the term **"a thousand years,"** it is very obviously using that term metaphorically to simply mean "a very long time."

We find this term used in this way in Psalm 90:4, Ecclesiastes 6:6, and twice in 2 Peter 3:8. So there can be zero question that the term **"a thousand years,"** as used in verses 2, 4, and 6 of this chapter, is not necessarily literal.

But the term **"the thousand years"** is distinctly different. This term, which the Bible uses only in verses 3, 5, and 7 of Revelation 20, is very specific. And in each of these verses, the word "the" is distinctly present in the Greek text.[59]

---

[59] The Greek word used in all three of these cases is τα, *ta* in our alphabet. This is the nominative plural neuter form of the Geek word ὁ, *ho* in our alphabet. (word number 3588 in Strong's Greek Dictionary) As this is the Greek definite article, it indeed translates literally as our English word "the."All three of these verses distinctly use the Greek phrase τα χιλια ετη, *ta chilia ete* in our alphabet. This translates literally as **"the thousand years."**

Why is this significant? Because the definite article is optional in Greek, as it is in Hebrew. So omitting it has no significance. But not so with including it. In Biblical Greek (and Hebrew,) when the definite article is explicitly stated, it is normally done for stress. That is, to stress the fact that it is referring to something specific. Not just *something*, but a particular thing. So the term **"the thousand years"** means a specific period of a thousand years. In Genesis 31:22, the prophet Joseph told Pharaoh that **"the dream was repeated to Pharaoh twice because the thing is established by God, and God will shortly bring it to pass."** But this passage first uses the term **"a thousand years,"** and then the term **"the thousand years,"** and then repeats this pattern twice more for a total of three times. If saying somethng twice means it is established by God, what does saying it three times mean? This is stressing that this is not just a long period of time, but a particular period of time, one which will last **"a thousand years."**

But as we noted earlier, the duration of this kingdom is only a detail. Even if these people were correct in claiming that the **"thousand years"** is only a metaphor for "a very long time," that would make no difference in the proper interpretation of this scripture. For many of the prophecies in the Bible explicitly state that when the Lord returns, He will establish a physical kingdom on this earth.

The fact that this kingdom will be physical, and not merely spiritual, is seen in the many scriptures that explicitly say that the ancient nation of Israel will be brought back to their ancient homeland, and will again be united there as a single nation, with a king. Some of these are:

> **"It shall come to pass in that day**
> **That the Lord shall set His hand again the second time**
> **To recover the remnant of His people who are left,**
> **From Assyria and Egypt,**
> **From Pathros and Cush,**
> **From Elam and Shinar,**
> **From Hamath and the islands of the sea.**
> **He will set up a banner for the nations,**
> **And will assemble the outcasts of Israel,**
> **And gather together the dispersed of Judah**
> **From the four corners of the earth.**

> Also the envy of Ephraim shall depart,
> And the adversaries of Judah shall be cut off;
> Ephraim shall not envy Judah,
> And Judah shall not harass Ephraim.
> But they shall fly down upon the shoulder
> of the Philistines toward the west;
> Together they shall plunder the people of the East;
> They shall lay their hand on Edom and Moab;
> And the people of Ammon shall obey them."
> (Isaiah 11:11-14)

And, "But you, O mountains of Israel, you shall shoot forth your branches and yield your fruit to My people Israel, for they are about to come. For indeed I am for you, and I will turn to you, and you shall be tilled and sown. I will multiply men upon you, all the house of Israel, all of it; and the cities shall be inhabited and the ruins rebuilt. I will multiply upon you man and beast; and they shall increase and bear young; I will make you inhabited as in former times, and do better for you than at your beginnings. Then you shall know that I am the LORD. Yes, I will cause men to walk on you, My people Israel; they shall take possession of you, and you shall be their inheritance" (Ezekiel 36:8-12)

And the fact that this restored Israel will be the center of a future earthly kingdom is seen in such scriptures as:

"And it shall come to pass *that* everyone who is left of all the nations which came against Jerusalem shall go up from year to year to worship the King, the LORD of hosts, and to keep the Feast of Tabernacles. And it shall be *that* whichever of the families of the earth do not come up to Jerusalem to worship the King, the LORD of hosts, on them there will be no rain. If the family of Egypt will not come up and enter in, they *shall have* no *rain;* they shall receive the plague with which the LORD strikes the nations who do not come up to keep the Feast of Tabernacles. This shall be the punishment of Egypt and the punishment of all the nations that do not come up to keep the Feast of Tabernacles." (Zechariah 14:16-19)

And,

> "Thus says the Lord GOD:
> 'Behold, I will lift My hand in an oath to the nations,
> And set up My standard for the peoples;
> They shall bring your sons in *their* arms,
> And your daughters shall be carried on *their* shoulders;
> Kings shall be your foster fathers,
> And their queens your nursing mothers;
> They shall bow down to you with *their* faces to the earth,
> And lick up the dust of your feet.
> Then you will know that I *am* the LORD,
> For they shall not be ashamed who wait for Me.' "
> (Isaiah 49:22-23)

But now, returning to the text of Revelation 20, and remembering that the end of the previous chapter had been the great battle in which **"the beast"** and **"the false prophet"** were taken and cast into **"the lake of fire,"** the very next words are:

"Then I saw an angel coming down from heaven, having the key to the bottomless pit and a great chain in his hand. He laid hold of the dragon, that serpent of old, who is *the* Devil and Satan, and bound him for a thousand years; and he cast him into the bottomless pit, and shut him up, and set a seal on him, so that he should deceive the nations no more till the thousand years were finished. But after these things he must be released for a little while." (Revelation 20:1-3)

It is remarkable that some try to pretend that **"Satan"** is currently **"bound,"** and unable to **"deceive the nations."**

For this is contrary to explicitly stated scripture. We are told that **"your adversary the devil walks about like a roaring lion, seeking whom he may devour."** (1 Peter 5:8)

And the effects of this future binding are seen in such scriptures as:

"No more shall every man teach his neighbor, and every man his brother, saying, 'Know the LORD,' for they all shall know Me, from the least of them to the greatest of them, says the LORD. For I will forgive their iniquity, and their sin I will remember no more." (Jeremiah 31:34)

And, "For the earth shall be full of the knowledge of the LORD As the waters cover the sea." (Isaiah 11:9b)

So it is very plain that the binding of Satan in that day will have an effect that is radically different from anything that exists in the present age.

Next, we read, **"And I saw thrones, and they sat on them, and judgment was committed to them. Then *I saw* the souls of those who had been beheaded for their witness to Jesus and for the word of God, who had not worshiped the beast or his image, and had not received *his* mark on their foreheads or on their hands. And they lived and reigned with Christ for a thousand years."** (Revelation 20:4)

This passage parallels several that we previously noticed in the book of Daniel. We see this first in Daniel 2:44, where we read, **"And in the days of these kings the God of heaven will set up a kingdom which shall never be destroyed; and the kingdom shall not be left to other people; it shall break in pieces and consume all these kingdoms, and it shall stand forever."**

Then we see it in Daniel 7, where Daniel said,

> "I was watching in the night visions,
> And behold, *One* like the Son of Man,
> Coming with the clouds of heaven!
> He came to the Ancient of Days,
> And they brought Him near before Him.
> Then to Him was given dominion and glory and a kingdom,
> That all peoples, nations, and languages should serve Him.
> His dominion *is* an everlasting dominion,
> Which shall not pass away, And His kingdom *the one*
> Which shall not be destroyed." (Daniel 7:13-14)

Then, in the interpretation of the vision, Daniel was told both, **"But the saints of the Most High shall receive the kingdom, and possess the kingdom forever, even forever and ever,"** (Daniel 7:18) and, **"the Ancient of Days came, and a judgment was made *in favor* of the saints of the Most High, and the time came for the saints to possess the kingdom."** (Daniel 7:22)

But this is not only found in Daniel, for David was told:

> **"Once I have sworn by My holiness;**
> **I will not lie to David:**
> **His seed shall endure forever,**
> **And his throne as the sun before Me;**
> **It shall be established forever like the moon,**
> **Even *like* the faithful witness in the sky."** (Psalm 89:35-37)

Again, as we just noticed, Isaiah 32:1 says, **"Behold, a king will reign in righteousness, And princes will rule with justice."**

Isaiah is also quoted in Romans.

> **"And again, Isaiah says: *"There shall be a root of Jesse;***
> ***And He who shall rise to reign over the Gentiles,***
> ***In Him the Gentiles shall hope."*** (Romans 15:12)

Due to translation differences, this reads differently in our version of Isaiah 11:10, from which this is quoted.

Many of the prophecies in the Psalms and Isaiah could be interpreted to speak of a "spiritual" reign. But not so what the Lord said through Jeremiah:

"And the word of the LORD came to Jeremiah, saying, 'Thus says the LORD: 'If you can break My covenant with the day and My covenant with the night, so that there will not be day and night in their season, then My covenant may also be broken with David My servant, so that he shall not have a son to reign on his throne, and with the Levites, the priests, My ministers. As the host of heaven cannot be numbered, nor the sand of the sea measured, so will I

multiply the descendants of David My servant and the Levites who minister to Me.'"** (Jeremiah 33:19-22)

While the term **"the descendants of David"** *could* be rationally interpreted to refer to Christ, not so the term **"and the Levites."** This cannot be rationally interpreted to mean anything other than what it so explicitly says.

And when the angel was sent to Mary, he was very specific in telling her, **"And He will reign over the house of Jacob forever, and of His kingdom there will be no end."** (Luke 1:33) While the name "Israel" can, in some places, be rationally interpreted to mean **"the church,"** not so the name **"Jacob." "The house of Jacob"** is not a spiritual entity, but a physical group.

In Romans 5:17, the Holy Spirit said, **"For if by the one man's offense death reigned through the one, much more those who receive abundance of grace and of the gift of righteousness will reign in life through the One, Jesus Christ."** This says we **"will reign in life."** But we most certainly are not reigning in *this* life.

In the same way, Titus 2:12 says, **"If we endure, We shall also reign with *Him*."**

And in Revelation 5, the glorified saints sing:

> "You are worthy to take the scroll,
> And to open its seals;
> For You were slain,
> And have redeemed us to God by Your blood
> Out of every tribe and tongue and people and nation,
> And have made us kings and priests to our God;
> And we shall reign on the earth." (Revelation 5:9-10)

We need to notice that this last passage explicitly says **"we shall reign on the earth."**

As we have progressed through these first few verses of Revelation 20, we have examined so many other scriptures to plainly see two things. First, that there will be a physical kingdom established **"on the earth."** And second, that this kingdom is not just a side detail of Bible prophecy, but is a major theme that runs throughout the prophetic scriptures.

But now we come to a very important statement. **"But the rest of the dead did not live again until the thousand years were finished. This *is* the first resurrection."** (Revelation 20:5)

We had just been told, in verse 4, of **"those that had been beheaded,"** that **"they lived and reigned with Christ for a thousand years."** Now we are very explicitly told, **"But the rest of the dead did not live again until the thousand years were finished."** This could not be more explicitly stated. This is a clear statement of two resurrections, which will take place at different times, with a thousand years between them.

Many imagine that the words **"this is the first resurrection"** disprove the doctrine of the pre-tribulation rapture. But in this, they are ignoring the context of this statement. This is said in contrast to the resurrection of **"the rest of the dead,"** which, we are explicitly told, will take place a thousand years later.

For next we are told, **"Blessed and holy *is* he who has part in the first resurrection. Over such the second death has no power, but they shall be priests of God and of Christ, and shall reign with Him a thousand years."** (Revelation 20:6)

Here we plainly see that those that have **"part in the first resurrection"** includes more than just **those who had been beheaded for their witness to Jesus."** For it says that they are **"Blessed and holy,"** and that **"they shall be priests of God and of Christ."** And it says, **"over such the second death has no power."** All of these details apply plainly to all the redeemed of God, to all who have truly trusted in the Lord Jesus Christ as their all sufficient and only Savior, So this clearly includes those that had been taken to be with the Lord, from all the ages, including those taken in the rapture.

These who have **"part in the first resurrection" "shall reign with Him a thousand years."** This is the same **"thousand years"** during which **"Satan"** will be **"bound,"** and **"shut up"** in **"the bottomless pit."** But after that, he **"must be released for a little while."** (Revelation 20:3) We passed over this statement when we were discussing verse 3 in favor of discussing it in connection with what comes next:

"Now when the thousand years have expired, Satan will be released from his prison and will go out to deceive the nations which are in the four corners of the earth, Gog and Magog, to gather them together to battle, whose number *is* as the sand of the sea." (Revelation 20:7-8)

Many imagine that it makes no sense to imprison Satan for **"a thousand years,"** and then release him. But that only shows that they do not understand the mind of God.

While others find this very perplexing, its purpose is obvious to a Dispensationalist. For the Millennium is the last of a series of demonstrations that God is making to prove that mankind will fail under every conceivable circumstance.

The first of these demonstrations was innocence, with man not knowing the difference between good and evil. (Genesis 3:5) But they disobeyed the only command they had been given. This ended with **"a flaming sword, which turned every way, to guard the way to the teee of life."** (Genesis 3:24)

The second demonstration was conscience, in which mankind was left up to his conscience. But **"every intent of the thoughts of his heart *was* only evil continually."** (Genesis 6:5) This ended with the great flood of Noah. (Genesis 6-8)

The third demonstration was human government, where God told mankind to avenge the blood of murder. (Genesis 9:5-7) This ended with mankind's language being confused at the tower of Babel. (Genesis 11:7)

The fourth demonstration was promise, where God called out one man, and gave him great promises for his descendants. (Genesis 12:1-2, 15:4-16, 17:4-8, 22:15-18) This ended with his descendants losing all hope in wretched slavery. (Exodus 5:20)

The fifth demonstration was law, where God gave mankind a righteous law. (Exodus 20-23) but none of them obeyed it. This ended with the only man that ever kept it hanging on a tree at Calvary. (Matthew 27:35-35)

The sixth demonstration, the one that is now running, is grace, where mankind is offered a free pardon for just believing. (John 3:16,

Acts 26:18) But we have already been told that this will end in apostasy. (2 Timothy 3:13, 2 Peter 3:3-4)

Even so, the millennium will be a seventh demonstration, a reign of righteousness so long that there is no man living who has any memory of a time when things were anything less than perfect. This will end with a test. Satan will be released from his prison, and will once again bring mankind into a state of rebellion.

The point of all this is to prove that mankind will fail under any conceivable situation. And to prove this, God chose the number of demonstrations that represents perfection, seven. That is, God is perfectly proving that man will fail under any system He might set up. And why prove this? To prove that the only solution is grace, unmerited favor, showered unconditionally on whoever chooses to believe.

Many imagine they can be saved by doing all kinds of good things, (helping others, donating to charities, etc.) but that is the opposite of what God says, in places such as:

"For by grace you have been saved through faith, and that not of yourselves; it is the gift of God, not of works, lest anyone should boast." (Ephesians 2:8-9)

And:

"For we ourselves were also once foolish, disobedient, deceived, serving various lusts and pleasures, living in malice and envy, hateful and hating one another. But when the kindness and the love of God our Savior toward man appeared, not by works of righteousness which we have done, but according to His mercy He saved us," (Titus 3:3-5a)

So our God instead says:

> "Seek the LORD while He may be found,
> Call upon Him while He is near.
> Let the wicked forsake his way,
> And the unrighteous man his thoughts;
> Let him return to the LORD,
> And He will have mercy on him;
> And to our God,

> For He will abundantly pardon.
> 'For My thoughts *are* not your thoughts,
> Nor *are* your ways My ways,' says the LORD.
> 'For *as* the heavens are higher than the earth,
> So are My ways higher than your ways,
> And My thoughts than your thoughts.' " (Isaiah 55:6-9)

So our relationship with God is based on pardon, or it does not exist at all. We can never do anything to merit this pardon, for He tells us that. **"we are all like an unclean thing, And all our righteousnesses are like filthy rags."** (Isaiah 64:6a)

Instead of good works, Our God says that **"the blood of Jesus Christ His Son cleanses us from all sin."** (1 John 1:7)

So, unless we simply seek His pardon, based solely on the blood our Lord Jesus shed at Calvary, the only thing we can expect from God is that **"anyone not found written in the Book of Life was cast into the lake of fire."** (Revelation 20:15)

But after this needful digression, we need to re-read the place in Revelation wher we were:

"Now when the thousand years have expired, Satan will be released from his prison and will go out to deceive the nations which are in the four corners of the earth, Gog and Magog, to gather them together to battle, whose number *is* as the sand of the sea." (Revelation 20:7-8)

So, even as we are explicitly told that the present age will end in apostasy, we are also explicitly told that the next one will end in open rebellion against Christ. The proof of mankind's failure will then be complete. For mankind has failed under innocence, under conscience, under human government, and under law. And it will fail under grace and under a reign of righteousness. Thus, God will have proved, with the perfect number of demonstrations, that mankind will fail under any system God might ever set up.

But what will happen in this final rebellion?

> **"They went up on the breadth of the earth and surrounded the camp of the saints and the beloved city. And fire came down from God out of heaven and devoured them. The devil, who deceived them, was cast into the lake of fire and brimstone where the beast and the false prophet *are*. And they will be tormented day and night forever and ever."** (Revelation 20:9-10)

This is unquestionably not the battle described in Ezekiel 38 and 39. Some have imagined a connection between these passages because **"Gog and Magog"** are mentioned here, as in Ezekiel 38:2. But here, it is **"Gog and Magog,"** rather than **"Gog, of the land of Magog,"** as it is stated in Ezekiel 38:2. But the difference in these attacks is far greater than just the designation of the attacker..

In Ezekiel 39, the Lord told Gog **"'You shall fall upon the mountains of Israel, you and all your troops and the peoples who *are* with you; I will give you to birds of prey of every sort and *to* the beasts of the field to be devoured. You shall fall on the open field; for I have spoken,' says the Lord GOD."** (Ezekiel 39:3-5)

So there, Gog would fall **"upon the mountains of Israel"** and **"upon the open field."** But these are only general. Specific detail is also given. **"It will come to pass in that day *that* I will give Gog a burial place there in Israel, the valley of those who pass by east of the sea; and it will obstruct travelers, because there they will bury Gog and all his multitude. Therefore they will call *it* the Valley of Hamon Gog."** (Ezekiel 39:11) So in Ezekiel 39, Gog would be buried in **"the valley of those who pass by east of the sea."** But a **"valley"** **"east of the sea"** cannot be in the area around **"the beloved city,"** which obviously means Jerusalem, as is explicitly stated in Revelation 20:9. Some translations read "east of the Dead Sea" instead of **"east of the sea."** This is based on a conclusion that the Hebrew text implies the Dead Sea, even though it does not explicitly name it. Only a few scholars have come to this conclusion. But if correct, this would only make this reason more extreme. But either way, whether this interpretation is or is not, correct, these two battles, although they both involve **"Gog and Magog,"** will definitely take place in different locations.

Also, in Ezekiel 39:22 the Lord says that **"the house of Israel shall know that I *am* the LORD their God from that day forward"** This fixes the date of that battle as after Daniel's seventieth week and before the millennium. That is because during the seventieth week they will be worshiping the antichrist. But during the millennium **"No more shall every man teach his neighbor, and every man his brother, saying, 'Know the Lord,' for they all shall know Me, from the least of them to the greatest of them."** (Jeremiah 31:34) So Ezekiel 39:22 places that battle at the time when they cease false worship and begin to truly worship the Lord. That is, at the beginning of the millennium. But the date of the battle in Revelation 20 is **"when the thousand years have expired,"** that is, after the millennium for that is explicitly stated in Revelation 20:7.

Nor can this be the famous "battle of Armageddon." For Armageddon is on the edge of the plain of Megiddo, about 55 miles north of Jerusalem. And this attacking army will surround Jerusalem, **"the beloved city."** (Revelation 20:9) So this will happen in a different place than Armageddon.

At the time of this battle, there will be nothing more to prove, no one to convince. So there is no word here of great signs like those at the battles before the millennium, such as the **"great earthquake in the land of Israel,"** as in Ezekiel 38:19, nor **"pestilence," "flooding rain, great hailstones, fire, and brimstone,"** as in Ezekiel 38:22, Nor do we read of **"rays *flashing* from His hand,"** or **"before Him went pestilence, And fever followed at His feet,"** as we read in Habakkuk 3:4-5. Instead of all this awesomeness, we simply read that **"fire came down from God out of heaven and devoured them."** (Revelation 20:9b) So, instead of making a big show of it, God will simply destroy them.

But then, **"The devil, who deceived them, was cast into the lake of fire and brimstone where the beast and the false prophet *are*. And they will be tormented day and night forever and ever."** (Revelation 20:10)

This passage strikes a death blow to the false doctrine called Annihilationism. There are some that insist that a loving God could not possibly be so cruel as to punish the wicked eternally. These evil pretenders claim that the scriptures do not teach the doctrine of an eternal hell. But here we read that **"the beast and the false prophet are"** still in **"the lake of fire and brimstone"** **"a thousand years"** after they had been cast there in Revelation 19:20.

And this punishment will not only last **"a thousand years."** For it explicitly says, **"and they will be tormented day and night forever and ever."** And a few verses afer this, it says, **"And anyone not found written in the Book of Life was cast into the lake of fire."** (Revelation 20:15) So the common concept of eternal torment in flames of fire, in a place we call hell, is indeed taught in scripture.

But now, after **"the thousand years"** are over, and after the final rebellion has been crushed, comes the second resurrection, the great white throne.

> "Then I saw a great white throne and Him who sat on it, from whose face the earth and the heaven fled away. And there was found no place for them. And I saw the dead, small and great, standing before God, and books were opened. And another book was opened, which is *the Book* of Life. And the dead were judged according to their works, by the things which were written in the books." (Revelation 20:11-12)

There will be no escape from this judgment for:

"The sea gave up the dead who were in it, and Death and Hades delivered up the dead who were in them. And they were judged, each one according to his works." (Revelation 20:13)

For those who had not trusted in Christ, **"in whom we have redemption through His blood, the forgiveness of sins,"** (Colossians 1:14) there can only be one result of being **"judged according to their works."** For **"all have sinned and fall short of the glory of God,"** (Romans 3:23) and **"He who believes in Him is not condemned; but he who does not believe is condemned already, because he has not believed in the name of the only begotten Son of God."** (John 3:18)

This is not **"the judgment seat of Christ"** mentioned in Romans 14:10. That is a judgment to determine the rewards to be received by the redeemed. For at that time, **"If anyone's work is burned, he will suffer loss; but he himself will be saved."** (1 Corinthians 3:15) and **"then shall every man have praise of God."** (1 Corinthians 4:5 KJV) But here, there is only unsparing judgement of the wicked. For it says:

"Then Death and Hades were cast into the lake of fire. This is the second death." (Revelation 20:14)

This shows us that none of the redeemed will be present at this judgment. For we read earlier in this chapter, that **"Blessed and holy is he who has part in the first resurrection. Over such the second death has no power."** (Revelation 20:6) But here, **"Death and Hades were cast into the lake of fire."** The evident meaning is that all those from either of these places was **"cast into the lake of fire."** But, as **"this is the second death,"** none of those who had **"part in the first resurrection."** can be there, for **"over such the second death has no power."** (Revelation 20:6)

It is indeed sad that so many have been deceived into imagining that they can be saved from this judgment by their own efforts. They seem totally unaware of the fact that God has said that **"we are all like an unclean thing, And all our righteousnesses are like filthy rags."** (Isaiah 64:6) And that is why He says that **"a man is not justified by the works of the law but by faith in Jesus Christ... that we might be justified by faith in Christ and not by the works of the law; for by the works of the law no flesh shall be justified."** (Galatians 2:16)

Instead of such worthless stuff, Jesus said, **"Most assuredly, I say to you, he who hears My word and believes in Him who sent Me has everlasting life, and shall not come into judgment, but has passed from death into life."** (John 5:24)

But the judgment and punishment here is terrible. **"And anyone not found written in the Book of Life was cast into the lake of fire."** (Revelation 20:14-15)

What is this **"Book of Life?"** It appears to be a register of those professing the name of Christ, because both Revelaton 3:5 and Revelation 22:19 indicate that the names of false professors will be removed from it. So in the end, it will contain only the names of those who have truly **"washed their robes and made them white in the blood of the Lamb."** (Revelation 7:14) and sadly, at this final judgement, **"anyone not found written in the Book of Life was cast into the lake of fire."** But those who are removed from **"the book of life"** can include no person who has truly trusted in Jesus as their all suufficient and only Savior, for many scriptures are very clear that those who have truly trusted in Him will never be lost. A typical example of these is, **"My sheep hear My voice, and I know them, and they follow Me. And I give them eternal life, and they shall never perish; neither shall anyone snatch them out of My hand."** (John 10:27-28)

# REVELATION 21

At this point begins a vision of a new time.

> "Now I saw a new heaven and a new earth, for the first heaven and the first earth had passed away. Also there was no more sea. Then I, John, saw the holy city, New Jerusalem, coming down out of heaven from God, prepared as a bride adorned for her husband. And I heard a loud voice from heaven saying, 'Behold, the tabernacle of God *is* with men, and He will dwell with them, and they shall be His people. God Himself will be with them *and be* their God. And God will wipe away every tear from their eyes; there shall be no more death, nor sorrow, nor crying. There shall be no more pain, for the former things have passed away.'" (Revelation 21:1-4)

This **"new heaven and a new earth"** is totally different from the millennial earth, even though they are often confused. According to 2 Peter 3:13, **"righteousness dwells"** in the **"new heavens and a new earth"**, as opposed to only reigning in the millennium, as is clearly stated in Isaiah 32:1 and Jeremiah 23:5. Sin is still present in the millennium, as we see in the fact that, **"the sinner, *being* one hndred years old shall be accursed."** (Isaiah 65:20) And Zechariah 14:17-19 specifies the punishment of any families that fail to **"go up from year to year to worship the King, the LORD of hosts, and to keep the Feast of Tabernacles."**

The fact that **"righteousness dwells"** in the **"new heaven"** and **"new earth,"** as opposed to only reigning in the millennium, shows us the reason for another great difference between these two times. For in the **"new heaven"** and **"new earth,"** **"there shall be no more death."** (verse 4) But in the millennium, since sin is still present, although suppressed, **"the child shall die one hundred years old."** (again, Isaiah 65:20) And **"as the days of a tree, so** *shall be* **the days of My people, And My elect shall long enjoy the work of their hands."** (Isaiah 65:22)

Again, in the **"new heaven"** and **"new earth,"** **"there shall be no more pain."** but in the millennium, there will be trees whose **"fruit will be for food, and their leaves for medicine."** (Ezekiel 47:12) The need for medicine implies the presence of pain or sickness in the millennium.

In addition to these less visible differences, the **"new earth"** will have significant physical differences from the present one, which will not exist in the millennium. One of these is that **"there was no more sea."** But also, in this **"new earth:"**

> "Every valley shall be exalted
> And every mountain and hill brought low;
> The crooked places shall be made straight
> And the rough places smooth;
> The glory of the LORD shall be revealed,
> And all flesh shall see it together;
> For the mouth of the LORD has spoken." (Isaiah 4:4-5)

This prophecy is quoted in Luke 3:5.

The **"new heavens and a new earth"** are also mentioned in Isaiah 65:17 and Isaiah 66:22. And the time at which this will take place is discussed in 1 Corinthians 15:24-28, where we read:

> "Then *comes* the end, when He delivers the kingdom to God the Father, when He puts an end to all rule and all authority and power. For He must reign till He has put all enemies under His feet. The last enemy *that* will be destroyed *is* death.

> For *'He has put all things under His feet.'* But when He says *'all things are put under Him,' it is* evident that He who put all things under Him is excepted. Now when all things are made subject to Him, then the Son Himself will also be subject to Him who put all things under Him, that God may be all in all."

Before leaving Revelation 21:1-4, we should notice that, as **"the holy city, New Jerusalem,"** comes **"down out of heaven from God"** to the **"new earth,"** she is **"prepared as a bride adorned for her husband."** This is after the millennium. And **"the marriage of the Lamb"** had been a thousand years earlier, before the Lord returned in power and glory to set up the millennium. (Revelation 19:7-9) But now, a thousand years later, she is still **"a bride."**

This last detail also answers two perplexing questions. The first of these is why do we see this city descending twice, once, here, as **"the New Jerusalem,"** and again in verse 10, as **"the holy Jerusalem"**? And the other question is, how will the righteous be preserved when **"the heavens will pass away with a great noise, and the elements will melt with fervent heat; both the earth and the works that are in it will be burned up"**? (2 Peter 3:10)

It is obvious that no living thing could survive such an event. So it was obvious that God would do something to preserve the righteous. We are not directly told how He will do this. But this coming down twice shows us that He will remove them from the earth before this happens. We are not explicitly told of this removal. But since this beloved city descends from heaven twice, she had to have returned to heaven in between these two descents.

This vision is summed up, **"Then He who sat on the throne said, "Behold, I make all things new."** " (Revelation 21:5a) And in connection with all this, we remember the words of Hebrews 1:10-12, quoting Psalm 102:25-27:

> *"You, LORD, in the beginning*
> *laid the foundation of the earth,*
> *And the heavens are the work of Your hands.*

They will perish, but You remain;
And they will all grow old like a garment;
Like a cloak You will fold them up,
And they will be changed.
But You are the same,
And Your years will not fail."

Next we read, **"And He said to me, 'Write, for these words are true and faithful.' And He said to me, 'It is done! I am the Alpha and the Omega, the Beginning and the End. I will give of the fountain of the water of life freely to him who thirsts. He who overcomes shall inherit all things, and I will be his God and he shall be My son. But the cowardly, unbelieving, abominable, murderers, sexually immoral, sorcerers, idolaters, and all liars shall have their part in the lake which burns with fire and brimstone, which is the second death.'"** (Revelation 21:5b-8)

The alternatives presented here are between a person being able to **"inherit all things, and I will be his God and he shall be My son"** or having **"their part in the lake which burns with fire and brimstone, which is the second death."** To the wise, the choice is simple. This is like a warning made long before, **"I call heaven and earth as witnesses today against you, that I have set before you life and death, blessing and cursing; therefore choose life, that both you and your descendants may live."** (Deuteronomy 30:19)

Here ends the series of visions that had begun in chapter 17, all of which have been sequential. But now the Holy Spirit goes back to pick up a few details that had been previously passed over.

> "Then one of the seven angels who had the seven bowls filled with the seven last plagues came to me and talked with me, saying, 'Come, I will show you the bride, the Lamb's wife.'" (Revelation 21:9)

The first indication that this vision is stepping back in time is who it is that comes to John. It is **"One ot the seven angels who had the seven bowls filled with the seven last plagues"** The visions of these bowls had ended in chapter 16. And now, one of the angels who had poured out the bowls returns. But as we progress through this vision, we will see a number of other indicators that we have stepped back in time.

> "And he carried me away in the Spirit to a great and high mountain, and showed me the great city, the holy Jerusalem, descending out of heaven from God, having the glory of God." (Revelation 21:10-11a)

The second indication that we have stepped back in time is the name given to the city. In verse 2 she had been called **"the holy city, New Jerusalem."** But now, in verse 10, she is called **"the great city, the holy Jerusalem."** The name **"New Jerusalem"** very obviously comes after the name **"holy Jerusalem,"** "not before it. For in both places, the city is called **"holy."** So this again shows a step back in time.

And **"Her light *was* like a most precious stone, like a jasper stone, clear as crystal."** (Revelation 21:10-11)

We remember that our Lord compared Himself to **"a merchant seeking beautiful pearls, who, when he had found one pearl of great price, went and sold all that he had and bought it."** (Matthew 13:45-46) Likewise, in the Old Testament, the Lord said of **"those who fear the LORD And who meditate on His name,"** that, **"they shall be Mine" "On the day that I make them My jewels."** (Malachi 3:16-17) So when the Lord compares His own to **"a most precious stone,"** He is indicating how very much they mean to Him. So much that He would give **"all He had,"** even His own life, for them.

"Also she had a great and high wall with twelve gates, and twelve angels at the gates, and names written on them, which are *the names* of the twelve tribes of the children of Israel: three gates on the east, three gates on the north, three gates on the south, and three gates on the west." (Revelation 21:12-13)

Here we have two more indicators that we have stepped back in time. For in **"heavens"** and **"earth"** where **"righteousness dwells,"** There is no need for **"a great and high wall."** Nor is there any need for **"gates,"** or for **"angels"** standing guard at the **"gates."** So this goes back in time to when **"righteousness"** only reigns, instead of dwelling.

Also, the **"names written on"** **"the gates"** again indicate that we have stepped back in time. For, even as roads are typically named for where they lead, so are gates. As the **"names written on them"** ***"are the names** of the twelve tribes of the children of Israel,"*** this indicates that this city is in close contact with **"the twelve tribes of the children of Israel."** This indicates that the time is the millennium, because that is when Israel will be restored, both to her ancient homeland and to her God.

But also, **"Now the wall of the city had twelve foundations, and on them were the names of the twelve apostles of the Lamb."** (Revelation 21:14) This shows us that, although this city is in close contact with Israel, yet it is the church, for we have **"been built on the foundation of the apostles and prophets, Jesus Christ Himself being the chief corner *stone*,"** (Ephesians 2:20) We also remember that the Holy Spirit inspired Paul to write, **"According to the grace of God which was given to me, as a wise master builder I have laid the foundation, and another builds on it. But let each one take heed how he builds on it. For no other foundation can anyone lay than that which is laid, which is Jesus Christ."** (1 Corinthians 3:10-11)

So **"the names of the twelve apostles of the Lamb"** being on the **"twelve foundations"** of **"the wall of the city"** not only indicate that this city is the church, but also remind us that the writings of the apostles, the New Testament, are the very foundation of our protection. If we abandon these writings, we lose our protection against the atacks of the enemy of our souls, Satan himself, through his willing servants.

> **"And he who talked with me had a gold reed to measure the city, its gates, and its wall. The city is laid out as a square; its length is as great as its breadth. And he measured the city with the reed: twelve thousand furlongs. Its length, breadth, and height are equal."** (Revelation 21:15-16) [60]

---

60 The Greek word here translated **"furlongs"** is σταδιους, *stadious* in our alphabet. This is the plural of σταδιον, *stadion* in our alphabet. (word number 4712 in Strong's Greek Dictionary.) We previously noted that this was 600 Greek feet, which are thought to equal 607 of our feet. 607 feet x 12,000 = 7,284,000 feet.

The city is represented as being a perfect cube, being the same perfect square no matter which way you might look at it. This speaks of God's view of the church, as perfected in Christ, thus being perfect, regardless of how you look at it. Likewise, the dimensions of each wall are twelve, the number representing completeness, times a thousand, a number representing beyond imagination. So the dimensions of the city represent a size far more complete than can be imagined.

The symbolic language continues, **"Then he measured its wall: one hundred *and* forty-four cubits, *according* to the measure of a man, that is, of an angel. The construction of its wall was *of* jasper; and the city *was* pure gold, like clear glass."** (Revelation 21:17-18) In scripture, as just noted, the number twelve represents completeness. So the thickness of the wall, **"one hundred *and* forty-four cubits,"** (twelve times twelve cubits) would represent a completely complete protection.

Again the city was pure gold, like transparent glass. As gold is not transparent, this, again, has to be symbolic. Gold, in the scriptures, symbolizes the righteousness of God. And the city being transparent would indicate that nothing is hidden, as we are told that **"all things are naked and open to the eyes of Him to whom we must give account."** (Hebrews 4:13)

> **"The foundations of the wall of the city *were* adorned with all kinds of precious stones: the first foundation *was* jasper, the second sapphire, the third chalcedony, the fourth emerald, the fifth sardonyx, the sixth sardius, the seventh chrysolite, the eighth beryl, the ninth topaz, the tenth chrysoprase, the eleventh jacinth, and the twelfth amethyst."** (Revelation 21:19-20)

Eight of these stones were used in the breastplate of the high priest, as specified in Exodus 28:17-20. But four, the **"chalcedony," "sardonyx," "chrysolite,"** and **"chrysoprase"** are different, replacing the **"turquoise," "diamond," "agate,"** and **"onyx"** of the breastplate.

This, divided by 5,280 = 1380 miles. So this city is represented as being 1380 miles (the distance from Dallas, Texas to New York City) square *and* high. This makes it obvious that the dimensions are symbolic.

"The twelve gates *were* twelve pearls: each individual gate *was* of one pearl. And the street of the city was pure gold, like transparent glass." (Revelation 21:21) Again, since pure gold is not transparent, this has to be symbolic.

But now we come to a part of the description that is obviously not symbolic. **"But I saw no temple in it, for the Lord God Almighty and the Lamb are its temple. The city had no need of the sun or of the moon to shine in it, for the glory of God illuminated it. The Lamb *is* its light."** (Revelation 21:22-23)

We remember that Ezekiel 48:35 says of the city in the restored Israel, **"and the name of the city from *that* day *shall be*: THE LORD *IS* THERE."**

"And the nations of those who are saved shall walk in its light, and the kings of the earth bring their glory and honor into it. Its gates shall not be shut at all by day (there shall be no night there). And they shall bring the glory and the honor of the nations into it." (Revelation 21:24-26)

Here is the fifth indication that we have stepped back in time. For all of this is clearly millennial. We see nations that heve been saved. According to Isaiah 19:22-24 this will include **"Egypt"** and **"Assyria."** According to Jeremiah 49:39 it will include **"Elam."** According to Jeremiah 48:47 it will include **"Moab."** According to Jeremiah 49:6 it will include **"Ammon."** According to Ezekiel 16:53-55, it will include **"Sodom and Samaria,"** And according to Zechariah 14:16 it will include **"everyone who is left of all the nations which came against Jerusalem."**

And finally, we are told that **"the glory of God illuminated"** the city and **"the Lamb *is* its light," "there shall be no night there."**

And, **"But there shall by no means enter it anything that defiles, or causes an abomination or a lie, but only those who are written in the Lamb's Book of Life."** (Revelation 21:27)

This does not need to be explained. It needs to be believed.

 # Revelation 22

T e vision continues.

> "And he showed me a pure river of water of life, clear as crystal, proceeding from the throne of God and of the Lamb." (Revelation 22:1)

This river is described in detail in Ezekiel 47:1-12, where verse 9 says, **"And it shall be *that* every living thing that moves, wherever the rivers go, will live. There will be a very great multitude of fish, because these waters go there; for they will be healed, and everything will live wherever the river goes."** And, like our verse here, verse 1 of that chapter says that **"there was water, flowing from under the threshold of the temple."** And the correspondence between these two passages that mention the river is the sixth indication that this vision has stepped back in time to the millennium.

But there is one more indication that we have stepped back in time. **"In the middle of its street, and on either side of the river, *was* the tree of life, which bore twelve fruits, each *tree* yielding its fruit every month. The leaves of the tree *were* for the healing of the nations."** (Revelation 22:2) This again corresponds to the vision of Ezekiel 47, where verse 12 says, **"Along the bank of the river, on this side and that, will grow all *kinds of* trees used for food; their leaves will not wither, and their fruit will not fail. They will bear** fruit every month, because their water flows from the sanctuary. Their fruit will be for food, and their leaves for medicine." So this again shows that this vision refers to the millennium.

So now we have seen a total of seven different indications that this vision has stepped back in time to the millennium, which will be over before the **"New Jerusalem"** will come **"down out of heaven from God"** in Revelation 21:2.

We remember that as a result of mankind's first sin, **"the LORD God said, 'Behold, the man has become like one of Us, to know good and evil. And now, lest he put out his hand and take also of the tree of life, and eat, and live forever'– therefore the LORD God sent him out of the garden of Eden to till the ground from which he was taken. So He drove out the man; and He placed cherubim at the east of the garden of Eden, and a flaming sword which turned every way, to guard the way to the tree of life."** (Genesis 3:22-24) But now, sin having been put away by the blood of Christ, and Satan having been imprisoned, mankind will again be allowed to eat of the tree of life.

But also as a result of mankind's first sin, the Lord had said, **"Cursed is the ground for your sake; In toil you shall eat of it All the days of your life. Both thorns and thistles it shall bring forth for you, And you shall eat the herb of the field. In the sweat of your face you shall eat bread "** (Genesis 3:17-19) But now, in the millennium, **"there shall be no more curse, but the throne of God and of the Lamb shall be in it, and His servants shall serve Him."** (Revelation 22:3)

And the vision ends with the words, **"They shall see His face, and His name** *shall be* **on their foreheads. There shall be no night there: They need no lamp nor light of the sun, for the Lord God gives them light. And they shall reign forever and ever."** (Revelation 22:4-5)

The Lord had told the great Moses, that, **"You cannot see My face; for no man shall see Me, and live."** (Exodus 33:20) But now, **"They shall see His face,"** And not only shall they see Him, but **"His name** *shall be* **on their foreheads."**

Then it is repeated that **"They need no lamp nor light of the sun, for the Lord God gives them light."** And then, as a grand finale, **"And they shall reign forever and ever."**

All this seems too good to be true, so, **"Then he said to me, 'These words *are* faithful and true.' And the Lord God of the holy prophets sent His angel to show His servants the things which must shortly take place. 'Behold, I am coming quickly! Blessed is he who keeps the words of the prophecy of this book.'"** (Revelation 22:6-7)

After assuring us of the truth of these words, He then certifies that He had himself **"sent His angel to show His servants"** these things. But then He adds two words. These things **"must shortly take place."** And **"Behold, I am coming quickly!"**

Our Lord's return is continually pressed upon as as an immediate expectation. That is, that He might return at any time. That is why we often say, "It could be today!" And that is why the doctrine of the rapture coming before the great tribulation is so important. For all other theories about the timing of the rapture mean it could not even possibly happen today, or at any time in the immediate future.

Our Lord does not teach us to be watching for the Antichrist, but to be watching for His coming, which He calls **"the blessed hope."** (Titus 2:13) But the Holy Spirit warned us through Peter, **"that scoffers will come in the last days, walking according to their own lusts, and saying, 'Where is the promise of His coming?'"** (2 Peter 3:3-4) And Jesus called the servant who says, **"My Master is delaying His coming,"** **"that evil servant."** (Matthew 24:48)

But then He said, **"Blessed is he who keeps the words of the prophecy of this book."** [61]

The effect of these visions on the prophet was more than he could bear. As was so common among those that received messages from God, he reacted inappropriately.

> "Now I, John, saw and heard these things. And when I heard and saw, I fell down to worship before the feet of the angel who showed me these things. Then he said to me, 'See *that you do* not *do that.* For I am your fellow servant, and of your

---

61   The Greek word here translated **"keeps"** is τηρων, *teron* in our alphabet. This is a present active form of the Greek word τηρω, *tereo* in our alphabet. (word number 5083 in Strong's Greek Dictionary) The word is here used in the sense of "observes," that is, "pays attention to," one of the many meanings of this Greek word.

> **brethren the prophets, and of those who keep the words of this book. Worship God.'"** (Revelation 22:8-9)

Those who are truly serving God are never seeking applause, but only seeking to exalt Christ and to teach the Holy Word. We saw this when the people of Lystra wanted to worship the apostles. **"But when the apostles Barnabas and Paul heard this, they tore their clothes and ran in among the multitude, crying out and saying, "Men, why are you doing these things? We also are men with the same nature as you, and preach to you that you should turn from these useless things to the living God."** (Acts 14:14-15)

> "And he said to me, "Do not seal the words of the prophecy of this book, for the time is at hand." (Revelation 22:10)

This is an obvious reference to the ending of the book of Daniel, where he was told to **"shut up the words, and seal the book until the time of the end,"** (Daniel 12:4) and **"the words are closed up and sealed till the time of the end."** (Daniel 12:9) Why the difference? **"For the time is at hand."** As we just noticed, imminence is critical to understanding Bible prophecy. If we do not understand the doctrine of imminence, that is, that Christ could return at any time, we cannot even begin to understand Bible prophecy.

But next comes an awesome declaration.

> **"He who is unjust, let him be unjust still; he who is filthy, let him be filthy still; he who is righteous, let him be righteous still; he who is holy, let him be holy still."** (Revelation 22:11)

This is not an excuse to continue as we have been doing. It is rather an awesome decree. When the Lord comes, it will be too late to change anything. We will be judged as we are at that time. It will be too late to repent. The time of grace will be over. And all will be judged on the basis of their works.

And now the Lord himself speaks:

"And behold, I am coming quickly, and My reward *is* with Me, to give to every one according to his work. I am the Alpha and the Omega, *the* Beginning and *the* End, the First and the Last." (Revelation 22:12-13)

Here, although the Lord will indeed **"give to every one according to his work,"** His stress is not on the punishment some will receive, but on the rewards His own will receive. For He says, **"My reward *is* with Me."**

And then the speaker plainly identifies Himself as the Lord God Almighty by saying, **"I am the Alpha and the Omega, *the* Beginning and *the* End, the First and the Last."**

And then He says, **"Blessed *are* those who do His commandments, that they may have the right to the tree of life, and may enter through the gates into the city. But outside *are* dogs and sorcerers and sexually immoral and murderers and idolaters, and whoever loves and practices a lie."** (Revelation 22:14-15)

This is not only a blessing and a curse. It also identifies those who are in the city, being **"those who do His commandments."** These, and these only, **"may enter through the gates into the city."** And only these **"have the right to the tree of life."**

And then He says, **"I, Jesus, have sent My angel to testify to you these things in the churches. I am the Root and the Offspring of David, the Bright and Morning Star."** (Revelation 22:16) This repeats what He had previously said in Revelation 1:1, where we are told that this book is **"The Revelation of Jesus Christ,"** that **"He sent and signified it by His angel to His servant John."**

And then we come to that great invitation, **"And the Spirit and the bride say, 'Come!' And let him who hears say, 'Come!' And let him who thirsts come. Whoever desires, let him take the water of life freely."** (Revelation 22:17)

The Lord has been giving this invitation to all for many ages, as He said through Isaiah so long before"

> "Ho! Everyone who thirsts,
> Come to the waters;
> And you who have no money,
> Come, buy and eat.
> Yes, come, buy wine and milk
> Without money and without price.
> **Why do you spend money for *what* is not bread,**
> **And your wages for *what* does not satisfy?**
> **Listen carefully to Me, and eat *what* is good,**
> **And let your soul delight itself in abundance.**
> **Incline your ear, and come to Me.**
> **Hear, and your soul shall live;**
> **And I will make an everlasting covenant with you--**
> **The sure mercies of David."** (Isaiah 55:1-3)

Then follows a most solemn warning and a curse.

> **"For I testify to everyone who hears the words of the prophecy of this book: If anyone adds to these things, God will add to him the plagues that are written in this book; and if anyone takes away from the words of the book of this prophecy, God shall take away his part from the Book of Life, from the holy city, and *from* the things which are written in this book."** (Revelation 22:18-19)

Sadly, in spite of this dreadful warning, the book of Revelation has been corrupted more than any other book in the entire Bible, which is part of the reason this was included here. But that is not the only reason we find this warning here.

This does not just come at the end of this book, but at the end of the entire Bible. For the Revelation is the last book of the Bible to have been given. So this warning does not just apply to the book of Revelation, but to the entire Bible. As God had said such a long time earlier:

> **"Every word of God is pure;**
> **He is a shield to those who put their trust in Him.**
> **Do not add to His words,**

Lest He rebuke you, and you be found a liar."
(Proverbs 30:5-6)

And God's final word, not only for this book, but for the entire Bible, is. **"He who testifies to these things says, "Surely I am coming quickly."** and the answer of the saints is, **"Amen. Even so, come, Lord Jesus!"** (Revelation 22:20)

And the book ends with John's blessing on the readers.

"The grace of our Lord Jesus Christ *be* with you all. Amen." (Revelation 22:21)

Appendix

Why Historians Date the Revelation to the Reign of Domitian

In recent years there has come to be a considerable amount of debate about when the Revelation was given. Almost all of this debate has been driven by arguments advanced by a group who call themselves Preterists. This word comes from the Latin word preterit, which was the Latin name for the past perfect tense. That is, it refers to events or actions that were completed in the past. These people insist that all (but some of them, who call themselves Partial Preterists, only say most) of the events prophesied in the Bible have already taken place. As a part of this doctrine, they insist that the main subject of the Revelation was the destruction of Jerusalem, which is believed to have taken place in the year 70 A.D. Thus, it is absolutely critical for a Preterist to insist that the Revelation was written before that time. The Preterists use the term "Futurists" to refer to those who believe that at least most of these prophesies remain to fulfilled in the future. They claim that only futurists think the Revelation was written after Jerusalem had been destroyed. But this is simply incorrect.

Futurists really could care less when the Revelation was written, for to them that date is completely irrelevant. To them, its meaning is exactly the same whether it was written before or after Jerusalem was destroyed. The same is true of secular historians. Their entire interest in when any event took place is historical accuracy. They could care less what the date was. They only want to correctly determine that date, whenever it was. So why, then, do essentially all scholars who are not Preterists agree that the Revelation was written more than twenty years after Jerusalem was destroyed? (I say *essentially* all, because there are a very few exceptions to this rule.)

This is so widely accepted among essentially all unprejudiced historians because an overwhelming majority of the earlier Christian writers, among those called the "Early Church Fathers" were in agreement about information that indicates that the Revelation was given a few years after A.D. 90.

The earliest such comment we know about is one by Irenaeus, who wrote, "We will not, however, incur the risk of pronouncing positively as to the name of Antichrist; for if it were necessary that his name should be distinctly revealed in this present time, it would have been announced by him who beheld the apocalyptic vision. **For that was seen no very long time since, but almost in our day, towards the end of Domitian's reign.**" ("Against Heresies," by Irenaeus, Book 5, Chapter 30, paragraph 3. From "Ante-Nicean Fathers," ed. Alexander Roberts, D.D. and James Donaldson, D.D., Edinburgh, 1884, in the American edition ed. by A. Cleveland Coxe, D.D, reprinted Peabody, 1996, vol 1.) This is thought to have been written between A.D. 186 and 188.

Preterists claim that the words "That was seen no very long time since, but almost in our day, towards the end of Domation's reign." Refer to John, rather than to his vision. But when we consider the point Irenaeus was making, we see that this cannot be correct. He told us why he had decided not to name the Antichrist. It was because if that knowledge was needed at that time, it would have been announced in "the apocalyptic vision." Further, it is important to realize that Irenaeus did not say, "for he was seen no very long time since..." He said "For that was seen no very long time since, but almost in our day." Using the word "that," rather than "he," clearly shows that Irenaeus was saying that John's vision had been so recent that if there was any need to know the Antichrist's name at that time, it would have been announced in the vision. This clearly demonstrates that Irenaeus was referring to the time the Revelation was written, not to the last time John had been seen.

Some of the more radical Preterists, determined to reject this testimony of Irenaeus, claim that his words, "For that was seen no very long time since, but almost in our day…" cannot refer to "the apocalyptic vision," because they claim that Irenaeus usually used the word "seen" in reference to persons, but not for things (like visions.) But this is clearly incorrect. For in this same "Against Heresies," Irenaeus repeatedly used the word "seen" with reference both to visions and to things seen in visions. He used it in book 4, chapter 20, paragraph 10, saying, "This, too, was made still clearer by Ezekiel, that the prophets saw the dispensations of God in part, but not actually God Himself. For when this man had seen the vision of God, and the cherubim, and their wheels…" He used it again in book 4, chapter 20, paragraph 12, saying, "However, it was not by means of visions alone which were seen, and words which were proclaimed, but also in actual works, that He was beheld by the prophets, in order that through them He might prefigure and show forth future events beforehand." He used it again in book 5, chapter 26, paragraph 1, saying, "He teaches us what the ten horns shall be which were seen by Daniel, telling us that thus it had been said to him: 'And the ten horns which thou sawest are ten kings, who have received no kingdom as yet, but shall receive power as if kings one hour with the beast.' " He used it again in the same paragraph, saying, "Daniel also says particularly, that the end of the fourth kingdom consists in the toes of the image seen by Nebuchadnezzar…" He used it again in book 5, chapter 28, paragraph 2 of this work, saying, "John has thus described in the Apocalypse: 'And the beast which I had seen was like unto a leopard…' "(All of these comments can be found in the same volume 1 of "Ante-Nicene Fathers" that was previously cited.) So, contrary to the claim made by these Preterists, Irenaeus often used the word "seen" in regard to things (like visions.)

But after claiming that Irenaeus did not say that the Revelation was seen "towards the end of Domatian's reign," Preterists then claim that all other ancient writers that say the Revelation was given in the reign of Domitian were simply relying on the word of Irenaeus. They do not even seem to notice the logical contradiction of claiming that this is not what Irenaeus said, and then claiming that everyone else who said the same thing was simply relying on his word. But aside from the logical contradiction, this claim is demonstrably incorrect.

For Victornius wrote, "'And He says unto me, Thou must again prophesy to the peoples, and to the tongues, and to the nations, and to many kings.' He says this, because **when John said these things he was in the island of Patmos, condemned to the labour of the mines by Cæsar Domitian.** There, therefore, he saw the Apocalypse; and when grown old, he thought that he should at length receive his quittance by suffering, Domitian being killed, all his judgments were discharged. And John being dismissed from the mines, thus subsequently delivered the same Apocalypse which he had received from God." ("Commentary on the Apocalypse of the Blessed John," by Victorinus, comments on Revelation 10:11, translated by Rev. Robert Ernest Wallis, Ph.D. From "Ante-Nicean Fathers," in the edition previously cited, vol 7.) This is thought to have been written in the late third century.

We need to notice two details in this statement. Victorinus said that "when John said these things he was in the island of Patmos, condemned to the labour of the mines by Cæsar Domitian," and that "John being dismissed from the mines, thus subsequently delivered the same Apocalypse." Since Irenaeus did not state either of these details, they are conclusive proof that this statement by Victorinus was based on information other than the statement by Irenaeus.

So there is an independent ante-Nicene source that confirms what Irenaeus said.

In addition to this, in the Post-Nicene period Jerome said concerning John that "**In the fourteenth year then after Nero Domitian having raised a second persecution he was banished to the island of Patmos, and wrote the *Apocalypse*,** on which Justin Martyr and Irenæus afterwards wrote commentaries. But **Domitian having been put to death and his acts, on account of his excessive cruelty, having been annulled by the senate, he returned to Ephesus under Pertinax** and continuing there until the time of the emperor Trajan, founded and built churches throughout all Asia, and, worn out by old age, died in the sixty-eighth year after our Lord's passion and was buried near the same city." ("Lives of Illustrious Men," by Jerome, chapter 9. - From "Nicene and Post-Nicene Fathers," Second Series, ed. by Philip Schaff,

D.D., LL.D. and Henry Wace, D.D., vol.3.) We must notice that neither of the earlier accounts mentioned John returning to Ephesus under Pertinax. Thus, Jerome's account was based, at least in part, on information that did not come from either of the ante-Nicene accounts we have examined. So now we have the same information from three ancient sources, every one of which included at least some details that none of the others contained. (None of the other accounts also mentioned Domatian's acts having been annulled by the senate or his excessive cruelty, but as these were commonly known facts of history, they would not have needed to come from information specifically about John.)

So we see that, contrary to the claims of Preterists, there were at least three independent ancient sources that indicated that the Revelation was written during the reign of Domatian. These three accounts have been presented together to demonstrate that every one of them contained at least some information that was not included in any of the others. But in addition to these three independent statements, there were also numerous other such statements made by these and other early Christian writers.

In addition to the statement quoted above, Victorinus also wrote, " 'And there are seven kings: five have fallen, and one is, and the other is not yet come; and when he is come, he will be for a short time.'] The time must be understood in which the written Apocalypse was published, since then reigned Cæsar Domitian; but before him had been Titus his brother, and Vespasian, Otho, Vitellius, and Galba. These are the five who have fallen. **One remains, under whom the Apocalypse was written—Domitian, to wit.** 'The other has not yet come,' speaks of Nerva; 'and when he is come, he will be for a short time,' for he did not complete the period of two years." ("Commentary on the Apocalypse of the Blessed John," by Victorinus, comments on Revelation 17:10, tran. by Rev. Robert Ernest Wallis, Ph.D. From "Ante-Nicean Fathers," in the edition previously cited, vol 7.)

Likewise, after Jerome's statement which we have already noticed, he also said, "John is both an Apostle and an Evangelist, and a prophet. An Apostle, because he wrote to the Churches as a master; an Evangelist, because he composed a Gospel, a thing which no other of the Apostles, excepting Matthew, did; a prophet, **for he saw in the**

island of Patmos, to which he had been banished by the Emperor Domitian as a martyr for the Lord, an Apocalypse containing the boundless mysteries of the future. Tertullian, more over, relates that he was sent to Rome, and that having been plunged into a jar of boiling oil he came out fresher and more active than when he went in." ("Against Jovinianus," by Jerome, Book I, chapter 26. From "Nicene and Post-Nicene Fathers," Second Series, in the edition previously cited, vol. 6.)

A work attributed to Hyppolytus, who wrote shortly after Irenaeus, said, "**John, again, in Asia, was banished by Domitian the king to the isle of Patmos, in which also he wrote his Gospel and saw the apocalyptic vision**; and in Trajan's time he fell asleep at Ephesus, where his remains were sought for, but could not be found." (From "Appendix to the Works of Hippolytus, Containing Dubious and Spurious Pieces," item 49, section 3. From "Ante-Nicean Fathers," in the edition previously cited, vol 5.)

Again, Sulpitius Severus said, "**Then, after an interval, Domitian, the son of Vespasian, persecuted the Christians. At this date, he banished John the Apostle and Evangelist to the island of Patmos. There he, secret mysteries having been revealed to him, wrote and published his book of the holy Revelation,** which indeed is either foolishly or impiously not accepted by many." ("The Sacred History Of Sulpitius Severus," book 2, chapter 31. - From "Nicene and Post-Nicene Fathers," Second Series, in the edition previously cited, vol. 11.)

We need to notice that none of these quotations contained any reference whatsoever to the statement of Irenaeus that is alleged to be the source of all of them. In actual fact, the only other source (from this general time period) that even mentioned that statement by Irenaeus was the famous church historian Eusebius, who wrote:

"**Domitian, having shown great cruelty toward many**, and having unjustly put to death no small number of well-born and notable men at Rome, and having without cause exiled and confiscated the property of a great many other illustrious men, finally became a successor of Nero in his hatred and enmity toward God. He was in fact the second that stirred up a persecution against us, although his father Vespasian had undertaken nothing prejudicial to us.

"It is said that in this persecution the apostle and evangelist John, who was still alive, was condemned to dwell on the island of Patmos in consequence of his testimony to the divine word.

"Irenæus, in the fifth book of his work Against Heresies, where he discusses the number of the name of Antichrist which is given in the so-called Apocalypse of John, speaks as follows concerning him:

" 'If it were necessary for his name to be proclaimed openly at the present time, it would have been declared by him who saw the revelation. For it was seen not long ago, but almost in our own generation, at the end of the reign of Domitian.'" ("Church History," by Eusebius, book 3, chapters 17 and 18. From "Nicene and Post-Nicene Fathers," Second Series, in the edition previously cited, vol. 1.)

There is only one source that is unquestionably previous to the sixth century and clearly said the Revelation was written before the reign of Domatian. That was Epiphanius of Salamis, who wrote a series of books called "The Panarion," which are thought to date from between 374 and 377. In this work Epiphanius first said, "Later, therefore, though from caution and humility he had declined to be an evangelist, the Holy Spirit compelled John to issue the Gospel in his old age when he was past ninety, after his return from Patmos, under Claudius Caesar, and several years of his residence in Asia." ("The Panarion," by Epiphanius, Section IV, paragraph 12.2, from "The Panarion of Epiphanius of Salmis, Books II and III, tran. by Frank Williams, ed. by J. M. Robinson and H. J. Klimkeit, pub. by E. J. Brill, 1994, pg 36. Available online at: http://www.ebooks-share.net/ the-panarion-of-epiphanius-of-salamis-books-ii-and-iii-de-fide-nag-hammadi-and-manichaean-studies/) Further on in the same volume, he also wrote, "St. John, who prophesied before his falling asleep, during the time of Claudius Caesar and earlier, when he was on the isle of Patmos." ("The Panarion," by Epiphanius, Section IV, paragraph 33.8, from pg. 66 in the volume previously cited.)

It is unreasonable to argue that this is even close to a reliable witness, for Epiphanius has John having prophesied not only during the time of Claudius, but perhaps even earlier, for he has him returning from Patmos "under Claudius Caesar." The Christian Classics Ethereal Library says of Epiphanius, "He was lacking in knowledge of the world and of men, in sound judgment, and in critical discernment. He was possessed of a boundless credulity, now almost proverbial, causing innumerable errors and contradictions in his writings." http://www.ccel.org/ccel/schaff/hcc3.iii.xiii.ix.html Even the Preterist website Bible.org says of these statements by Epiphanius, "Unfortunately, Ephiphanius is also another example of inconsistent credibility in historical matters, in one place, for instance, making the unusual claim that Priscilla was a man! Therefore, this witness, too, must be taken with a grain of salt." https://bible.org/seriespage/chapter-3-dating-apocalypse So this lone voice of any writer provable to be previous to the sixth century is widely recognized as historically unreliable.

Preterists make much of one other ancient document which includes a statement that, if it were correct, would prove the Revelation was written very early, even though it does not say that. This is called the Muratorian Canon, and says, "the blessed Apostle Paul, following the rule of his predecessor John, writes to no more than seven churches by name, in this order: the first to the Corinthians, the second to the Ephesians, the third to the Philippians, the fourth to the Colossians, the fifth to the Galatians, the sixth to the Thessalonians, the seventh to the Romans. Moreover, though he writes twice to the Corinthians and Thessalonians for their correction, it is yet shown— i.e., by this sevenfold writing— that there is one Church spread abroad through the whole world. And John too, indeed, in the Apocalypse, although he writes only to seven churches, yet addresses all." ("Canon Muratorianus," author unknown, paragraph 3. From "Ante-Nicean Fathers," in the edition previously cited, vol 5.) As the last of Paul's epistles is thought to have been written around A.D. 64, this implies that the Revelation was written before A. D. 64.

This document is usually dated to the late second century because its fourth paragraph said, "The Pastor, moreover, did Hermas write very recently in our times in the city of Rome, while his brother bishop Pius sat in the chair of the Church of Rome." But what do we really know about the Muratorian Canon? It is actually a single sheet from a codex style manuscript. This single sheet obviously does not contain the entirety of the original document, so it is called the Muratorian Fragment. And the codex in which it is found is called Codex Muratorius, or sometimes the Muratorian Manuscript. In the nineteenth century this manuscript was examined in detail by Brooke

Faust Wescott. This is the same Wescott of Wescott and Hort fame, who has pronounced favorably on manuscripts that numerous others, including myself, completely reject. But here his judgment was exactly the opposite. He wrote concerning the "Muratorian Fragment:"

"The fragment from Ambrose (*De Abrahamo*, 1. 3. 15) which follows the Fragment on the Canon furnishes a fair criterion of the accuracy to be expected from the scribe. And by a remarkable accident the piece is more than usually instructive, for the whole fragment is repeated. Thus we have two copies of the same original and their divergence is a certain index of the inaccuracy of the transcriber which cannot be gainsaid. The second copy differs from the first in the following places:... [Here Wescott gave a line by line list of the differences in these fragments.]

"Thus in thirty lines there are thirty unquestionable clerical blunders including one important omission, (p. 11^b 29), two other omissions which destroy the sense completely (p. 12^a 11 *merito*, I9 *dicitur*), one substitution equally destructive of the sense (p. 12^a 9 *decem et octo* for τ), **and four changes which appear to be intentional and false alterations** (p. 12^a 6 *scivit*, 11 *populosu exercitu*, 23 *filii*, 25 *sacrificat*). We have therefore to deal with the work of a scribe either unable or unwilling to understand the work which he was copying, **and yet given to arbitrary alteration of the text before him** from regard simply to the supposed form of words...

"On the other hand the text itself as it stands is substantially a good one. The errors by which it is deformed are due to carelessness and ignorance and not to the badness of the source from which it was taken. **But these errors are such as in several cases could not be rectified without other authorities for comparison.**

"In the sheet which precedes the Fragment on the Canon the same phenomena appear. There is in that also the same ignorance of construction: the same false criticism: the same confusion of letters and terminations. If we now apply the results gained from the examination of the context to the Fragment on the Canon, part of it at least can be restored with complete certainty; and part may be pronounced hopelessly corrupt. It has been shown that a fragment of thirty lines contains three serious omissions and at least two other changes of words wholly destructive of the sense, and it would therefore be almost incredible that something of the like kind should not occur in a passage nearly three times as long. **Other evidence shows that conjecture would have been unable to supply what is wanting or satisfactorily correct what is wrong in the one case, and there is no reason to hope it would be happier in the other."** ("A General Survey of the History of the Canon of the New Testament," by Brooke Faust Wescott D.D., London, Macmillian and Company, 1866, 4th ed., 1875, pp. 522-524. - original not highlighted as shown here) The entirety of this book can be viewed online at: http://archive.org/stream/ageneralsurveyof00westuoft#page/522/mode/2up

So we see that the famous textural critic, Wescott, who has been widely criticized for accepting questionable manuscripts, concluded that the scribe who copied out the Muratorian Canon was "given to arbitrary alteration of the text before him," and that the known errors in the Manuscript "are such as in several cases could not be rectified without other authorities for comparison."

But what "other authorities" do we have "for comparison"? The only known other copies of any portion of this Canon are twenty-four of its eighty-five lines included in a Prologue to the Epistles of Paul. This Prologue is contained in three eleventh century and one twelfth century manuscripts of the *Corpus Paulinum* at the Benedictine monastery on Monte Cassino, and was first published in *Miscellanea Cassinese*, ii (1897). These can be found in "The Muratorian Fragment and the Development of the Canon," by Geoffery Mark Hahneman, Clarendon press, Oxford, 1992, pp. 9-10. Unfortunately, this book has not been published online, but it can be purchased online at: http://www.amazon.com/exec/obidos/ASIN/0198263414/peterkirby

The actual facts about the Muratorian Manuscript were cited by Wescott as: "The Manuscript (*Bibl. Ambros.* Cod 101) in which the Canon is contained was brought from Columban's famous monastery at Bibbo. It may therefore probably be of Irish origin or descent, though there is nothing in the Manuscript itself, as far as I could observe, which proves this to be the case. It was written probably in the eighth (or seventh) century, and contains a miscellaneous collection of Latin fragments, including passages from Eucherius, Ambrose, translations from Chrystosom, and brief expositions of the Catholic Creed." (pp. 514-515 of the volume previously cited.)

So, all we really know about the date of the Muratorian Canon is that its earliest known example was supposedly copied out in the seventh or eighth century. That is, it came out of the third or fourth century of the Medieval period of ignorance, long after the facts of history had been forgotten, and myth and superstition reigned supreme. And no other scribe copied out any portion of this document until three or four hundred more years of this same Medieval darkness, although four copies of that work were made. These four other copies did include the comment about Paul "following the rule of his predecessor John." But they did not contain the sentence "The Pastor, moreover, did Hermas write very recently in our times in the city of Rome, while his brother bishop Pius sat in the chair of the Church of Rome." **That sentence, which is found in *only one* manuscript, is the *sole* basis of the presumed early date of this canon, yet it comes from an ignorant and careless scribe "given to arbitrary alteration of the text before him."** So in truth, there is no solid logical basis for assuming that this document originated in the late second century. It is thus seen to be sheer nonsense to even pretend that the Muratorian Canon is a reliable witness as to the date of the Revelation.

Again, Preterists claim that the writings of Clement of Alexandria prove that the Revelation was written in the time of Nero, not Domitian. But what did Clement actually say?

"For the teaching of our Lord at His advent, beginning with Augustus and Tiberius, was completed in the middle of the times of Tiberius.

"And that of the apostles, embracing the ministry of Paul, ends with Nero. It was later, in the times of Adrian the king, that those who invented the heresies arose; and they extended to the age of Antoninus the elder, as, for instance, Basilides, though he claims (as they boast) for his master, Glaucias, the interpreter of Peter." ("The Stromata, or Miscellanies," by Clement of Alexandria, book 7, chapter 17, paragraph 4, from "Ante-Nicean Fathers," in the edition previously cited, vol. 2.) This is the only apparently reliable and provably early quotation advanced by Preterists that even seems to be a denial of what the others said, but that is not necessarily the case. For Clement only explicitly said the epistles of Paul ended with Nero. And he could have been considering the Revelation to be a subsequent teaching directly from the Lord himself, (Revelation 1:1, 22:16) and that John was simply acting as a secretary who recorded what the Lord had said. (Revelation 1:11,19).

In addition to this statement by Clement, Preterist build great arguments based on another of his statements. For he also said, "And that you may be still more confident, that repenting thus truly there remains for you a sure hope of salvation, listen to a tale, which is not a tale but a narrative, handed down and committed to the custody of memory, about the Apostle John. **For when, on the tyrant's death, he returned to Ephesus from the isle of Patmos**, he went away, being invited, to the contiguous territories of the nations, here to appoint bishops, there to set in order whole Churches, there to ordain such as were marked out by the Spirit." ("Salvation of the Rich Man," by Clement of Alexandria, chapter 42, tran. by Rev. William Wilson, M.A. From "Ante-Nicean Fathers," in the edition previously cited, vol. 2.)

Preterists claim that Clement's words "the tyrant" in this statement have to mean Nero, claiming that it was primarily Nero who was called "the tyrant." In defense of this claim they sometimes quote Tertullian as having said, "For any one who knows him, can understand that not except as being of singular excellence did anything bring on it Nero's condemnation. Domitian, too, a man of Nero's type in cruelty, tried his hand at persecution; but as he had something of the human in him, he soon put an end to what he had begun, even restoring again those whom he had banished." ("The Apology," of Tertullian, tran. by the Rev. S. Thelwall, chapter 5. From "Ante-Nicean Fathers," in the edition previously cited, vol 3.) Preterists like to stress the words, "he had something of the human in him," and the words "he soon put an end to what he had begun, even restoring again those whom he had banished." But among the ancient Christian writers, Tertullian stands alone in using such soft words concerning Domitian. And even in this same account, Tertullian said Domitian was "a man of Nero's type in cruelty." But let us examine what others said of Domitian.

Remember that Eusebius said, "**Domitian, having shown great cruelty toward many**, and having unjustly put to death no small number of well-born and notable men at Rome, and having without cause exiled and confiscated the property of a great many other illustrious men, finally became a successor of Nero in his hatred and enmity toward God." ("Church History," by Eusebius, cited above.)

"The Marterdom of Ignatius" said, "When Trajan, not long since, succeeded to the empire of the Romans, Ignatius, the disciple of John the apostle, a man in all respects of an apostolic character, governed the Church of the Antiochians with great care, **having with difficulty escaped the former storms of the many persecutions under Domitian**, inasmuch as, like a good pilot, by the helm of prayer and fasting, by the earnestness of his teaching, and by his [constant] spiritual labour, he resisted the flood that rolled against him, fearing [only] lest he should lose any of those who were deficient in courage, or apt to suffer from their simplicity." ("The Martyrdom of Ignatius," author unknown, chapter 1. From "Ante-Nicean Fathers," in the edition previously cited, vol 1.) Although the author is indeed unknown, the last chapter of this work said, "Having ourselves been eye-witnesses of these things…" (chapter 7 of the work cited above.) Again, in the portion of the account that describes their voyage to Rome, the pronoun "he" was twice changed to "we." (Toward the end of chapter 5 and the beginning of chapter 6.) So the author of this account plainly represented himself to have been a companion of Ignatius and an eye-witness of his martyrdom, and thus someone who had actually experienced "**the many persecutions under Domitian.**"

Lactantius said, "After an interval of **some years from the death of Nero, there arose another tyrant no less wicked (Domitian)**, who, although his government was exceedingly odious, for a very long time oppressed his subjects, and reigned in security, until at length he stretched forth his impious hands against the Lord. Having been instigated by evil demons to persecute the righteous people, he was then delivered into the power of his enemies, and suffered due punishment. To be murdered in his own palace was not vengeance ample enough: the very memory of his name was erased. For although he had erected many admirable edifices, and rebuilt the Capitol, and left other distinguished marks of his magnificence, yet the senate did so persecute his name, as to leave no remains of his statues, or traces of the inscriptions put up in honour of him; and by most solemn and severe decrees it branded him, even after death, with perpetual infamy. Thus, **the commands of the tyrant having been rescinded**, the Church was not only restored to her former state, but she shone forth with additional splendour, and became more and more flourishing." ("Of the Manner in Which the Persecutors Died," by Lactantius, chapter 3, tran. by Rev. William Wilson, M.A. From "Ante-Nicean Fathers," in the edition cited above, vol. 7.)

Augustin called hin "the cruel Domitian," saying, "He who gave power to Marius gave it also to Caius Cæsar; He who gave it to Augustus gave it also to Nero; He also who gave it to the most benignant emperors, the Vespasians, father and son, gave it also to **the cruel Domitian**; and, finally, to avoid the necessity of going over them all, He who gave it to the Christian Constantine gave it also to the apostate Julian, whose gifted mind was deceived by a sacrilegious and detestable curiosity, stimulated by the love of power." ("The City of God," by Augustin, tran. By Marcus Dodss, D.D., book 5, chapter 21. From "Nicene and Post Nicene Fathers," First series, ed. by Philip Schaff, D.D., LL.D., in the edition quoted above, vol.2.)

And Melito the Philosopher said, "**Nero and Domitian alone of all the emperors, imposed upon by certain calumniators, have cared to bring any impeachment against our doctrines.**" ("Apology Addressed to Marcus Aurelius Antoninus," by Melito, the Philosopher, part II. From "Ante-Nicean Fathers," in the edition cited above, vol. 8.)

So there can be zero question that the early Christians **often** called Domitian a tyrant.

Preterists also argue that a statement by Tertullian ties John into the persecutions under Nero, rather than Domitian. For they claim Tertullian has John persecuted at the same time as Paul. But that is not what Tertullian said. His words were, "Since, moreover, you are close upon Italy, you have Rome, from which there comes even into our own hands the very authority (of apostles themselves). How happy is its church, on which apostles poured forth all their doctrine along with their blood! where Peter endures a passion like his Lord's! **where Paul wins his crown in a death like John's where the Apostle John was first plunged, unhurt, into boiling oil, and thence remitted to his island-exile**! See what she has learned, what taught, what fellowship has had with even (our) churches in Africa." (The Prescription Against Heretics," by Tertullian, tran. by the Rev. Peter Holmes, D.D., chapter 36. From "Ante-Nicean Fathers," in the edition cited above, vol 3.) Saying that Paul suffered the same persecution as John does not even so much as imply that these persecutions took place at the same time. This can be seen in the last sentence before the one about Paul and John. For it says that "Peter endures a passion like his Lord's." This author obviously knew that Peter was not persecuted at the same time as his Lord. So the claim that Tertullian tied John into the persecutions of Nero is only nonsense.

Finally, Preterists argue that in the two oldest Syriac versions of the New Testament, the title of the Revelation says, "written in Patmos, whither John was sent by Nero Caesar." This sounds significant, until we realize that the oldest of these two versions is the Philoxenian Version, which is thought to have been made by Polycarpus of Mabug in about 508 A.D., and the other one is the Harclean version, thought to have been made by Thomas of Harkel in about 616 A.D. That is, they date from around four and five centuries after the Revelation was written! None of the older Syriac versions even contained the Revelation at all.

In conclusion, during the second through the fifth centuries at least six Christian writers clearly stated facts that date the Revelation to within the reign of Domitian, including details that demonstrate at least three independent sources of information. Two early writers said things that could be interpreted to mean it was written earlier, but that is not a necessary conclusion from any statement made by either of them. There are only two clearly stated comments about an earlier date. One of these was made by a writer noted for historical errors. And the other comes from an eighth or seventh century copy made by an ignorant and careless scribe "given to arbitrary alteration of the text before him." So all solid and reliable evidence points to the Revelation having been given in the later years of Domitian.

At the time Jerusalem was destroyed, the emperor of Rome was Vespasian. About nine years later he was succeeded by his son Titus, the one who had previously conquered Jerusalem. Titus ruled from approximately A.D. 79 to 81, to be succeeded by Domitian about eleven years after the destruction of Jerusalem. Domitian ruled until approximately A.D. 96, some 26 years after Jerusalem was destroyed. "Toward the end of Domitian's reign," as Irenaeus put it, would be a few years earlier. And that is why most scholars conclude that the Revelation was written sometime between A.D. 92 and 94, with most favoring the later date.

Dispensational Publishing House is striving to become the go-to source for Bible-based materials from the dispensational perspective.

Our goal is to provide high-quality doctrinal and worldview resources that make dispensational theology accessible to people at all levels of understanding.

Visit our blog regularly to read informative articles from both known and new writers.

And please let us know how we can better serve you.

Dispensational Publishing House, Inc.
PO Box 3181
Taos, NM 87571

Call us toll free 844-321-4202

www.DispensationalPublishing.com

www.ingramcontent.com/pod-product-compliance
Lightning Source LLC
Chambersburg PA
CBHW071954110526
44592CB00012B/1079